ZENITH MAN

McCracken Poston Jr.

CITADEL PRESS
Kensington Publishing Corp.
www.kensingtonbooks.com

Some names have been changed to protect the privacy of individuals connected to this story.

CITADEL BOOKS are published by

Kensington Publishing Corp.
900 Third Ave.
New York, NY 10022

All Kensington Titles, Imprints, and Distributed Lines are available at special quantity discounts for bulk purchases for sales promotions, premiums, fund-raising, and educational or institutional use. Special book excerpts or customized printings can also be created to fit specific needs. For details, write or phone the office of the Kensington special sales manager: Kensington Publishing Corp., 900 Third Ave., New York, NY 10022, attn: Special Sales Department, Phone: 1-800-221-2647.

Library of Congress Card Catalogue Number: 2023947404

ISBN-13: 978-0-8065-4279-9
First Kensington Hardcover Edition: March 2024

ISBN-13: 978-1-4967-4281-2 (ebook)

10 9 8 7 6 5 4 3 2 1

Printed in the United States of America

This book is dedicated to my father, McCracken King Poston Sr., who did his best under the toughest circumstances, winning in the end; and to my mother, Barbara Sumners Poston, for being there for us and doing everything else.

AUTHORS NOTE

This is a true story, told to the best of my recollection and verified through interviews, court documents, and newspaper articles. All quoted dialogue is as accurate as memory can allow. Alvin and I have revisited our conversations often during our weekly lunches as I wrote this book. Because the facts are so important to me, I have tried throughout to be as accurate as possible.

PROLOGUE

October 4, 1997

Emerging from his late parents' run-down house on Inman Street, itself for years the target of local innuendo, Alvin Ridley, failed television repairman and the town bogeyman, abruptly turns to lock the door. Glancing around to see if his perceived tormentors are watching him, he pulls open the formidable homemade gate and then slowly drives a thirty-two-year-old Chevrolet pickup truck through it. Then he jumps back out and quickly closes and locks the gate with chains and a padlock.

Two-tenths of a mile down Evitt Street, he carefully drives the 25 mph speed limit right past the local volunteer fire department, visibly staffed with an ambulance and professional EMTs always on the ready, and turns south on U.S. Highway 41, away from town. Thinking better of it less than half a mile later, he pulls into the roadside monument for the 1863 Battle of Ringgold Gap and turns around.

Continuing to drive slowly, as if it were a usual lazy Saturday morning, he pulls into the ShopRite parking lot and tries the pay phone on the exterior wall. Unsuccessful with this attempt, he gets back into the truck and drives through two parking lots to a pay phone located along LaFayette Street, behind the Catoosa County Courthouse Annex and Jail. He puts coins in the phone and calls, if you believe the later speculation, a funeral home to retrieve a dead body from his house. He most certainly calls Erlanger Hospital in downtown Chattanooga, Tennessee, but is instructed that this is a matter for the Catoosa County authorities.

Reluctantly he dials 911. The Catoosa County 911 office is just across the street. The operators could look out the single window facing LaFayette Street and see the stooped figure making the call.

"Catoosa 911. Where is your emergency?"

A pause, and then he answers flatly, giving his home address.

"What's the problem?"

Again, lacking emotion, he says, "I think my wife's passed out."

The operator confirmed the address.

"Yeah."

"Is she breathing?"

"I don't think so—it's behind the steel plant there." He adds matter-of-factly, "I'm calling from a pay phone booth."

"You don't have a phone at your house?"

"There's no phone there."

This is the portion of the 911 call, in the detached voice of the caller, that is instantly spread around the world upon the revelation that a dead body was found in the ramshackle house on Inman Street. The immediate problem for investigators is, who was this soul? Certainly not the alleged spouse of the infamously solitary Alvin Ridley. Ridley said it was his wife, but can produce no identification for her. The body of the woman he calls his wife—Virginia— is declared dead by the coroner Vanita Hullander, who plans to take it to the hospital across the county in Fort Oglethorpe, and the next morning, deliver it to the state crime lab in Atlanta.

The portions of the 911 call not shared with the public or played on the news stations were the parts where the caller shared that his wife was, in his words, "*epi-letic*", or that he ended the call with a request: "Please hurry."

Later that morning, five miles to the south, an extremely hungover failed politician, failed husband, and marginally failing lawyer, rises. Too down and broken to even drive to Athens to see his beloved University of Georgia Bulldogs play, and seeking something for his blinding headache, he drives slowly into town.

1

Flashback eleven months, to November 6, 1996, past midnight

*T*hat night, as I locked up the little storefront campaign office, still wearing my suit and tie, I thought, *I need to get drunk.* I'd partied pretty hard in high school, in college, and in law school, a secret drunken legend to my friends and cohorts. Now that I had lost an election for the United States Congress, and just about everything else that mattered to me, I was ready. First, though, I had to make a phone call.

Reva and I hadn't announced our separation, as I was in the middle of an election when she received the job offer, but I didn't want to be responsible for her losing a major career opportunity in Chicago. We were still friends, and although "friendly divorce" seemed like an oxymoron, ours was just that. "We didn't have any business getting married" was her mantra. I had become a neurotic micromanager, frozen, distant, and didn't quite know what was wrong with me.

My opponent's team members tried to use Reva's absence to their advantage. Late in the campaign, his staffer called my staff members and asked, "Where did he hide the body?" Once the word got out that Reva wasn't around, my opponent's very nice wife suddenly seemed to be everywhere he was, seated next to him when both he and I were scheduled to be on the same stage. Next to me, now an empty chair appeared, as if waiting for a woman who would never again appear, either on the campaign trail or in my life. It seems cruel, but I was fair game. I had played hardball politics myself over the years. Touché, Congressman.

The numbers spoke volumes. I didn't even win Catoosa County, my home, where less than eight years before, I had won my state house seat by 70 percent. I thought I had done everything right. I had sacrificed what could have been a long, comfortable career in public service to follow the dictates of my conscience, and this is where it got me.

Although I had given my televised concession speech, emphasizing that I was conceding *this one,* I knew better. The red tide of the new Georgia Republicanism had washed up deeply in the northwest corner of the state. Devastated by the depth of the loss, I walked to the middle of the desolate U.S. Highway 41, the Dixie Highway, and called Reva in Chicago.

"It's over," I told her. "I lost. I'll file the divorce agreement papers tomorrow."

Walking to my truck, I was already hearing from around the state that colleagues from the state capitol were considering their own party switch from *D* to *R,* just as my opponent had done after winning his last election. I was the bellwether, apparently. Although there would be talk of great change, it's funny that the faces wouldn't change much.

Just then, I saw a figure in a shop doorway: "Creepy Alvin Ridley," "Crazy Alvin Ridley." *Crap.*

Alvin and I had a history, one I didn't want to think about right then. I had once chastised him for taking a percentage for simply cashing the disability check of an impaired man, John Howard. Howard had hitchhiked to the state capitol "to see his representative and governor" about it. I handled it, advising him to go to the bank. Then I came home and confronted Alvin Ridley, only getting a menacing stare for my trouble.

For now, let's just say Mr. Ridley was out there well past midnight, a guy who posted conspiracy missives on the inside of the windows of his dilapidated, padlocked shop—rants that I often secretly checked out to be sure my name wasn't among the many listed. In fact, he'd probably been posting one of those diatribes before he caught sight of me. Or maybe he had been guarding his decaying building, which had been closed for fifteen years. Other times, he lurked around the front door. If any activity occurred downtown, he was convinced people were breaking into this ruin of a store.

The sides of the windows showcased its plight, and as I passed them, he was just inside the alcove, standing in shadows.

"You got beat, didn't you?" he said.

"Yeah. I did."

I kept going, not wanting to engage him, remembering the time years ago he'd appeared, the subject of ridicule and amazement at an all-candidates rally, running for sheriff of Catoosa County in 1984.

Please, God, I thought. *Let my vote percentages be higher than his were.*

Eleven months later, Virginia, the wife that nobody knew he had, would be dead, and he would be ultimately arrested for her murder.

His defender? That would be this once-golden boy, now failed husband and politician, walking down this nearly deserted street, headed for a destination that not even I could imagine.

I'd dreamed of a political career since childhood in Graysville, although I didn't imagine it in those terms. I was just comfortable with it, since the age of twelve when my father's employer had given him a copy of Dale Carnegie's *How to Win Friends and Influence People.* I took it and never gave it back. Now, Ringgold, Georgia, and Catoosa County didn't want me, and the rejection was so devastating at a soul level that I considered leaving town.

The Alvin Ridley I remembered from my childhood was a bit on the strange side, but I never felt threatened. He was the same age as my oldest sister, and they were high school seniors when I was born. Furthermore, he was the guy who once sold and serviced televisions and took the task very seriously. He was one of the few TV repairmen with whom my dad liked doing business, because like him, Alvin liked to barter. Between my father sharpening Alvin's lawn mower blades and purchasing or trading something for a Zenith color TV set, they got along well.

My father, McCracken King Poston Sr., or "Mac," a Chattanooga foundryman by trade, was responsible for providing for my mother and us kids, which, by the time I arrived, numbered six, when he was only thirty-six years old. They fed us from a huge garden in which we all worked. Daddy never bought a new car in his life and always haggled, even when it was neither appropriate nor warranted. One of Daddy's deals was buying our color Zenith console television from Alvin, already by then a very strange individual who seemed to be paranoid about the world around him. Alvin was somewhat of an outsider, and seemed a little slow on the uptake, but in the 1970s he was going at his new Zenith TV Sales & Service franchise with great gusto.

Back in the day when we could get only three Chattanooga channels (3, 9, and 12), my dad purchased the television set from Alvin, and in our exuberance, my sisters and I wore off the plastic tuner knob. Pliers worked just fine for me, but Daddy had other ideas. Alvin visited our home, replaced the tuning knob, and gave me what I remember as a scolding lecture on how to turn a tuner knob on a TV. I was twelve or thirteen years old, and all I can recall now about that encounter is that I thought he smelled funny, and when he saw I was watching live wrestling, he claimed to have met Andre the Giant.

Years later, Alvin's brief attempt at local politics branded him as even more of an outsider. In 1984, in the midst of his angst about his father's passing and his displaced blame for it, he ran for sheriff of Catoosa County. In 1981, his father, Bill Ridley, was in a seemingly minor accident while driving Alvin's company truck. When Bill died of pancreatic cancer within two years, Alvin created a theory of causation that would have made Rube Goldberg proud, claiming that the minor accident had "killed" his father, by "worrying him to death." Litigation ensued, and then Alvin ran for Sheriff in 1984 after a deputy levied on Alvin's 1977 Chevy van for one of the defendant's counterclaims in the bizarre litigation.

*   *   *

I was already working in other campaigns, so the love of politics was already in my blood. I remember him very earnestly mounting the podium at the big 1984 candidate rally on the courthouse steps, carrying a tape recorder. I was actually impressed how at first he silenced his would-be hecklers by playing the national anthem, which he had recorded from WDEF-TV's nightly sign-off. Even his detractors became silent and removed their hats. But then, as Alvin spoke and his conspiracy theories unwound, the snickers resumed. Predictably, Alvin lost. He got fewer than three hundred votes.

2

On the way to the courthouse to file the divorce papers as promised, I instinctively grabbed a copy of the *Catoosa County News*. GOP SURPRISES DEMOCRATS HERE was the headline. I scanned the article: "Poston, challenging incumbent Nathan Deal (*R*-Lula) for the 9th Congressional District, failed to win Catoosa County by almost 300 votes." Catoosa County, my own home.

But momentarily, another door of opportunity seemed to be opening up.

I was invited to President Clinton's second inauguration by my good friend—the newly elected U.S. senator Max Cleland. Max and I had worked together when I was in the Georgia House of Representatives, and he was Georgia's secretary of state. We both ran in 1996 on the issue that I sponsored and he championed, the "Ethics in Government Act of 1992." It brought groundbreaking, for Georgia, new lobbying registration and reporting laws. He won running on the issue, and I lost. We met at the beautiful Northwest Washington, DC, home of Bill Stuckey, a former congressman from Georgia.

Max, a triple amputee from the Vietnam War, told me as the Democratic senator, he got to make appointment recommendations to the president. A mutual friend, his body man William Perry, witnessed our conversation in one of Congressman Stuckey's parlors.

"United States Attorney for the Northern District of Georgia is one of those appointments," he continued. "And you are the best person I could think of for the job."

I told him on the spot that I would do it. I didn't even need to think about it. I still had an Atlanta apartment. In the ten weeks since the election, I had yet to try to start up my moribund law practice.

"Well, it's a process that has to take place," Max said, "but you need to put in for it."

My spirits were lifted, but not for long. While it somehow got out that Senator Max Cleland had encouraged me about the appointment, forces in Atlanta clearly didn't want to see the young man who took on his own leadership at the state capitol for ethics reform be vested with the powers of a federal prosecutor.

"I'm getting a lot of pushback," Max told me in a call later.

Although I knew that something or someone or scores of "someones" were pushing me out of contention, I was only halfway expecting the cold reception that I got in the meeting with the committee to recommend a short list of candidates to the senator, who then would make recommendations to the president.

"Sit down, Mr. Poston," the committee chair said.

The committee chair, a man whose law firm had made untold amounts of money doing business with Max when he was our former Georgia secretary of state, led the few questions I got with one I couldn't believe I was hearing.

"Mr. Poston, I remember reading in the newspaper that at some point during the battles for the ethics bill, you had been stricken with diabetes"; then he asked, "So, do you think you are up for the rigors of this job?"

I uttered something like a yes, but mumbled also that I found it odd that a committee appointed by a triple amputee would lead with a disability question. I left, knowing that I had nowhere to go but Ringgold, Georgia. I needed to start actually practicing law again.

I was used to jump-starting my law practice because I had done it every year at the end of each session of the Georgia General Assembly. Assessing my own situation, Catoosa County had gained ten thousand new citizens since my first election. Development was going full blast. It was becoming a different place than when I grew up. I was different now, too, with a line running from my right front pocket to a port and cannula that put synthetic insulin into my body. This gave me something I should micromanage, but of all things, I was less compliant with my health—drinking to excess, then ricocheting to avoiding alcohol, for weeks or months even. I couldn't even be a consistent alcoholic, if that's what I was setting out to achieve.

At some point, I met Alison Vaughn, out in Chattanooga where she was with a friend. We started dating, but as these things usually went with me, it did not last beyond a few weeks. I slowly started up my law practice, which had been dead for over a year since I ran for congress.

October 4, 1997, began as a rare lazy Saturday. My team, the University of Georgia Bulldogs were playing, but I was too hungover for the two-hour drive to Athens. An early riser by genetics, I drove into Ringgold to continue reintroducing myself to my community, starting with the coffee gang at Hardee's on Alabama Road.

The news was already buzzing—about a dead woman found at Crazy Alvin Ridley's house. As the news came in waves throughout the day, I heard Ridley was saying that she was his *wife*. I had no idea he had a wife, but I really hadn't given it much thought. The Ringgold folks who seemed to know everything about everyone were shocked, though.

What did surprise me, however, was seeing the elusive Alvin Ridley as he walked right by me on LaFayette Street, the following Monday morning, the first time I had seen him in the light in the few years since I had confronted him about John Howard's monthly check. Dressed in sagging, dirty clothes, he looked pitiful. We only made brief eye contact, but I nodded as he went toward the post office, and I headed to the back of the courthouse complex.

The next morning, Tuesday, I saw him again, launching from the phone stand on LaFayette Street, the one they were saying he called 911 from, the previous Saturday morning after driving right by an ambulance at the fire station one-half of a mile from his front door. This morning, he headed my way again. I let him pass in front of me, again nodding to him.

Wednesday came, and the same interception of our paths was about to happen a third time. I realized that he was leaving the phone stand at the exact time he would need to meet me. It seemed he was waiting for me. I tested this theory by stopping in my tracks, which caused him to stop and awkwardly turn around. He looked confused. I resumed, and he turned back on track. This time, at the corner of Nance Lane and LaFayette Street, I spoke.

"Mr. Ridley, I'm sorry for your loss," I said, expecting no response and for him to pass by.

He stopped dead still. "I can't take it anymore. The sheriff has worried us all to death, my father, my mother, and now my wife!"

"Well, I'm sorry," I repeated, not knowing what else to say.

"Now they's harassing me and searching my place. Her family's talking and getting them to harass me. People are talkin' about my wife."

"I know exactly how you feel," I said, remembering the congressional campaign.

He stopped. My inside joke seemed to change his demeanor from anger to hurt. His face screwed up like a child's as he lamented the slights he and his wife allegedly took from untold numbers of "officials," apparently in local government.

I offered to provide legal advice, pointed back toward the converted ranch home-now-law office that I shared with Kevin Silvey and Mike Giglio, and invited him to come see me. "Just don't talk to the detectives if they try to turn this thing against you." I didn't know then that it was too late, and that he would go meet with them again today, or that his wife of thirty-one years was to be buried that afternoon.

The next time I heard from him was a series of wild phone calls at home, sometimes very late at night. He said my father had given him my number. I told him I would only meet him at the office, and that he needed to make an appointment. As the weeks went by and nothing seemed to be happening, the calls tapered off. In our last conversation, I promised I'd come see him if I learned he had been arrested.

Alison came back into my life and into my home in late October

1997. My practice was never to reveal whom I was even speaking to, professionally, so I never mentioned my talks with Alvin Ridley.

As with any new relationship, I had to broach some embarrassing family situations. I had the sister with whom I had not spoken in a while, ever since I hyper-controlled and micromanaged my congressional campaign into the ground after letting her son, my nephew, go from the campaign. And for what? I still lost, and now I had lost connection with family as well.

The second one was more apparent, even obvious.

"It was nice to meet you, Melanie," my dear father said after being introduced to Alison as he reeled out of the room.

"I don't even know a Melanie!" I insisted to Alison.

It was hard even in my late thirties to disclose my father's alcoholism. It had affected all of us in different ways. I left my U.T. Chattanooga college dorm in 1979 to come home and help my mother manage him. Two years later, in my internship at the local district attorney's office, I learned that my father was about to be indicted for commodity fraud. A child of the Great Depression, he drunkenly used my grandmother's name and applied for and received more "government cheese" for her than she was allotted. Horrified and embarrassed, I worked out a deal for everyone charged with that to pay back the overage and avoid indictment.

At least the tragic issue of our father and his distressingly deteriorating condition gave my five sisters and me something to talk about. We needed to act, and act fast. And for the first time, we did an intervention. We admitted our father to a hospital just across the state line in East Ridge, Tennessee. I made up with my sister and nephew and we presented a united front.

During the hospitalization, Alison and I, now making future plans, went to Graysville to have a traditional New Year's Day dinner with my mother. We had just sat down to dinner when the hospital called.

"Oh no," said my mother, the sweetest person in the world, especially to strangers on the phone. "Oh, my, yes, I will come there soon," she said, and put the phone receiver down on its cradle. "It's your father," she said. I followed her into another room. "Some things are happening," she told me. "They said we have to have someone with him at all times now."

I insisted that I take the first shift of babysitting my father, who was apparently having some strange acting-out issues. As much as I had ever seen him drink in my whole life, he was never an out-of-control drunk, never the Hollywood stereotype trope of a Southern alcoholic male: drunk in the white wife-beater undershirt. He was a sweet, kind, and loving man—a sad, slurred-speech, falling-asleep drunk, who never got physically or verbally abusive toward a soul. That didn't make it any easier. In fact, it made it harder.

When I got to the hospital, the first thing I noticed was that they had him restrained in the bed. He was very disturbed.

I opened the conversation with a simple, "What's wrong, Daddy?"

He winced and pulled at the restraints. "I don't know why they have me here, or what I'm doing here!"

This concerned me. He knew before that he was in the hospital.

"Well, your drinking had gotten bad, and—"

"But why am I in a bowling alley?" he interrupted.

I didn't have an immediate answer to that one.

We argued for a while, something we had been doing all of my life when he was drinking. At some point in my early teens, I decided if you can't beat 'em, join 'em, and had been swinging between extreme periods of binge drinking and strict sobriety ever since.

He finally calmed down enough for me to loosen the restraints to let him go to the bathroom.

"I just want to show you one thing, son." He bolted toward the door and opened it before I jumped up. He stopped at the open door and asked, "Why is there a bowling alley out here?"

I looked down the long institutional hallway, halfway hoping to see a set of ten-pins to justify this nonsense.

"What in the hell is he on?" I asked the nurse. "He's *never* acted like this before."

"Well, he was given Ambien," the nurse said, "He apparently doesn't tolerate it well."

"You think?" I could not help the sarcasm.

"By the way, what's his wife's name?" the nurse asked.

"My mother's name is Barbara," I told her, "but he calls her 'Bobbie.' Has he been calling for her?"

"The reason we called," she said, "was that he walked into another patient's room, and started saying 'Scoot over, Bobbie' as he tried to squeeze into bed with her."

I felt bad for the traumatized patient, but could not suppress a laugh.

With the Ambien out of his system, the next day and night were wonderful with my dad. I shared with him that I'd been "meeting" with Alvin Ridley: "Not like in the office, just on the street."

"Alvin is a good man," my father said. "He's odd now, very odd, but I don't think he would ever hurt a fly." He added, "He just thinks differently."

"I'm not even sure anything will come of it," I shared. "I haven't heard any word on the street about him in weeks."

He was more clearheaded than he had been in a long while, particularly for this hour of the day. We had some honest conversations together.

I had probably the first long adult conversations that I ever had about my father's drinking with him when he wasn't already drunk or getting there. He was amenable to treatment, and Dr. William Findley was going to try a new drug on him, one that would hopefully curb his addiction.

3

*A*lison and I married in the first week of May 1998, a second marriage for each of us. We both wanted to make having a family our priority. Suddenly it seemed all her close friends were popping up pregnant. With every month passing, our frustration grew. But we enjoyed travel, and, settling into the house that I had owned for seven years, we hosted lots of pool parties, and bought a new light green Ford Explorer, primarily for my wife's use, which was brand new from the factory, with good-looking Firestone Wilderness AT tires.

These were, of course, the very tires that were eventually recalled by Bridgestone, the owner of Firestone, after scores of fatal tread separation accidents, but not before one blew out on us in Atlanta on the way to a Braves game. Considering ourselves fortunate, on Monday, June 29, 1998, we limped the car on its spare to Ken Abney's tire place in Ringgold.

An old truck was being towed away as we pulled in.

We started talking about tires, but Ken Abney couldn't contain himself. "Do you know whose truck that is?"

I said I did not.

"It's Alvin Ridley's truck! He was just arrested out there for locking up and killing his wife!"

I felt a sudden queasiness.

"I've got to go into the office," I told Alison. I took her home, explaining I wanted to shop around for the tires. I hadn't told her about my earlier encounters with Alvin Ridley. I drove to the Catoosa County Jail.

When I pressed the intercom button at the metal door, it was answered by someone in the control room. "It's Poston from across the street. I'm here to see Mr. Alvin Ridley," I said over the intercom. I waited for the buzzing that indicated the electronic door bolt was opening.

Instead of the irate man whom I saw on the street several times, Alvin was quiet.

"I promised I would come, and here I am," I told him. He still said nothing.

I got out of him that while he had assets, none of them, unfortunately, were in his actual name, never having been transferred from his deceased parents.

"My shop is in my name," he suddenly seemed to remember. That building was a mere shell, with a giant hole in the roof that you could see looking in the windows. It was a disaster.

"What's its tax value?" I asked.

"I don't know," he said.

"Are the taxes paid up?"

This clearly offended him. "I pay my taxes!"

I told him if the district attorney didn't agree to a bond, it could take up to a month to get a superior court judge to hear a motion for one. I also told him I would have to get a court order that allowed him to post his own property bond, which is usually not allowed unless ordered.

"I've got my cats inside," he said.

"Okay, maybe you could sign your keys out to me, and I'll make sure they're fed."

"Naw." He shook his head. "Just get me a bond and get me out."

Now I felt real pressure, knowing he had cats that were stuck in his house.

I called our district attorney, Herbert E. "Buzz" Franklin. I had known Buzz from before I was a lawyer, as he was an assistant district attorney here when I was a college intern, both of us working under the then–district attorney David L. "Red" Lomenick. I was even closer friends with Buzz's younger brother, Jim, from our time together in Athens at the University of Georgia School of Law.

Buzz agreed to a conference call with Judge Ralph Hill. On it, I managed to convince them both that Mr. Ridley should get a bond he could afford, and that he needed to use his building to make it. But I had to wait until the morning to get proof he paid his property taxes.

The next morning, I delivered a filed copy of the signed bond order to the jail. Alvin Ridley was given his few belongings, in a clear plastic bag. He said little as we walked out.

"I'm taking you to get your truck," I said. He said nothing on the short drive to the impound lot at Sexton's service station.

I went home to explain to my wife of six weeks that I had not only been advising Alvin Ridley for eight months, but that I had just gotten him out of jail. She would have known soon enough, later that night, when I got one of the old late-night screaming calls, like the ones that I used to get from him the previous October.

Even from a distance from the handset, Alison could hear him screaming and berating me.

"Listen, I got you out in less than twenty-four hours!" I reminded him.

"Twenty-six hours," he responded.

Finally I found a moment. "Mr. Ridley, I know that you and your wife were very private people, right?"

"Yeah," he said.

"Well, you are disrespecting my wife's privacy by calling us late at night and screaming at me," I said. "Our attorney-client relationship, if there is to be one, has some ground rules. Number one, no calls at night at home, got it?"

"Yeah," he reluctantly answered.

"Okay, and in exchange, here's what I'm going to give to you," I told him. "You don't have to make an appointment. Just come by the office anytime you think I'm there. I'll stop whatever I'm doing to see you. You will be my most important client—that is, if I'm appointed to represent you."

This seemed to satisfy him. I wasn't sure that it satisfied Alison, who, having heard this exchange, looked terrified.

After another media deluge regarding Ridley's release, claiming that Alvin had threatened a deputy, Buzz wanted to revisit the issue of bond. I quickly agreed to new conditions on behalf of my not-yet client.

August 1998

The *National Examiner* tabloid screamed SICKO HOLDS HIS WIFE HOSTAGE FOR 30 YEARS THEN KILLS HER . . . COPS CHARGE. It was mostly allegations from Virginia's sister Linda Barber, but some of the descriptions hit too close to home for my comfort. Calling Alvin Ridley "a hard faced loner," the article restated an allegation that he had first called the funeral home to come get his wife's body.

I read on, with the coroner and sheriff also piling on the bad news. Sheriff Phil Summers hinted that the investigation might include the exhumation of Alvin's mother, Minnie Ridley.

The article ended stating that the trial was scheduled for September, next month. From the perspective of the first week of August, to me this was more horrifying than any of the allegations I was reading.

I had very little to go on at this point. I finally got him to come into my office, in early August. He still wouldn't make an appointment, but my granting him special "drop-in" status had done the trick. We discussed having a psychological evaluation, and that I would take him to the judge to sign up for an appointed lawyer. Since we had a working relationship, he could request that it be me.

I took Alvin to Judge Ralph Van Pelt's office to do just that. But the court had more information than I did. "I'm sorry, Mr. Ridley, the detectives just left. They told me about your quarter-million-dollar piece of property near the lake in Chattanooga. You do not qualify for appointed counsel."

I was dumbstruck, and looked to Alvin. *There must be a mistake,* I thought.

"Mama didn't ever want me to sell that property," he said.

We were going to have to make other arrangements.

On Thursday, August 6, Alvin again dropped in, repeating the same things that he was saying every other day. Benita Jay, the shared secretary for all three lawyers in the building, stuck her head into my office.

"Congressman Deal just called you, and said he wanted to talk to you."

This was a complete surprise, a call from my last political opponent, Congressman Nathan Deal. Former Democrat Nathan Deal, now Republican Nathan Deal. I had not spoken to him since conceding the race after he dispatched my challenge in November 1996. Oddly, that same night, I also encountered this strange man now sitting across the table from me. I took the message slip from Benita.

Alvin sat up straighter, as if this call was about him. I could tell from his rants and what he used to post on the missives that for every ounce of suspicion he had for local and state government, there was always a counterweight of hope from the three branches of the *federal* government.

Alvin said, "Ain't you goin' to call the congressman back?"

I had no idea what my former opponent was calling me about. Maybe he wanted to make peace by asking my opinion on some big issue, or to ask me to serve in some citizen capacity to advise him on some matter. Then I thought, *Who am I kidding?* I had somehow accomplished pissing off the entire political spectrum of Georgia, both sides.

"Let's call him back right now," I told Alvin, assuming that maybe he would be impressed that his lawyer was getting a call from a U.S. congressman.

I held the phone to my ear as I called the number he had left with my receptionist. When I got through to the operator, the familiar voice of the man I had known for a decade came on.

"Congressman," I said. "It's good to hear from you."

Never being known for pleasantries, Nathan Deal got directly to the point of his call. "I need you to keep Alvin Ridley away from my congressional offices," he said sternly.

"Well," I awkwardly fumbled, not wanting Alvin to hear the reason of the call. "I'll certainly pass that along."

"This is notice to keep him away, please," he said. "He scares the ladies there."

I thanked him for his call, not revealing that the subject was eagerly waiting on the other side of the table from me. Then it occurred to me, Alvin was probably hoping that his U.S. representative was calling about his troubles and was going to come riding up on a white horse and fix everything.

"Alvin," I said, "let's walk out to your car."

I walked him out, struggling to find the words. I could break his spirit if I said this wrong. *How do I tell him he can no longer count on help from that branch of the federal government?*

I paused, thought, and said, "Alvin, you know that damn Nathan Deal guy *hates* me, don't you?"

"He does?" Alvin stared.

"Yes, he does," I said, "and I'm afraid that it is now starting to affect you."

"Really?" Alvin asked, bewildered.

"He hates me so much," I said, "you know, from the election two years ago." Alvin looked a bit confused, as he knew that I had been routed.

"He hates me so much that he said if me or you ever came to his congressional offices again, he would have us both arrested." I felt that misery might love some company.

As Alvin looked down, I said, "But you know what?"

"What?" he asked.

"Please stay away from his offices and work hard to help me represent you in this case, and after we win . . ."

He leaned in, listening as my voice softened to an almost whisper, as if I were telling him something special, and secret.

"After we win," I promised, looking around to make sure no one was within earshot, "I will tell you where he *lives,* and you can go right up to his door and see him at his house!"

This seemed to satisfy him, for now. He got into his car and left.

The next day, Friday, August 7, was a big day for Alvin Ridley. It was the day his home phone that I was providing would be reconnected. I took my camera, hoping that in the hubbub of having a phone reinstalled in his house, I could slip in and get critical photos of where Virginia lived and died. Alvin, of course, had other plans, making me wait outside until the guy from the Ringgold Telephone Company came. Then he insisted that the phone be installed on his enclosed porch. None of us were going into the house, it appeared. I was paying the bill, so it was now possible for him to call my Atlanta-based cellphone directly.

Sure enough, over the weekend, and on Monday, I got phone calls every few hours from Alvin, who was increasingly complaining of "chest pains." I knew it was likely just anxiety over what was scheduled for Wednesday, the psychological evaluation, followed by the preliminary hearing in the afternoon.

On the morning of Wednesday, August 12, 1998, I was pleasantly surprised to see Alvin's Dodge K-car parked at my office before anyone else was there.

Dr. Sam Perri arrived. The state psychologist had a disarming manner, and he asked Alvin a series of questions to determine basic competency to stand trial. At the end of the half hour or so for the evaluation, I talked alone with Dr. Perri.

"He's clearly competent to stand trial," Dr. Perri said before I could even ask him. "But," he added, "he's also clearly paranoid." I thanked Dr. Perri, then saw him out to his car, advocating for my client for any sentencing mitigation he might consider putting in the report.

I took Alvin to lunch, mainly just to keep him from disappearing before the preliminary hearing scheduled for that afternoon. I tried to lessen the drama and importance of it to him by saying, "You aren't going to testify. You can sleep through it."

Deputy Magistrate Judge Anthony Peters was the presiding judge. Technically, this hearing was about if the state had probable cause for the case to go to the grand jury for consideration for indictment. For us, it was to see what they had.

The prosecution was the only side the grand jury got to hear. With the rumor mill running so rampant in the media, they'd be ready to indict Alvin before even hearing the evidence.

Buzz was there, but Assistant District Attorney Melodie Bedford called the case: "For purposes of a preliminary hearing, we'd sound the *State* versus *Alvin Eugene Ridley*, charged with murder." She called Detective Dan Bilbrey to the stand.

Detective Bilbrey described that the body had already been removed by the coroner, adding, "And she advised me that upon taking the body up to the morgue, she found signs of petechiae, which are—It's a condition that is found . . . It's associated with asphyxia or some type of smothering, something like that."

Bilbrey related from the coroner, "She indicated that she had known Mr. Ridley for twenty years and had never known him to be married or living with another female."

Almost all of his testimony was based on what the coroner had told him, which was allowed. A good lawyer will never object to hearsay at a preliminary hearing. You want it all to get in so that you have a better idea of the case. Alvin stared ahead, silently. I would have to work on that—his glaring, obvious discomfort.

A cloudburst outside sent torrents of rain on top of the building, making it harder to hear the witness. This was typical for a hot Georgia afternoon.

"She advised me that she was going to have an autopsy performed on Virginia Ridley." Bilbrey continued relating what he learned from the coroner. "She also advised me that Mr. Ridley was very—did not want the autopsy done. However, one was scheduled for the following day down at the Georgia Bureau of Investigation Crime Lab."

The prosecutor asked, "Do you know who performed the autopsy?"

Bilbrey said louder, over the thunderstorm outside, "Dr. Fredric Hellman."

The prosecutor asked, "What does he conclude, as far as his opinion regarding cause of death?"

Bilbrey answered, "His opinion stated that Virginia Ridley died due to asphyxia, and that the petechiae that were found on Mrs. Ridley, even with resuscitation, the petechiae were so excessive that the resuscitation would not account for the amount of petechiae that were present on Mrs. Ridley."

I wrote down "petikei," knowing that it was likely misspelled. I looked over, and Alvin was writing "P.T. Key Eyes," which was actually closer to the way it was being pronounced.

Then the ADA asked her witness about Dr. Hellman's opinion about cause of death.

"Yes, ma'am, he did," Bilbrey answered. "His opinion was Virginia Ridley died at the hands of another person. Further, that she died from either a soft strangulation or a smothering, as in with the aid of a pillow or something like that." He then confirmed that, in his investigation, there was no one else with Virginia at the time of her death other than Alvin Ridley.

Then it was my turn.

"Okay"—I wanted to nail Bilbrey down now, under oath, to keep his description from changing before trial—"did you find anything unusual or remarkable that would give evidence that someone had been barricaded or held hostage or held there? Did you find any evidence that indicated that?"

"No, sir," he answered. *Perfect.* I pressed on. "Okay, you found no evidence of restraint or material evidence of a barricade or anything?"

"No, sir," he answered.

I was ready to move on, feeling good about the cross-examination and nailing the investigator down on these issues.

"I would comment on restraint," Bilbrey interrupted. "What I thought was odd, as well, is upon entering the house, Mr. Ridley had cats, and these cats were all tied around the neck by a string tied to the table, which I thought was very unusual."

What? I thought. *Cats tied to the table?* I tried to maintain a poker face. This could be a problem.

"Okay," I said, hoping to find my footing again. "How many?"

"I believe I saw two," Bilbrey answered.

I pivoted, "Did the medical examiner mention anything about the physical effects of a grand mal seizure?"

"Yes, he did," he said.

Essentially, I was able to determine from Bilbrey that the impetus of the arrest warrant was Dr. Fredric Hellman's crime lab report. That meant after today I needed to start studying these conclusions of Dr. Hellman to see if any part of his decision could have been prejudiced by the onslaught of sheer rumor coming from Northwest Georgia.

"This is a probable cause hearing," Judge Peters said. "Therefore, the court finds the state has, by a probable cause standard, shown the allegations of the warrant. Therefore, the case of the *State of Georgia* versus *Alvin Ridley* is bound over to the grand jury of Catoosa County for indictment." *Not even for the consideration of indictment,* I thought, *bound over for indictment.*

While I considered the preliminary hearing somewhat of a success, to Alvin, it was the opposite. For the next week, he delved into his now predictable delusions of all the conspiracies against him.

The following Wednesday's arrival of the *Catoosa County News* helped. It had an extremely positive spin about the preliminary hearing. All of my comments in the article were directed to one reader, Mr. Alvin Ridley. He brought the article to me at my office, his first visit in a week. POSTON NOT IMPRESSED WITH D.A.'S EVIDENCE AGAINST MR. ALVIN RIDLEY was the headline, and I could not have asked for a better one, as to its effect on the spirit of my client.

Alvin handed me a copy of the newspaper. Evaluating the hearing, I was quoted saying, "I learned that a Ringgold man has been much maligned." Alvin read the whole article to me, and he seemed renewed.

He appeared up for the fight again, but that didn't mean he would let me in his house. "I'll think about it" was his constant refrain when I would ask for access to take photos.

This same week, I also dove into research about petechiae, the tiny little red ruptured blood vessels we had all butchered the name of. Every doctor I spoke to indicated that they could occur even after a hard coughing fit. I had to get some definitive word on these tiny red devils.

I knew of only one place to go, the one local source I knew would have some forensic pathology books. I drove to Summerville, Georgia, to the law office of Bobby Lee Cook. He was by far the most famous lawyer I knew, and was hailed as one of the best criminal defense lawyers in the country. The Matlock character on television was said to have been based on him.

I was graciously received, and in his usual manner, he made me feel welcome. He ushered me to his beautiful law library, a rounded room with two stories of bookshelves, with custom ladders to climb to reach the top shelves. He knew just where to look, and he quickly handed me three forensic pathology books. Full of actual photos of the dead, with heinous wounds and various states of decomposition, these were not books you would leave open on the coffee table.

"Do you mind if I copy some of these articles?" I asked.

"I want you to *take* the books, and use them as long as you need them," Bobby Lee said.

I excitedly thanked him and lugged the huge books to my car.

In each one, I found warnings to forensic pathologists about jumping to conclusions about petechiae. Back at the office, I showed Alvin the provisions and suggested that we might want to consider finding our own forensic pathologist to put on the stand to counter Dr. Hellman.

"What's that?" he asked.

"A forensic pathologist," I answered, the first of many times. Alvin dug into his shirt pocket, always stuffed with his reading glasses, several folded pieces of paper, and various receipts. He put the glasses on, grabbed a pen from the same pocket, and took out one of the folded-up papers.

"Can you spell that?"

And this was the first of countless times that he would ask me to spell it. *"F-O-R-E-N-S-I-C P-A-T-H-O-L-O-G-I-S-T,"* I would dutifully spell out, time and time again.

Alvin insisted that I focus on multiple civil cases he was involved in from 1970 to the mid-1980s. Incredulous about this, I nevertheless promised him I would look at them. Over the next several days, I spent hours in the clerk's office, one day just poring through the bound volumes of the *Catoosa County News*. There I found Alvin's 1984 campaign ad in his run for sheriff of Catoosa County. His entire campaign was a reaction to the sheriff's department's role—their legal duty, actually—in the execution of the writ used in the seizure of Alvin's van. And this occurred due to a counterclaim from Ringgold's chief of police, Charles Land, after being sued by Alvin and his mother over his father Bill's seemingly minor accident in the company truck. The van was returned, as it was taken prematurely, before a judgment. But again, Alvin still hadn't "accepted it back"—now fourteen years since the return of the gray van, it was slowly returning to the earth, on four flat tires, right next to the house.

I found the article, so now I could put a date on it, where Virginia's parents were trying to flush her out by claiming she was "missing." It ran in the local paper in December 1969. An identical article had been put in the Chattanooga afternoon newspaper.

On the last day of August, I stopped by Judge Van Pelt's office and asked his secretary, Cindy Hall, if the judge had left an envelope for me. It was Dr. Perri's evaluation of Alvin Ridley.

I did take immediate exception to one part: ". . . it does appear that he is competent to assist his attorney." *Bullshit!* I thought, as so far that had not been the case.

"His profile also suggests the possibility of a chronic conflict with social rules and other people. Interpersonally, people with similar profiles are reclusive, shy, and insecure in social situations. These individuals relate poorly, feel isolated, lack involvement, and may be withdrawn." He additionally wrote: "It does appear, however, that he does harbor some paranoid ideas."

Nailed it! I thought.

Suddenly my heart turned. Alvin *really* could not help himself, and he had apparently been this way a long time. Maybe he'd been this way all his life?

When I got back to the office, I immediately looked up the word "somatization" from the report. A psychiatric term, it basically means complaining of physical problems when there doesn't seem to be a cause for them, medically.

Wow. That's my client.

I immediately changed my thinking regarding Alvin's constant complaining of his "head-neck-spine-back-tailbone" pain. I better tolerated these issues from there on, but that's not to say that I didn't try, for my own sanity, to show him sometimes that he was physically fine.

Now we were on the cusp of September 1998, with certain indictment, arraignment, motions hearings, and, ultimately, a jury trial looming.

And I had absolutely nothing to work with. However, I suddenly felt a renewal of purpose, thanks to that call from Congressman Nathan Deal. Alvin was now my sole constituent, and I was back in a campaign of sorts.

4

I had been warned by Judge Sam Dills that "people are saying you two deserve each other." Judge Dills was politically adept and had managed to avoid Alvin's ire by buying a television. I did not take his comments as anything but him giving me the truth.

But I was distracted, with a client who rarely showed any confidence in my representation, and with a growing law practice that needed some reorganization. All three lawyers sharing the building on Nance Lane had been sharing a single secretary, Benita Jay. I hired Tammy Hardin away from all three of us to run the juvenile court after I was appointed part-time juvenile court judge. Benita's only help was a high school intern who worked after lunch in a vocational program for seniors. I sat down with Kevin Silvey and Mike Giglio and told them that I needed to get my own secretary, but that I would continue to pay my portion of Benita's salary for the rest of the year.

I asked Kaye Vaughn, my new mother-in-law, if she knew anyone who might be available because she knew a lot of people in office work. She recommended Lori Duckworth, and I asked her to come in for an interview.

Lori was very interested in working as my legal secretary. She was capable and seemed to understand the new office technology. The new desktop computers with monitors were replacing typewriters.

After I offered her the job, Lori shared with me that in the past she had been a victim of domestic violence. I worried a bit, since I didn't want any case or client to trigger any past trauma for her. I asked her, using Alvin's case as an example, if she felt she could give 100 percent to the job, even if a client's case included allegations of domestic violence. She said she could.

Alvin was more wary of Lori than she was of him, as it turned out. Lori's personality was not one to sugarcoat things, and not one to coddle clients—particularly noncompliant ones. And that was exactly what I needed. Alvin, however, kept asking where Benita was, and why Benita wasn't coming back to help us. I explained that Benita was still here, but shifting to work exclusively for the other two lawyers. Before the year was out, Benita would go on to other ventures, and Kevin's and Mike's law offices were then covered by Misty Walker. But Benita and Alvin had formed a special bond, as she had a calming effect with Alvin and I often had her remain in the office during his visits. She promised to continue to help however she could.

As expected, Alvin was indicted by the grand jury on September 14, 1998, the very first day that they were in session. I pored over the document in the clerk's office: *State of Georgia* vs. *Alvin Eugene Ridley, Criminal Action Number 98-CR-00836.* It was interesting how the State of Georgia had decided to charge Alvin. He was charged with: Count One, Murder, alleging that he "did unlawfully and with malice aforethought cause the death of Virginia Ridley, a human being, by suffocating her"; Count Two, Felony Murder, alleging that he "did unlawfully, while in the commission of a felony, to wit: Aggravated Assault, cause the death of Virginia Ridley, a human being, by suffocating her"; and Count Three, Aggravated Assault, alleging that he "did unlawfully make an assault on the person of Virginia Ridley with his hands, deadly weapons in the way and manner used, by suffocating her . . ."

There was no mention of the prevailing rumors of Alvin holding his wife against her will in the basement for decades. *Those were the sensational allegations that directed the world's attention to tiny Ringgold, Georgia,* I thought, *and when they got around to indicting him, these allegations aren't even there?* I was relieved.

The potential sentence was life in prison. Alvin could not survive prison, so even though there was no death penalty being sought in this case, any sentence would be a death sentence to him.

I tried to spin the news to Alvin that afternoon. "The good news," I said, trying to force a smile on my face, "is that there is no false imprisonment charge!" All Alvin saw was murder, felony murder, and aggravated assault. He wasn't impressed. "But you see, Alvin," I begged him to understand, "now this is just a straight-up murder and aggravated assault case."

"I've had it!" he screamed. "They falsely robbed me of any recovery on my wrecked business truck!" A few breaths later, "They illegal seized my business van!" Then some more of his greatest conspiracy hits, including the Division of Family & Children Services (DFCS) trying to take his mother away. "My head-neck-spine-back-tailbone hurts! And they can't force me to go to court if I'm hurtin'—the Constitution says that, and you ought to know that!"

And this was all on Lori Duckworth's first day of work.

Exasperated, I cried, "Oh, *Lord*!" Suddenly silence filled the room. I looked up, and he was bowing his head, his hands clasped. He thought I was starting a prayer. A new strategy was born. I began "praying" my advice to him.

I knew it was just a matter of time before my effectiveness as his lawyer would be challenged. I tried not to take it personally, considering what I had just recently read in his psychological evaluation.

"Let's look at the indictment," I said, in part as diversion. I went over each count, trying to convince Alvin that this case was going to come down to science. "I've been studying these petechiae things," I told him, "I've got some books from Bobby Lee Cook that are going to help us." I tried to make it feel like a team effort, by saying "us" instead of "you."

The rest of the week, we managed the wave of new media reports reacting to the formal indictment, and finally we got back down to trying to work on the case, attorney and client. I thought it might be a good idea to find articles about epilepsy, death, and petechiae. Most of the articles were abstracts, references to medical journal articles that I didn't have access to.

"SUDEP is sudden death in epilepsy," I informed him. Alvin seemed quite sad to learn that this was a thing.

A name was repeated in the most prominent abstracts, and it was quite a name: Braxton Bryant Wannamaker, MD. I read the name aloud to Alvin.

"This is the kind of guy we need." I put him on my list to find later.

But first, we needed to create and file motions. To get all the state discovery, we had to "opt in" to the law, obligating us to share all the defense discovery with the prosecution. I informed Alvin that we were going to "opt in" and very much needed to gather all the discovery we planned to use at trial, every *photograph,* expert report, everything. I used this in my continuing effort, sounding like a broken record, about how I needed to get inside Alvin's house, and inside his long-shuttered business as well.

"I'll think about it" was Alvin's recurring move to put me off.

On Tuesday of the week after indictment, Alvin was already deeply into his now-routine "illness" and citing nonexisting provisions of the U.S. Constitution as it related to his illness. Arraignment was Friday, September 25, and he did not want to go.

On September 21, there was some sad national news about the death of Florence Griffith Joyner, the famous Olympic gold medalist track star. I was always impressed with "Flo-Jo," as she was nicknamed, as a champion on the field and with an incredible style off it. We were almost exactly the same age, and now she was dead at thirty-eight. There would, of course, be an autopsy. I had actually seen Flo-Jo, although she was not competing, at the Atlanta Olympic Games just two years before. I did not know it at the time, but the tragic death of the track star was going to be a very significant development.

Thursday, September 24, the day before arraignment day, Alvin left a phone message that he was "sick and can't come to court tomorrow."

I created forty-four motions, more than I had ever filed in a case before, to file at arraignment. There were the usual demands for preserving and giving us certain evidence, such as reports and statements. However, I feared the only motion the world would notice was one that Alvin had insisted on, a Motion for Disclosure of Electronic Surveillance, because he had convinced himself that the government was listening in on him.

This explained the resumption of late-night phone calls from phone booths. I had to pick my battles, and it was just easier to file it and take the embarrassment than to endanger what little attorney-client relationship that I had managed to build. I did draw the line and told him that I would not file a motion based on his false view that the detectives illegally searched his home—because he had signed a consent for them. Alvin signed a security deed on the old TV shop to secure my representation. I was about to have to pay out money for experts too.

The night before arraignment, I went to Alvin to ensure that he understood that nothing significant was going to happen to him to-morrow. He was in his midfifties, but walked like a man who was close to ninety. His old neck brace was back on, amplifying an odor that was hard to be around.

Friday morning came, and I drove to Inman Street. I was re-lieved to find him there.

Alvin and I drove to the small back lot of the courthouse com-plex. As I pulled up and went around to assist my barely mobile client in getting out of my Jeep, I saw WRCB-TV cameraman Tommy Eason, and he was headed our way. Tommy lived in Ring-gold and went all over for the Chattanooga station. His police scanner gave him an incredible edge on getting to the scene of local breaking-news stories. While he wasn't a reporter, he was often there before his reporter showed up, so he would bark ques-tions from behind the camera, which struck some of his subjects as acerbic, even threatening. He didn't care. His reputation pre-ceded him.

As I opened the door for Alvin, I started to caution, "Here comes Tommy Eason. Make sure you don't . . ." In my peripheral vision, I saw Alvin, neck brace flying off behind him, in a full run, *fast*, going around the right side of the complex. Eason, who was al-ready fiddling with his heavy television news camera, saw this and took off after him. I followed suit, my case file pressed to my side.

Tommy, his camera, and I showed up on the front of the old court-house. Alvin was not to be seen. Tommy couldn't take his camera into the courtroom, so he was trying to figure out where to set up to get us on the way out.

"Well, you know where my Jeep is . . ."

He winked and walked back around the outside of the building.

Before I went inside to look for my client, I saw the familiar image of "Turnaround," the nickname for Ralph Greene, a famil-iar local man who seemed to be constantly walking, always turning at right angles. Today, though, he was standing uncharacteristi-cally still, directly facing in my direction, with both hands clasped together in front of him. A single finger was raised, pointing to-ward his left. I saw part of Alvin's shirt and pants sticking out from behind a tree along Jail Street. I went over, collected my client, re-united him with his neck brace, and walked him into the court-house.

Alvin sat uncomfortably among all the other defendants who showed up for arraignment. When his name was called, we quickly walked up to the bench. Judge Van Pelt was presiding.

I filed my forty-four motions and wrote "NOT" in all caps in the blank on the indictment just before the word "guilty," to show Alvin for certain that we were in the fight. He signed as the defendant with all three of his names, Alvin Eugene Ridley, presumably be-cause all three were on the indictment.

Judge Van Pelt informed us that he would hear our motions and, since there were so many, rule on them at a specially set motions hearing on the following Tuesday, September 29.

Without any state discovery yet, the weekend after arraignment was a relatively quiet weekend. Alvin's seemingly baseless ailments, which Dr. Perri had called "somatization," were increasing in sever-ity and in volume. The night calls started up again, only this time to my cellphone, which I had to keep on for juvenile court emergen-cies.

On Monday morning, I walked to the district attorney's office and picked up the state discovery for the case. Before long, Alvin was limping into the office, barely able to walk, singing the tired old tune about the Constitution and what it supposedly said about getting to skip court if you are "feeling badly."

He did make one request—that he be allowed to drive himself to my office before the motions day hearings. That was fine with me.

The morning of September 29 was warm, and rain was in the morning forecast. I tried to call Alvin on my drive to the office, but wasn't concerned that he didn't answer. He might already be there, I hoped. None of his vehicles were around the office, but I was early, so I left Lori with instructions to walk him straight over when he came. He did not show at 9:00 a.m.

"Your Honor," I said when Judge Van Pelt entered the room from the door behind the bench that led to his chambers. "I'm having a client problem, but I can attest that he wasn't feeling well last night."

Judge Van Pelt had certainly warned me what he wanted to do about a client who doesn't show up to court, but the more likely relief would be to dismiss all forty-four motions I had filed, and that could create a potential appellate mess.

"It's a little after nine a.m.," the judge said. "You have until the afternoon session at one-thirty p.m. to find him and get him here. Otherwise, he will be staying at the jail, where I will always have access to getting him to court, and he will be staying in the jail until we have his trial."

Lori and I started scrambling to find him, going to his house first.

Finally I thought to call the Chattanooga VA Clinic. When I had first taken him there earlier this year, he had signed a form that allowed me to call and discuss his treatment with the staff there.

"Yes, sir, he's here," whispered an operator, as if she didn't like the idea of telling me, or maybe he was within earshot.

"Can you tell me why he's there?" I asked.

"His chief complaint is that he was bitten by a giant spider," she said, "but he keeps saying something about court."

"Yes, he's supposed to be in court today," I said. "Please delay letting him go, because if I don't have him back to Ringgold by after lunch, he'll be put back in jail."

I sped up I-75 N to I-24 W and was at the clinic in less than thirty minutes. I walked in to find him sheepishly sitting in the waiting room, looking at me in resignation.

"Get in my car, and I'll bring you back to your truck after court," I said. "Either that, or plan on going back to jail. It's that simple, Alvin."

He winced with every move, seeming to stumble with his first few steps, and got into my car.

I pretty much let him have it the whole way down to Ringgold. I attribute some of my over-the-top reaction to my dropping blood sugars. I did grab a copy of his intake to show the court that he had complained of a spider bite, although it didn't identify it as either a "giant" spider, or a giant figment of his imagination. We were in the courtroom before 1:30 p.m.

When Judge Van Pelt entered the courtroom, I thought it best to explain my client's earlier absence.

"Your Honor, I found Mr. Ridley at the VA Clinic in Chattanooga," I said, "and he reported to them that he was there because he was 'bitten by a giant spider.' I have proof here of the complaint he gave them." I think I might have used finger air quotes on the spider part. I braced myself to take some of the heat.

Before Judge Van Pelt responded, while looking at Alvin he seemed to lose the color in his face. I turned around to see my client, standing there making his own case, his shirt pulled up, revealing near his navel, a huge, volcanic-looking insect bite wound. It was most definitely a bite, and from what I could assess with a layman's diagnosis, it must have been a big-ass spider. Perhaps even "giant".

"Mr. Ridley, I'm going to let you go home and rest and recover," the court pronounced. "We can reconvene on this case for the hearing of Mr. Ridley's motions on Thursday, October 1. Mr. Ridley, be here on Thursday to hear those motions."

I was still aghast at what I had just seen, but I felt worse about the berating I had been giving him the whole ride down from Chattanooga and up until we sat down in the courtroom. That made for a long, quiet ride back to the VA Clinic to get his truck. I apologized again.

The next morning, I got permission from the court for Alvin to waive his appearance at the motions hearing. "It would have to be a very well-drawn waiver, in writing, and filed with the clerk," the judge said.

I called Alvin excitedly. "Alvin, I've got a way for you to miss court tomorrow, so you can stay in and take care of yourself an extra day." He didn't sound as interested as I hoped he would have, that he could skip out on a court date.

"All right," he finally said. I told him I would be working on the necessary waiver that he would need to sign and asked if he could come by the office before the end of the day to sign it.

"All right," he said again.

I began working on the "waiver" that would purportedly allow him to miss motion hearings. I couldn't find a form exactly on point, so I just started drafting one. Mostly, it was an affidavit for Alvin to sign. To get his signature, I added lines like "That I was bitten by a spider, and that I have a number of other ailments that might jeopardize my attendance at the motion hearings now rescheduled for October 1, 1998." As I waited on him to come to the office to sign it, I added a few more lines. I made a signature line for Alvin, and since it was to be an affidavit, I would have to serve as the notary.

Still, no Alvin, and the office was closing. I called his phone and got a busy signal. I waited a couple more hours, not wanting to push him, looking over the motions that would be heard in the morning. His home phone, the one that I was paying for, was still giving a busy signal.

I called home and told Alison why I wasn't there yet.

"Just don't go to his house, okay?" was her only request. While I no longer feared Alvin, at all, others still did. I promised that he was coming to the office, and I would not be going to his house.

I called the operator and asked if she could test his phone line. She reported that the line was off the hook. *Damn.* I had to strategize. If he simply failed to appear in the morning, the court would surely order him to jail. I needed to resolve this issue.

But at the same time, I thought, *What if something is wrong with him?* I didn't want to do a law enforcement–led "welfare check," as they did to him when they just wanted to interrogate him the day after his wife died. I decided to call for an ambulance, through the

911 operator, but insisted that there be no law enforcement involved. "And no sirens," I insisted.

That day I was in the green Ford Explorer, Alison's car, and I
drove slowly to Inman Street, to wait on the ambulance. When it
did come, with lights flashing but no sirens, I introduced myself to
the two emergency medics, Thomas Sainthill and Christopher Guf-
fey, who were very nice and understanding that I had a "difficult"
client. I'm not sure if they knew who he was, but I explained the situation.

"Basically," I told them, "he's complaining of several ailments, so
we need to check him out." Then I added, "But he's also paranoid,
so I may end up being the patient if we don't handle this just
right."

Meanwhile, in Graysville, six or so miles to the north, just inside
the Georgia state line, my father was listening to his police scanner,
as he did throughout each night as he slept. He called my house
number and got Alison on the phone. "Well, I just heard they just
sent an ambulance to Alvin Ridley's house," he told her, "and they
said there was a green Ford Explorer there." *Busted.* I ignored the
calls on my phone. I was mainly worried about getting shot.

I walked very slowly up the crumbling steps, and when I got to
the door, I stepped to the left of it, while knocking loudly, calling,
"Alvin? Alvin, it's *me!*" I could hear something inside. Slowly the
door opened, and the red and blue lights from the silent ambulance reflected on his face. His hair was all disheveled, which was
unusual. He had obviously fallen asleep.

"Alvin, your phone is off the hook," I said.

"No, it ain't," he responded, while staring past me at the ambulance lights.

"Alvin, look at it," I said, pointing into the porch to the wall-
mounted phone, with its receiver off the hook.

I walked Alvin to the street, where the ambulance waited.

Taking advantage of the situation, I turned to the ambulance at-
tendants. "While you guys are here"—I pulled out the affidavit for
Alvin to sign—"would you witness his signature?" I drew two extra
lines on the sheet of paper.

Alvin, bewildered, went ahead and signed the document, with

my assurances that he could now "sleep in" and not worry about coming to court in the morning. The medics signed as witnesses, and I signed and applied my notary seal when I left and dropped it off at the office before heading home, to explain myself.

But I felt good for the first time in months. I was going to get to represent my client tomorrow morning, October 1, 1998, perhaps for the first time without his direct interference.

5

October 1, 1998

I woke up with a sense of renewal. I had to apologize to my wife
again for going to Alvin's house at night after promising her that I
would not. I also figured the fact that my father was up late listening to his police scanner and called her meant that he was probably
in good shape. I drove to the office and picked up the case files for
the motion hearings. I had the freshly signed affidavit of Alvin Ridley, which waived his presence, on the top so I could file it as soon
as I got there.

I walked over with Lori and made sure I had everything where I
needed it on the defense side of the adjoining counsel tables in the
small courtroom. Several other lawyers, all waiting to have their
motions for their cases heard, sat in the jury box and on the pew directly behind the counsel tables.

Because Judge Van Pelt had specially set our hearings for Tuesday, September 29, two days ago, we would not be getting in the
way here if things had gone as planned. Thanks to one convincing
"giant spider bite," my forty-four motions were now crashing the
regular motions day calendar.

My colleagues from the Lookout Mountain Judicial Circuit Bar
were not envious of me with this case or with this client. Many

shook their heads, smiling as they passed, realizing from just the stories they were hearing around the courthouse that I had been suffering greatly.

I kept Alvin's waiver in hand. As soon as the court called the day into order and announced, "I'm going to hear these Ridley motions first," I jumped up and presented the affidavit by which Alvin could miss these hearings, sharing with the court some sense of how difficult it had been to obtain.

The judge looked confused as I handed him the waiver of Alvin Ridley's appearance, saying, "He's here, Mr. Poston."

I was at once hit with simultaneous optical and olfactory senses. Alvin had come in while my back was turned and was sitting at counsel table. He handed me a document, saying only, "File this."

More giggling rippled around the courtroom as I stared at the single sheet of white paper that had been processed through his typewriter, bearing the same worn typeface many of us were familiar with from reading his postings on the old TV shop. In the uneven, familiar type, written in all caps, it was styled and spelled incorrectly as a MOTION OF DISMISSAEL; it alleged, with numerous misspellings, that an illegal search had occurred, an "ILLEGAL TAKING MERCHANDIST AND ARTICLE'S OUT OF THE HOME."

Lowering my voice just to keep the certainly delighted persons at the prosecution table from hearing this attorney-client communication, I gritted my teeth, emphasizing key words, and seethed, "You *signed* a *waiver* and *invited* them *in*!"

"Just file it," he said.

"Just stay in your seat," I told him. "You left off the certificate of service," I smarted off to him. "Here, let me *help* you." I handwrote, *I certify that I am giving Buzz Franklin a copy as soon as I get one* on the bottom of the page, and handed it to the clerk to my right after I signed my name. The deputy clerk smiled as she took it from me and left to make stamped copies for everyone.

I was rattled, and it took me a while to settle down. How was I going to get through a trial with this client? Normally, things that I would let slide were now lying on the edge of my last nerve.

We went through the numerous motions and, predictably, we

lost most of them. Of course, the court *granted* the one about electronic surveillance, which made Alvin act even more smug. I think the court did it as a joke. It was an easy request, telling the government not to do what all but one knew they were not doing.

I was exhausted and drained at the end of all the hearings on the various motions, having been active in hearings all day. I walked with Alvin to his car, still smarting a bit from my wasted time the night before and his out-of-time late motion.

"At least you didn't call it an *emotion*," I said to him, referring to his pleadings in the 1980s litigation. Alvin had demanded me to study the old civil litigation on file in the Clerk's Office. I argued that it had nothing to do with a murder case. "But I didn't kill my wife," he would protest, adding "but they did illegal-sieze my van in that civil case!"

"I won the one about them not putting me under surveillance," he crowed, as if he had argued it, and proud that he brought it up and convinced me to include it. Funny thing, when it did come up, Judge Van Pelt just smiled and said, "Granted." I was becoming the butt of jokes in the legal community.

I thought I might become just another of the long history of lawyers who started trying to represent Alvin Ridley for one thing or another in cases that always ended with them leaving or being fired. I was fed up and exhausted.

"Look, Alvin, we have to do some things differently from here on," I told him. "First I don't know why you aren't letting me in your house. You let everyone in last October, and they're the ones working against you. The one person who is working for you hasn't been able to get inside, and I need to get inside with my camera."

At least he seemed to be listening.

"And I'm going to ask for a continuance, and I hope the court grants it," I said, "but . . . we can't operate this way."

Then my frustration got the better of me, and it got personal. "And, Alvin, I know down at Truck City, they have showers, and you know where the Laundromat is. I need you to go to both. I'm not sure you've bathed since I've been working with you, and it'll be a year next Tuesday. It's just hard to sit there next to you and breathe . . . buddy." I added the awkward term of endearment at the end because I immediately wished I hadn't said these things as they were coming out of my mouth. I swore to myself that I would never bring up his personal hygiene again.

"Hey, I've got a rat that lives in my car!" he said, transitioning as if we had been just exchanging pleasantries. This somehow made me feel even worse for jumping on him.

"Oh, really?" I asked. "How do you know you have a rat that lives in your car?"

"Well," he started explaining, "I've seen him in it, and he eats any food I have left in here, and he does number twos all over the place."

Wondering how he knew the gender of the rodent, I asked, "I don't know. Should you put a trap in there?"

"Oh no, I've got it all figured out," he said.

There was silence, until I broke it, asking, "Oh, okay, what do you do then?"

His expression became serious, as if he were walking me through something very technical that I had to follow, point by point.

"You sit down in the car, and you get real quiet," he started to explain. "Then, all of the sudden, you just scream as loud as you can. That rat will get right out. It happens every time now, and he waits on me to get back home before he gets back in the car."

I was thinking maybe Dr. Perri needed a demonstration, and then he might change that opinion on competency.

The next day, a Friday, I called Alvin to come in to see new material that I'd just been served. He hadn't changed, literally, wearing the same clothes again from yesterday. I was almost happy that he'd ignored my outburst about his hygiene. I still felt bad about it.

The district attorney had served on me a great deal of new material. One, a supplemental state witness list, added forty-five new witnesses that I needed to learn about. Another, and the one I dreaded the most, a document titled "Notice of Prosecution's Intent to Present Evidence of Similar Transactions." This was giving us notice that Buzz intended to bring in some evidence of arguably extraneous and definitely troubling matters to the attention of the jury.

There were three issues listed on the notice of evidence that the prosecution intended to introduce at trial:

1. On or about the last ten years, the Defendant did, in violation of the personal liberty of Minnie Ridley, confine said person without legal authority in Catoosa County, Georgia.

2. On or about the last thirty years, the Defendant did, in violation of the personal liberty of Virginia Ridley, confine said person without legal authority in Catoosa County, Georgia.

3. On or about the 4ᵗʰ day of October 1997, the Defendant did cause unjustifiable suffering to living animals, to wit: two cats, by keeping them tied with little freedom of movement.

"So," I summarized for Alvin, sitting across the table from me in my office, "Buzz is planning to try to get in evidence about you holding your mother, your wife, and two cats in the house, against their will."

"The housecats," Alvin said, flying right over the first two allegations. "Mama didn't want them havin' no babies!" He explained to me that he was always bringing things into and out of the house, and leashing the cats only happened when the door was going to be opened a lot. I knew when Dan Bilbrey brought it up at the preliminary hearing in August that we might be having to deal with this. "When all those people came over after Virginia died, I started tying them up again, just until they all left," he offered.

"Alvin," I said, looking him straight in the eyes, "we must get these cats to the vet. If they are okay, then I think I can keep this one out." He did not protest, but I wondered if he would ever follow through. I added, "One crazy cat lover on the jury might vote to send you away, just because of these damned cat allegations!"

I told him that we needed to address the first two subjects as well, and he started telling me the story of his mother, Minnie Ridley, who was well up in her years, and how she suddenly became the subject of social services inquiries.

"Mama didn't want to see those people," he said. "When they told me they was gettin' a court order to see her, I took her up to

Erlanger Hospital in "Chattanoogee," and they checked her out. They tested her and found she was able to decide on her own what she wanted, and she wanted to go home with me."

"Why do you think they started looking into your mother's situation, Alvin?" I asked.

"I guess it was Virginia's folks, hoping to get us all out in the open," he said.

"And, of course, here's the allegation that you held Virginia captive for thirty years." We had talked about this issue for a year now. "Alvin, I *must* get into your house." I told him that I had to take detailed pictures of each window and each door to show that Virginia, and Mama Minnie, for that matter, could have, as Alvin put it, "walked out anytime."

The giving of the notice itself did not get the evidence in. We would have to endure a pretrial hearing on the issues, and the court would rule on each allegation, just before trial.

Alison was very understanding of all the time I was having to spend at the office with Alvin, or at least she did her best not to add to my woes by complaining much about it. But if we were going to trial in ten days, she knew I wouldn't be home much at all. I just had to get a continuance. These forty-five new state witnesses were a gift, in a way. Judge Van Pelt wouldn't want to give us an appeal ground of forcing us to trial with so many witnesses given at such short notice. I started poring over a draft for motion for continuance.

On the Sunday night before the calendar call on October 5, I went to see Alvin and make sure he was going to be in court in the morning. "You *will* be locked up for missing calendar call," I reminded him. He was now used to driving himself to my office and then walking over to the courthouse, and he had even managed to find his way in and to the defense table for the motions hearings, and that was fine with me.

I went to the office Sunday night to work on the case. As I sat at the computer desk putting the finishing touches on my new Motion for Continuance, which I would file first thing at calendar call tomorrow, I thought it was a good one. I was asking that the trial be moved from the two weeks of trials this month to the next term, which would be in March/April 1999.

As I worked to improve what I thought was a killer argument for a continuance, I began to hear something scratching and moving around, like an animal, under the floor of my office. The scratching was loud, and I wondered if damage was being done by a raccoon just under where I was sitting. I put up with it for a while, but then it just was so distracting that I quietly lay down on the floor, partially covered by a rug, to listen. Soon I realized that the clearest sound was coming from the register. Something was in the vent, I realized.

Taking a page from Alvin's book, I decided the best thing I could do would be to scare off whatever it was. I slowly crawled on my elbows and put my ear just above the register. As the sound came closer and closer, I decided to go full-Alvin, and I turned my head toward the vent and let out the loudest scream I could muster.

Big mistake. A mist billowed from the register, just barely missing my face. I felt that I had been maced, as if someone had sprayed my face with pepper spray, only worse. It was obviously a skunk. The scent fell over all the files, on me, and throughout the office. I went home, threw my clothes outside the house, and went straight to the shower. My long-suffering wife just seemed to think it was par for the course of representing Alvin Ridley.

The next morning, I met Alvin in court and showed him a copy of the Motion for Continuance.

"Hey, did you have a fallin'-out with a skunk?" he asked.

"Yes, Alvin." I was embarrassed to say more, because others were also picking up on the scent from either me or the files.

"I don't know if I'm going to be able to sit here," he said, seemingly completely unaware of the irony. Or maybe *very* aware.

I learned a big lesson. We can't always know someone's circumstances completely. Sometimes you just can't help things.

When the prosecutor called out the calendar and reached Alvin's name, I answered for him and asked him to stand so the court would see he was actually there. I then walked Alvin to his car. He kept talking about how I smelled like a skunk. I couldn't be upset with him. I found a way to laugh at myself, then promptly asked Lori to get an exterminator to come over. When they arrived, they showed me a straight tear, suspected to be where the skunk had entered the soft, flexible bend of the air duct, close to the ground and very close to an inexplicably opened access hatch door at the back of the house, one that was usually closed and latched.

Could he have . . . ? I thought briefly.

Fortunately, on Wednesday, the court listened to my many arguments and veiled threats of appellate review of any decision short of a continuance. No judge likes to be overruled, but I also had good arguments here. A continuance was approved, "but not to the spring, Mr. Poston," the court cautioned. "We are having two special jury trial weeks set for January 4 and January 11, 1999," he said, "and Mr. Ridley will go to trial in those weeks."

It felt good to win a contested continuance motion against the district attorney, even though it was for only twelve weeks.

"Alvin, we won today." I tried to boost his spirits. "Now, the only thing is, if you are going to still keep me from fully investigating this matter, we're going to be in the same shape in late December, with nothing. You must let me in your house, and soon."

He answered as he always did, saying, "I'll think about it."

As for me, I decided that I was going to have a blowout of a birthday party for myself. My birthday was on a Saturday in a couple of weeks, and I would drink in celebration of not having to try this case. I would drink in sadness of us not being pregnant yet. I would drink because I hadn't in a long while, it seemed. I would drink because it was what I always did.

As I continued to research the usual terms of epilepsy, death, and petechiae, I got a call the following Tuesday from Catoosa County coroner Vanita Hullander.

"Guess what I found in my desk drawer?" she said. "I found Virginia Ridley's ring!"

I couldn't believe it. And bless her heart for telling me about it. She indicated that she would involve the district attorney to release it to Alvin or me. I thanked her, but I didn't tell Alvin right away. The fact that this ring was even unintentionally withheld before burial from the hand of the woman who wore it for thirty-one years, reportedly without ever taking it off, was too good not to mention at trial. If I rushed to give it to Alvin, no one on earth would ever see it again.

For the next week and a half, I handled a few other cases to pay the bills, but every day I worked on some aspect of Alvin's case. I got Minnie Ridley's hospital records, which confirmed the story Alvin had told me with pride about how he and his Mama had "outsmarted" those "damn government social workers."

As my birthday approached, I ordered a keg of beer from a distributor in Chattanooga and got a bunch of wood to make a huge bonfire. My one-hundred-CD jukebox in the house was loaded up with plenty of dance music, from my favorite Athens, Georgia, bands, Pylon, Drivin'n'Cryin', the B52s, Cracker, and REM, to all the songs people like to sing when drunk, like David Allan Coe's "You Never Even Called Me by My Name." Hopefully, I was really going to forget Alvin Ridley for the weekend and let my wife see again the fun man she thought she had married.

Of course, as the guests arrived, every partygoer wanted to talk about the case, so there was no escaping it. Jeff Keith, one of Alison's high school friends, came up and said, "Hey, I've been enjoying watching you represent the 'Zenith Man.'" I had always known him as Alvin Ridley, the TV repairman, and later people called him Crazy Alvin, but this generation was too young to have encountered him much. Nevertheless, the giant Zenith sign still loomed over Nashville Street, where his shop of oddities remained, shuttered from the public but displaying the conspiracies weekly from the inside of the glass windows and door. *Zenith Man.* I liked it. He definitely needed rebranding, even though the actual Zenith brand had long left him. *I'm sure they won't mind the continued association,* I thought jokingly.

The party was an overall success, and Alison had a lot of fun with her nonpregnant friends and kept good company with her pregnant friends. As I often did, I drank to excess, but danced to even greater excess, sweating it all out, so I was mostly sober and still up at 2:00 a.m. as I began to clean up the house.

I switched on the TV to CNN, just to catch up with the world as I cleaned, and I heard something that caught my attention. I waited another half hour to hear it again. The autopsy report of Olympic champion Florence Griffith Joyner, or Flo-Jo, had been released. She died, it had been determined, of a seizure disorder that it turns out she knew about, but had managed well over the years. It had kept her out of the 1996 Atlanta Olympic Games, which explained why she wasn't competing the one day I had attended the event.

I grabbed a pen and wrote down as much information as I could: *Florence Griffith Joyner, Flo-Jo, seizure death, Orange County, Medical Examiner.* I ran to the stack of *Chattanooga Times* newspapers that I had mostly ignored the past several weeks. I saw an article from two days ago, October 23, and caught the name of the medical examiners who performed the Olympian's autopsy, Dr. Richard Fukumoto and Dr. Barbara Zaias.

The following Monday, October 26, 1998, I was on the telephone trying to call the Orange County Medical Examiner's Office. I had been having great difficulty finding an autopsy of someone who had died from a seizure disorder, mainly because they rarely happen in the manner, or to anyone, that would have brought my attention to them. But I also had to follow the rules of the various state and federal bars I belonged to. I decided to take a minimalist approach, being extremely sparse in what information I gave about myself, but to be honest in everything I said. If asked a direct question, I would honestly answer it. But I wasn't going to tell them everything going in.

I asked for either Dr. Zaias or Dr. Fukumoto, and the receptionist/screener asked, "What is the nature of your call?"

"This is Poston from Catoosa County, Georgia," I said, every word of it a true statement. "We have a case here"—also a true statement, if you counted *we* as me *and* Alvin—"that involves a seizure death just like yours with Ms. Griffith-Joyner, the Olympic star." Truth. I finished with, "We'd like to take a look at that autopsy"—again me and Alvin—"and run it by our pathologist," when we hire one, of course. Again . . . all true.

I braced for a barrage of questions. "Hold for Dr. Fukumoto" was the one response I wasn't quite expecting. When Dr. Fukumoto came on the line, I used the exact same script. I didn't want to mess things up, and assuming he was on a recorded line, I was very careful with my words. I intentionally tried to make myself sound *busier* than he was, just to get to the point, basically, that *we* had what looked like a seizure death from a woman who was sleeping on her front, and there were petechiae—hoping I pronounced it properly—and *we* want to run his autopsy report by our pathologist. Dr. Fukumoto was very kind and shared, "She essentially had a seizure and smothered herself." This was his assessment of the death of, arguably, the greatest athlete of all time. Thanking him, but not too profusely, I gave him my post office box address in Ringgold, and he assured me he would send that autopsy out that day.

"Now we have to find some experts," I told Alvin. I looked for the uniform resource locator, or URL, which I had carefully handwritten on a note that I had left on my computer desk, still slightly reeking of skunk. I found it, handwritten on an old sheet from a Georgia House of Representatives notepad. I tried several variations of it until I finally keyed it in correctly. Not surprisingly, the most on-point articles involved Dr. Braxton Bryant Wannamaker, of Orangeburg, South Carolina. I found a Dr. Wannamaker in Orangeburg by using directory assistance.

On the other hand, Alvin became captivated by the website of a forensic pathologist right here in Georgia. Dr. Robert Goldberg's website had some computer-generated music and a small sixteen-bit animated item as well. Alvin had not been engaged about much in the criminal case because he was still obsessed with all the ancient civil cases, so I would dial up Dr. Goldberg's site for Alvin to click on and navigate on his own.

At the end, Alvin would inevitably ask, "How do you spell that again?" And I would dutifully spell out "forensic pathologist," again and again. I noted that for the pathologist's name he would always write down "Gold Bird," and I never corrected him. I didn't have the funds quite yet to hire Alvin's favorite. I felt Dr. Wannamaker was the more critical witness. The idea of "Gold Bird" made Alvin more engaged, so if it was at all possible, I'd try to get them both.

We were just over eight weeks from the special jury trial term. I had very little to go on, but was learning more about my client and what motivated him. I could literally "buy" his cooperation at some level, taking him to lunch every day and giving him grocery money. I tucked all this away to utilize when needed, just as I did our "prayer meetings" when I had to give him information in the form of an evangelical-style prayer. The more urgent the need for Alvin to do something, the more like the Rev. Ernest Angley I had to be, I figured. And it had worked on everything except getting me access to his house.

6

*T*uesday was Election Day, which had always been a holiday of sorts to me. Not this year. I was in a mad scramble to try to lessen the possibility of another big loss. Two years had passed from the debacle of my last campaign. Congressman Deal wasn't even opposed this time. I guess due to the thrashing that I had gotten two years ago, nobody wanted to run after seeing my example of how things were in Northwest Georgia. For the past sixteen or seventeen years, until the last cycle, which found me walking alone on Nashville Street, I spent this night in Atlanta, watching results come in. Not tonight, perhaps not ever again.

On a positive note, this week I had my first conversations over the phone with Dr. Braxton Bryant Wannamaker. He was very dry and hard to engage in any banter.

"The prosecution is putting a lot on the presence of petechiae," I said, and he told me that he had living patients who walked in to see him after a seizure with just as much petechiae.

I received Dr. Fredric Hellman's curriculum vitae, which was very impressive. I focused on his education and even called up some of his medical school professors for information on which books they used to teach him, particularly on the one subject on which he had staked his claim of homicide: the presence of petechiae on Virginia Ridley.

On November 18, we were about six weeks out from the special term. I got three autopsy photos of Virginia Ridley and decided it was finally time to talk to Alvin about Dr. Hellman's findings. Sparing him the nude photos made on the pathologist's table, I did show him what he had already seen: Virginia in her clothes lying on her deathbed, arms bent upward toward her upper chest. A faint red line appeared on her left arm, almost mid-forearm. I was picking up that Buzz wanted to make this faint line out to be a "ligature mark."

"She had a watch," Alvin said. "They took it with her ring." I still hadn't told him that the ring had been found, because he would want it back then and there. I didn't have it yet myself. No word on the watch, though, but the possible presence of a watch being pushed up her forearm during her seizure would explain the faint red mark. And Dr. Hellman said nothing about seeing such a mark, so it must have faded.

Alison and I had planned to go to both of our families' houses on Thanksgiving Day, and, of course, the big case always came up in conversation. I felt that some family members on both sides were just tolerating it. I was barely tolerating it. We went to Graysville last, and I was pleasantly surprised to find my father sober on a major holiday, for the first time in my memory. He was really trying, with the help of his doctor. It was this time last year that my sisters and I began to plot the intervention that would happen a month later, between Christmas and New Year's.

"Son, your mother and I want you to take Alvin a plate for Thanksgiving," my father said. It crossed my mind that I was finally enjoying a day that didn't revolve around Alvin Ridley, and that would be the last way that I wanted to spend any part of it.

As we said our goodbyes, I dutifully took the brown paper grocery bag that my mother had loaded up with a tinfoil-covered aluminum pie plate packed with the offerings of the Thanksgiving table.

I took Alison home first and drove back to what I felt would be our usual conditions of engagment at his house, either me being told to leave it outside the gate or on the top of the steps outside his door. But those were the times that I called first. I was lost in thought and didn't do that, instead driving straight to Inman Street and up to the giant gate.

I went around the left of the gate, and in just a few steps, I was once again climbing the crumbling stone steps. This door was as far as I had ever gotten.

I knocked loudly. I could hear shuffling and the door cracked open.

"Happy Thanksgiving, Alvin," I said. "My folks wanted you to have a turkey plate for dinner."

He looked at the brown bag in my hand. The aroma of my mother's cooking was powerful.

"Just wait here," he said, closing the door. I didn't know if he felt he needed to give me something in return, which was his transactional nature sometimes, or if he just wanted to turn down the television, which was blaring in the background. I did hear the television sound go off, but then I heard his voice again, as if he were talking to someone. Finally he came back to the door, opened it, and said the words I was not at all expecting, but had been wanting over a year to hear. "Come on inside."

I followed him into a very cluttered room that was once, he had told me when the phone was being installed, a front porch. At some point, the sides were walled in, and I'm certain this helped insulate the next rooms from the winter cold. As I turned to the right and followed him into that next room, it appeared to be totally darkened by the dark cloth "drapes" that covered the single window. I could barely see anything, but what I could see was bathed in an eerie red glow, the source being a large older-style Christmas tree bulb that was somehow connected with an adapter to the light in the ceiling. A single pull of a string, which Alvin performed, ignited a single forty-watt light bulb.

From the coroner's pictures, I recognized Virginia's deathbed to my immediate left. There was a furnace with a stovepipe leading to a vent on the far wall, which seemed to be almost completely covered in paper. A passage in that wall, I later learned, led to a kitchen and to another room he didn't want me to see. There was a door to the right that led to another bedroom, and another door that led down to a full basement.

As my eyes adjusted, I saw something also familiar. Two cats, although I could not see them well, sitting and watching me from under a table. Sure enough, I could see that they were on little leashes made of twine.

"Alvin," I said, "remember, we have to get these cats to the vet." Then I asked, "Why did you tie them up for my sake?"

"You were comin' in, and Mama didn't want them gettin' out and havin' no babies. We only tied them when folks was comin' in and out of the house."

I couldn't see the two cats very clearly, but they were calm as Alvin unleashed them from their temporary bondage.

"Remember, we have to get them to the vet, and soon," I said, not really believing he would ever allow it.

As he untied the cats, I turned to the almost totally covered far wall. There were papers of all types, including cardboard, the reverse of cereal box fronts and backs, receipts, all types of paper; and they were all attached to the wall and a portion of the left wall with tape, nails, tacks, and even staples. I tried to focus, the shadow of my own head getting in the way of being able to clearly read them. Finally my eyes adjusted, and I was able to read. All the papers looked as if they had been written on by the same person, one with a real flourish on how the letters with lower reach, or descenders, were finished. I read one aloud, hoping he would explain what all of this was. It was an old Laura Ingalls Wilder poem, or a derivation of it:

> Remember me with smiles and laughter,
> For that's how I'll remember you all,
> If you remember me with tears and sorrow,
> Then don't remember me at all.

Most of the writings were written with strong religious themes:

> When you are having troubles,
> you use the strength the Good Lord gave you
> and do the best you can.

And many of the writings were a record of a banal existence, watching television, cooking supper, and interpreting and recording the world through Alvin's experiences on the outside: *First day Alvin ever rode motorsicle was about 6 o'clock Saturday December 23, 1978.*

"Alvin!" I called out. "Who wrote all this?" At once, I suspected, hoped, and prayed it was the mystery woman, Alvin's wife.

"Virginia wrote all of them," he said, "I'm just puttin' them up because I miss her."

As I was trying to process the impact of this discovery, I asked, "Are there more?"

Alvin continued to talk. "She loved the Lord, and that's what she wrote about a lot."

"Are there any more writings, Alvin?"

"Yeah, there's more in that room," he said, pointing to the door to the right. I asked to see them. As he opened the door, I thought I saw a rat scamper away. Along a wall to the left were stacks of papers, loosely stuffed into boxes, trays, and just stacked up almost to the ceiling in boxes.

"Alvin, why didn't you tell me about this? We've got to use all of this to explain that she was here writing poems, writing about the Bible," I said. "I've got to have all of this to use at trial, Alvin!"

Without even pretending to think about my request, he said, "Naw, you can't have any of it. It's all I've got left of her."

"Don't you realize that this could turn the jury's thinking about you?"

He said nothing.

"Alvin," I said, "let's pray together." This time, I grabbed his hands and held them, to give a little boost to my instructional prayer. "Dear Lord, help your child Alvin understand that Virginia wrote all of these things to help him, and that she wants him to use everything that she wrote to help the jury understand that Alvin deeply loved her and would never hurt her."

Alvin's eyes were closed tightly, and he held both of my hands as strongly.

"And Lord, if Virginia does not want Alvin to use her writings, give us a sign right now!" I held my breath that the cats, rats, and other creatures would stay quiet. I counted to myself, *One, two . . . seven, eight, nine, ten!*

"Oh, thank you, Lord, for just now letting us know definitively that we need to use all of Virginia's wonderful works from her time with Alvin. Amen!" I sped through the closing. God had let pass my self-imposed statute of limitations on any sending of a sign *not* to use them.

"I'll think about it," Alvin said, and that was good enough, for now.

I noted to myself that it was a turkey plate that broke the stalemate on my getting into his house. Alvin was so transactional that he needed to reciprocate my gift. Now that I had passed the sacred threshold of getting in, it was easy to get him to agree that I was coming back tomorrow, the Friday after Thanksgiving, to take pictures of the absence of locks and bars on the windows, to show that it was not likely there ever were any of these things, because this house obviously had never been repainted since its original coat in the 1940s.

I went home and told Alison, still worried about me going over to Alvin's house, about my discovery. From Ringgold, she had grown up with all the stories about him. She was touched, however, by my description of Virginia's writings and the shrine Alvin was making with them.

I could hardly sleep. I realized that I would soon need to prove that Virginia wrote these, and that Alvin, Minnie, or Bill Ridley did not. I remembered once meeting Brian Carney, a handwriting expert in Atlanta. I would call him soon. He would tell me what to do.

I spent the last four work days of November inside Alvin's house, trying to identify and put some organization into Virginia's writings. Trying to match stacks, I estimated that there were possibly twenty thousand individual items that bore her writing, but many were already succumbing to age, fragility, and being ripped apart to line a mouse's nest or to become food for the scores of silverfish I had seen. The house was so unpleasant, and the lighting was terrible, but I was motivated by what I had found, and for the first time, Alvin was cooperating, somewhat.

The discoveries in Alvin's house were a collective game changer. The district attorney was trying to prop up a questionable death with creepy and lurid allegations of false imprisonment and years of captivity. Now my work was really cut out for me. It would come down to the question of whether my client would permit me to help him.

We were now five weeks from the special jury term.

7

December 1998

*T*he discoveries at the Ridley house were overwhelming. From the thousands of writings, it became clear that Virginia was a very religious woman. We're talking Old Testament religious, with the vengeful God and all the hard rules. She had filled the margins of more than one Bible with notes and definitions, like a perennial student in Sunday school. Then, occasionally, a work of art in pencil or pen would emerge from the piles. Lyrics of popular songs from the late 1960s through the 1990s were printed by hand.

Brian Carney, a handwriting expert from near Atlanta, told me over the phone, "You need known writings or signatures of everyone else who lived there in those years." That meant I had to round up "known," or official, writings or signatures of Alvin's parents, Bill and Minnie Ridley, as well as Virginia. Over the past few months, I had already been looking for evidence of her existence in the community. She wasn't registered to vote and never renewed her first driver's license.

Amidst all her writings, I came upon something that looked very familiar to me: campaign material from my 1996 race for the U.S. Congress, and deeper, campaign material from my state representative campaigns going back to 1988. No other candidate's material was here, save some cards from Alvin's 1984 sheriff's campaign. There was way more there than I would have left at their door. It was obvious that Alvin had picked it up from store counters.

"Alvin," I finally asked, "why do you have so much of my campaign material here?"

"Well," he answered, "we was with you."

"Wait," I stopped him. "Virginia never voted. I've looked at the records."

"Well," he adjusted, "I was with you."

"Alvin," I countered, "you never voted, either, at least since you ran for sheriff."

"We was still helpin', though, you know, influencin' folks."

I almost laughed.

I began to have a feeling, and was reminded of it time and time again, that these two had been perfect for each other. They shared the same conspiracy theories, the same sense of self-pity, and injustice. And the only real difference was that Virginia wrote it all down, and she was prolific in this task.

"Why did she write so much, Alvin?" I asked him.

"She just did," he said. "I guess the Lord told her to write it all down."

Negotiations began immediately as side talk as I went through her voluminous loose-leaf journal, or diary. I needed to use these in court, and because of the best evidence rule, I needed the originals. Alvin had already told me that I could not have the originals, and I understood his reluctance to part with all he felt that remained of his wife.

But as I had already learned, Alvin was, if anything, very transactional. He had to have a price, I figured.

"Look, Alvin," I reasoned, "if you go to prison, they aren't going to let you take these." I immediately wanted to pull those words out of the air and eat them. "Alvin, how about this . . .", and thus began the great negotiation. I offered to pay him one hundred dollars just to copy them.

The next day, he came to the office, walked in, and said, "How about two hundred dollars to rent them papers just to make copies, but I keep them originals with me?"

I said, "It's a deal!"

"But I ain't decided yet if you can use them," he cautioned.

"I know, but we have to get on to copying them and serving the DA if we ever want to use them, so, for now, it's a deal."

We shook hands on it, and back at Alvin's house I dove back into the piles of Virginia's records, creating a smaller pile of documents that I wanted to copy and, hopefully, use at trial.

I found a letter that was from the U.S. Department of Housing and Urban Development (HUD), obviously a reaction to another letter from Senator David Gambrell, and clearly from another high authority. It started:

> *Dear Mrs. Ridley:*
> *Your correspondence to the President of the United States, Mr. Richard M. Nixon, concerning your having been required to vacate your apartment in the low-rent public housing project in Ringgold, Georgia has been referred to this office for reply . . .*

So the woman who the district attorney wants to tell the jury was held captive for thirty years was corresponding during this time with a U.S. senator and President Richard M. Nixon. There were similar pleas to the administrations of Presidents Carter and Reagan.

In the evenings after these full-day excursions in Alvin's house, I would go home and, by agreement with Alison, drop my clothes at the door before coming in to shower and then go wash and dry the clothes, separate from our other clothes. She was showing great patience for the sake of the case.

On Tuesday, December 1, I got an extension on the deadline to serve discovery on the state. This allowed us a little more breathing room to process the new discoveries that the Thanksgiving turkey plate gift had caused to happen.

On Thursday, December 3, I finally got Alvin to lug the first big stack of documents, mostly Virginia's writings, to my office for copying. He fussed over them as if he were a Brinks armored car driver making a pickup at the bank. The copying machine was in the back of the converted ranch home turned law offices. We stayed almost joined at the hip, Alvin watching every original being placed on the scanner and ensuring that it came off. I could immediately tell that he had gone through the pile of what I had deemed important and had second-guessed my decision on several documents, pulling them from the copying file. I tried to remember a few of them and advocated that I needed them to copy and to use at trial. "I'll *think* about it" was his go-to reply.

I tried to sort through the pile that he did bring and make small stacks of ones that I felt were critical. For organization purposes, I got several large mailing envelopes, the green-and-white ones made of a hard-to-tear substance and with an adhesive flap. For days, I would make copies, and then put the originals in an envelope with the date of copying marked on the envelope. Then I would put one set of the two copies made in a correlating file, also marked with the date of copying. This way, I thought, I could simply speed through a file, and if I found my copy, the original would be in the correlating envelope. The second copies would all go in one big pile, undated, to be served on the district attorney. This was the best way I could come up with to be able to quickly find an original at trial.

We repeated the copying the second day, on Friday, but I cut the day short. Alison and I had planned to come to downtown Ringgold to the annual "Down Home Christmas," where the shops stayed open late, and a holiday parade went down Nashville Street toward the old depot. The giant electric star on White Oak Mountain would be lit, symbolizing the holidays were upon us. I was spending so much time on the case that I felt the need to do something "normal" tonight.

Alvin seemed to understand, and we planned to get together the next day, Saturday, to continue the copying. "And I need those documents back that you have pulled out, Alvin," I chided him.

The darkened main street of Ringgold, U.S. Highway 41, or Nashville Street, usually was buttoned up tight at 5:45 p.m., this time of year. We gleefully enjoyed the camp aspect of much of a small-town parade, including seeing who Little Miss Range of Motion would be, sponsored, of course, by a chiropractic clinic; and how long the Volkswagen Club or the International Harvester Tractor Club was going to make the parade be this year.

An actual taxidermic deer head came by, mounted on the front of a truck like a giant hood ornament; it was akin to a nautical figurehead on an old ship. Bizarrely, a nostril had been drilled out, allowing a bright red light bulb to stick out of it, giving the unfortunate impression that the real Rudolph the Red-Nosed Reindeer had been bagged in a buck hunt this deer season. A couple of younger children I saw looked traumatized, one lamenting, "Rudolph's head is cut off!"

Seeing all the young children only brought our dream of having our own kids closer to mind. "As soon as I'm through with this case," I would always promise, "we are going to check all of our options!"

At some point, a Santa Claus passed by, not part of the parade, but on the sidewalk. I caught a whiff of him as he quickly passed, after handing me a piece of cheap hard candy wrapped in clear cellophane. When I saw his hands, the same rugged hands that I had recently held on to while recently trying to pray some common sense into the man attached to them, I knew who it was—Alvin, dressed in full moth-eaten Santa regalia, beard, cap, and the works, four weeks before his murder trial.

I followed him with my eyes as he walked up the street. People would get excited by the fact that another Santa was walking around, but after they had been around him a bit or got too close, they would move away. He made a critical mistake, stopping in front of the darkened, locked, and chained door of Ridley's Zenith TV Sales & Service, and he lingered a moment too long there under the giant Zenith sign that extended over the sidewalk from the roof. People started realizing who he was, and children were being snatched away from him, their candy ripped away by panicked parents and grandparents.

I walked up to him, and whispered, "Please go home, before we have an issue."

He sadly walked away, around the corner of the Georgia Power Company building, down Depot Street toward Inman. Apparently, he had been doing this for years in relative anonymity. There were always plenty of Santas and, more recently, Grinches. He blended in. Now I felt like the Grinch for sending him home. I wanted more than ever to win his case, if for nothing else than to vindicate old, smelly Santa.

The next day, Saturday, I tried to avoid mentioning the embarrassing outing of Santa Claus. He brought an unopened bag of the cheap hard candy to give to the folks in my office.

"They aren't here, Alvin, but they sure will appreciate it. I might even get into it if my blood sugar gets too low," I said as I tried to be appreciative of this newfound kindness in his nature. Then I asked, "Did you bring the other documents I had put in the pile at your house?"

He shook his head. "I forgot them."

I looked at him to make sure he knew I was serious.

"Why did you pull them out of my stack?" I asked. "It was some of the best stuff!"

"Well, 'Salesman Sam' said you didn't need all of them," he said.

That was a derisive nickname for Benjamin McGaha, an older man in a full gray beard who both pedaled and peddled his wares, selling merchandise from catalogs in his bicycle basket.

"*What?*" I made him repeat it.

My plan to be gentle after the debacle on the street the previous night went out the window. "What in the hell are you talking about?" I demanded. "Salesman Sam is advising you about what evidence I need in this case?"

He nodded sheepishly.

"I don't care what you need to do, but you need to get Salesman Sam here on Monday, Alvin. We have one week to get all our discovery copied and served on the DA. I need to have my system ready so I can find the originals during the trial. If you want to stay out of prison for the rest of your life, get his ass *here* on Monday morning!" I couldn't believe it.

While copying from the file a little longer, I found a document that I first thought the dynamic legal minds of Alvin Ridley and Salesman Sam had culled.

"Alvin," I said, "I'm sorry I overreacted. I just want to win your case so badly. Please forgive me."

He grinned and said, "That's all right. Sam told me you wouldn't like me taking his advice."

"He was right," I said; then I requested, "Alvin, while I copy these next few, can you go to the kitchen and get you a Coke and me a Diet Coke?"

Alvin jumped to the task, while I discreetly dropped the document that I thought was lost behind the copying machine. I'd get it and make the copies later, after he left. I just needed to secure it and not leave it to the whims of Alvin or Salesman Sam as to whether I had it to use.

If a document had major evidentiary importance, I developed a secret file I marked in all caps "GOLD." Whenever I saw such a document float up to the top of the copying file, I would send Alvin for a free Coke out of our fridge, or to "see if the sheriff is in the parking lot watching us!" The first entry into the GOLD file was by Virginia, and its evidentiary value to our defense was significant. Handwritten, with her familiar flourishes, it read as follows:

> Earl McDaniels asked me, Virginia Ridley, why don't you and your husband ever go out? He also let himself + the Orkin Man in unexpectedly one day and they frightened me because the Orkin man had allready frightened me because he asked me to go riding with him. I did personal things like changing clothes, taking a bath + when I am doing something personal I feel I should have my privacy so it really would scare me when Mr. Earle McDaniels would come + let himself in and his maintenance man in my house without knocking. From the Fall of 1968 until the Spring of 1970 Sheriff Lee Roy Brown talked to me while I was living at 130 Circle Drive in the Spring of 1970.

In this single document, self-identifying as written by Virginia Ridley in the first part of the long run-on sentence, it is established that the head of the Ringgold Housing Authority, whose name she spelled different ways, had noted and asked her about their secluded manner. She also detailed the subsequent event that triggered the "fallin'-out," as Alvin put it, with the Ringgold Housing Authority. It told about the flirty, imposing exterminator who came into the apartment unannounced while she was bathing, and who then had the audacity to ask her to "go riding with him." Finally she referenced Sheriff Lee Roy Brown, who was sheriff during the period of time mentioned, the spring of 1970, just before their eviction trial in September of that year.

If there was one document of the thousands that I needed, this was it. I had no qualms about "rescuing and securing" it from the whims of Alvin and his "other" legal counsel, Salesman Sam.

The following week was our last full week to get the rest of our discovery copied. We finished copying any that Alvin would allow.

Judge Van Pelt finished his in camera, or private/in chamber, review of the Department of Family & Children Services, or DFCS, file on Alvin's mother, Minnie Ridley, which was required because the agency must protect its sources. Listening to Alvin's paranoid rants led me to assume that it was Virginia's family, the Hickeys, who had triggered that investigation. The biggest surprise after the review was that it was Minnie herself who caused the investigation. In a 1986 letter to the Division of Family & Children Services, someone had obviously typed out a letter for his mother to sign, and basically she was begging them in what was termed a "Mother's Day request" for financial aid, which said she was "living in a home that is badly in need of repair," went through the story of Bill Ridley's fender bender accident, but said that he "wanted his claims settled while he was alive" because he "planned to rebuild my deteriorated home, buy me two new dresses and a new refrigerator." It was signed "Sincerely, From a Mother, Mrs. William Ridley." I read it again. The wording was very much like that in many of Virginia's writings.

While it wasn't on Monday, as I had demanded, Alvin eventually appeared that week at the office with Benjamin McGaha/Salesman Sam. I had gotten over it and had forgotten that I had demanded that he bring the character who was constantly second-guessing my legal strategy.

As a peace offering, I suppose, Salesman Sam brought me a draft of a new chapter of his book he was "writing on a computer." A "new" chapter he had just added detailed the two times he had seen Virginia Ridley.

"Are you sure about this?" I asked.

He replied, "I never forget anything."

I decided I could try to make Salesman Sam an asset. I ended up ordering some promotional pencils for my office from him, and a pair of shoes for Alvin. I negotiated with him an agreement from Alvin to use all the writings that I selected, that I would give Alvin two hundred dollars, and I ordered the pencils and shoes so that the erstwhile "co-counsel" would get something in the deal.

Had I been taken in now by *two* con men? I was literally paying Alvin to focus on this case. And today I was ordering useless items from Sam, who was now claiming to have seen Virginia many times. I wasn't really sure about his claims to have met Virginia, but Alvin backs them up. It was worth ordering all of that junk just to enlist him to calm Alvin down and make the decision to let me have and use the originals of Virginia's voluminous writings.

The autopsy of Florence Griffith Joyner had come in from Orange County, California, just in time for me to serve on my district attorney, and to send a copy to Dr. Wannamaker. It was fascinating for the similarities between the deaths of the two women, one perhaps the most famous and greatest athlete ever to live, and the other essentially known to only one person, Alvin.

By the end of the thorough autopsy done by the professionals in California, and certainly by the time Dr. Fukumoto talked to me, the decision there was unanimous. Flo-Jo had died from a seizure, positionally asphyxiating herself while being facedown in bed during a seizure. Her clean toxicology report, showing only therapeutic amounts of Tylenol and Benadryl, checked the irresponsible performance enhancing drug rumors by people who did not want to acknowledge her sheer greatness as an athlete.

Even the description of the arms of the Olympian sounded very similar to the position of Virginia's arms, but the athlete had much more petechiae and Tardieu spots than Virginia did. The details of her passing could potentially help vindicate a lonely widower, a town eccentric who had very few people in his cheering section.

Monday, December 14, was one day before the discovery deadline to get our defense discovery to the state, or risk not being able to use it. That included adding witness names. I was busy binding Virginia's writings together with wire to deliver another small bale of copies of it to the district attorney's office.

Suddenly Alvin burst through the door, shouting, "Ain't we taking the cats to that vet?" I just assumed that he was not going to allow it, as I had been reminding him over and over until I had decided that it wasn't going to happen.

Looking at the clock, I yelled to Elizabeth Cheek, my high school intern, "Elizabeth, get a couple of file boxes and get in the car. We're going to Alvin's house." Only as we followed Alvin home did I realize, *I'm bringing a high school kid to the house of an alleged killer.*

"Elizabeth," I said, "just stay outside with the car and put these boxes together."

In the driveway, I laid out the plan.

"Alvin," I said, "I'm not bringing anyone into your house." I pointed to the boxes Elizabeth Cheek was unfolding and forming into file boxes. "I'm going to give you one box at a time, Alvin," I said, "and you can go in and get one cat, then we'll give you the other box to get the other cat."

He nodded.

"And, Alvin," I lowered my voice, "by the time we get to the vet's office . . . these cats better have names!" I was always trying to humanize Alvin, but I had never heard him call them anything but "the cats."

Alvin dutifully took the first box in the house, and before long, he was back at the door, carefully holding a file box. He handed us the box.

"This is Meowy. Mama named her Meowy."

Elizabeth had something to hold the lid on, and we put the box in the back of Alvin's Dodge K-car. I took the next box to Alvin at the top of the steps and handed it to him. As he went inside, I thought that I saw movement under the fabric of a small sofa across from the door on the enclosed former front porch.

I got down on my knees to call out what I thought was the cat under the sofa, batting at and trying to raise the fabric panel. A giant rat scampered out, turned right, and I was the only thing between it and getting outside. Out of surprise, I let out a short yell. I heard a similar sound come from Elizabeth outside. I had the notion that she probably thought I was getting murdered. I came flying out of the house, and so did the rat.

When it all died down, and Elizabeth and I had a laugh at my expense, Alvin reappeared at the door, again gently carrying the second box.

"This is Kitty. Mama named her Kitty."

We put Kitty's box into Alvin's car, next to Meowy's box, and made sure the lids were secure.

"It's as simple as this, Alvin," I said. "You're in complete control. The cats are in your car, and we will have you follow us, and we'll help you get them into the veterinarian's office. We will get Dr. Sutton to look at them, and I'll pay the bill."

Dr. Cynthia Sutton had taken my call and had agreed to evaluate the cats. If they didn't have any ligature marks indicating their being tied up long-term, then she would testify as to her findings. If the verdict by the vet was not good, then Lord help us, and especially those poor cats. I had not really seen either of them in good light, so I didn't know what to expect.

When Dr. Sutton came into the examination room, one box was on the table, and one was on the floor. Elizabeth and I were standing with Alvin, and I made all the introductions.

"Let's see what we have here," Dr. Sutton said as we removed the lid of the box on the table. A medium-sized calico cat appeared.

"That's Meowy," Alvin said. "Mama named her Meowy."

As Dr. Sutton examined Meowy, she asked Alvin a few questions about her, starting with "How old is Meowy?"

Alvin stared down and then said, "Mama got Meowy in 1990."

"Well, that looks about right, eight or nine years old," Dr. Sutton said, looking in the cat's ears. "We have some ear mites, but I can treat those."

I positioned myself behind Alvin and was sending hand signals to the doctor, flipping my fingers up my own neck. "Check the neck, please."

Dr. Sutton fluffed the cat's neck on all sides, pulling fur against the grain so she could see the skin. "Looks fine," she said.

Alvin, without prompting, pointed to the box on the floor, "Mama got Kitty in 1977." That was the year between my junior and senior years at Ringgold High.

"Alvin, I think you're mistaken," I said. "That's twenty-one, almost twenty-two years."

Alvin's voice rose. "I'm right. Mama saved her from a shotgun death in 1977!"

I decided to leave that alone, when I saw a single black toe and claw come through the handle hole of the box.

We raised the box to the examination table, once Meowy was back in her file box. When the lid came off, I felt queasy. A scrawny black cat was there, and it appeared she was cross-eyed. But what was the most shocking was the appearance of her upper fangs. They were freakishly long, seemingly having grown down below her lower jaw and chin. I didn't know what to think. I didn't want any more strangeness in this case.

"Mr. Ridley," Dr. Sutton said as she took Kitty's temperature, which if anything gave me the impression that it made her eyes more crossed, "I think you're right. This is an extremely old animal." Alvin looked at me smugly.

"Check the neck," I said out loud, and Kitty Ridley passed that test as well. There was no evidence or indication that Alvin had excessively tied up his cats. We followed Alvin home and made sure he got the cat boxes to his door. The next day, I went out and bought a fancy and delicate "cat leash" from a pet store, to cross-examine the investigator with, should the judge let this so-called "similar transaction" in.

The next day, when all discovery was due to the state, I supplemented our witness list, adding Dr. Sutton, if needed.

In mid-December, I had found known, or official, signatures of Bill and Minnie Ridley, and, of course, Alvin, whose name was signed scores of times in the voluminous civil litigation. Virginia was the problem, but I did find a beautiful official signature on the marriage license application of Virginia Gail Hickey, with fortunately a *y* in her maiden name as well, to show the flourish that she gave the letter in both her maiden and married names.

Judge Van Pelt informed us for certain that trial would be in the two-week special term that started January 4, 1999, just three weeks away. I had been appointed to assist Mike Giglio in another murder case, Joe Canada, an inmate at the Catoosa County Jail. Under the rules, that case would be called first, as that defendant was in custody. I could be forced to try two murder cases back-to-back. Nobody seemed to be in the mood to put Alvin Ridley's case off any longer.

While I started working feverishly on jury lists and questionnaires, we still needed to hire the witness Alvin was most excited about, Gold Bird. We were both somewhat mesmerized by his multimedia website, with music and sixteen-bit animation, and many references to the Vidocq Society, which sounded like a mysterious and exclusive crime-solving group of sleuths.

CourtTV, the cable and satellite station that featured trials on its national network, reached out to the court, making the request to broadcast the trial. Judge Van Pelt denied the network's request, citing that he didn't know how the defendant would react. This, of course, got into the press.

Part of my deal to motivate Alvin was to buy tombstones for his wife and both of his parents. I took him to the Ringgold Monument company, helped him fill out the forms with the vital data, such as names and dates of birth and death. There was a space on each stone that he could personalize, and he solemnly added sweet sentiments to all three stones, such as "Loving Helpful Father," "Loving Mother," and "Beloved Wife and Friend." A few days later, when I needed something else or more cooperation out of him, I went ahead and told him we should go back and order his own stone, to mark the spot next to Virginia where his body would one day be.

We went back to the monument place and I paid for Alvin's stone. Before I left him, I suggested that he choose his own personalized line, and that he put something like "An Innocent Man," or "Loving Husband," or even "Wrongfully Accused." Something profound, for how he wanted to be remembered. I left him to make up his own mind and to write on the form what he wanted on there.

I hired a local young woman, Karen Benton Mandall, as our investigator. I figured Alvin would be calmer if a woman was on the job, and he was. Mainly, she served subpoenas and helped me try to keep my client at ease.

On Christmas, Alison and I spent time with both of our families in Ringgold and Graysville, and on the way back, we stopped by Alvin's house to give him a plate of food. He gratefully accepted it, and I handed him a wrapped package. Inside were some new pants, new shirts, and an electric blanket. He seemed very appreciative, thanked me, and waved at Alison in the car.

On Sunday, December 27, I got an order signed by Judge Van Pelt, allowing the defense to independently inspect what remains were still at the state crime lab. Now I had to hire Dr. Goldberg, even though I could not afford his full retainer, to get him to examine whatever of Virginia was retained at the crime lab. He agreed to a partial payment. Now we were on to go to Atlanta to the state crime lab on Wednesday.

I was also going to go by handwriting analyst Brian Carney's office with examples of found writings, Alvin's handwriting exemplar, and the known writings of the four people who had lived in that house on Inman Street.

On Wednesday, December 30, I finally met Dr. Goldberg in Marietta, while picking him up to go to the crime lab. He was a big man, balding, but with a long-established comb-over and a full beard. I liked him. He certainly sounded as if he knew what he was talking about. He wore a white lab coat.

I knew months ago what our defense would be: Virginia Ridley died after a seizure, which she had while sleeping facedown. I just needed him to opine about that and little else, but Alvin was counting on him for something else, insisting that Gold Bird come to his house. I figured I could use him to describe the side of the bed being also used as a sofa/chair, explaining the dip in the outside edge that I had heard was being discussed by the prosecution. Alvin was finally engaging in his defense.

As we pulled up to the state crime lab, we were told we would be received by Dr. Fredric Hellman, the pathologist who performed Virginia Ridley's autopsy. Dr. Hellman approached us professionally. Youthful, tan, and fit, in his late thirties, he looked familiar, like someone famous.

Dr. Hellman was circumspect, engaging in no small talk. He seemed somewhat dismissive of Dr. Goldberg, which I thought odd. He led us to part of the crime lab where defense evaluations of evidence happen, and delivered a white plastic bucket, filled with liquid and very few other items, and then he left us to ourselves. It was just me, Dr. Goldberg, and the bucket of what was left of Virginia, which appeared to be only her heart, her interior throat, and upward, including her tongue.

Dr. Goldberg dove right in, spouting opinions right and left. There seemed nothing unusual about the tongue and throat structure that was in the bucket. I was glad that the autopsy mentioned an intact hyoid bone, a delicate bone in the neck that very often is broken in strangulation cases. I knew that much. Other than that, we were just checking Dr. Hellman's work.

On the way out, I told Dr. Goldberg I needed to run some material to handwriting analyst Brian Carney's office. I was paying Goldberg by the hour, but to take him home, then drive back to this side of Atlanta again, didn't make sense. He seemed eager to go with me, so I drove on to Carney's office.

I was delivering to Carney a score of samples of Virginia's writings, from the GOLD file and others that were representative from her loose-leaf journal. I could not afford to have everything analyzed. These would each be called "questioned writing of Virginia Ridley," and numbered for later reference in his report. I brought an exemplar, where Alvin wrote things over and over in the fashion that Carney had instructed. Since Bill and Minnie Ridley were dead, I gathered up what known writings of theirs I could find: notarized documents, government forms, legal pleadings, and other signatures that by virtue of their official nature supported legitimacy.

While I was trying to talk to Carney, Dr. Goldberg was asserting himself with him, asking one question after another to the handwriting analyst. I left a check for Carney to evaluate these documents. It did not cover a trip to Ringgold to testify.

When we got back in the car, Dr. Goldberg quickly offered to be the handwriting analyst witness for the defense. Baffled, I politely declined this offer.

Brian Carney's report came in on December 31. It was his learned opinion that all the questioned writings of Virginia Ridley were actually written by Virginia Ridley, and not Alvin or her in-laws. I put him on call to testify to this.

On New Year's Eve, I learned that Joe Randles, the senior official court reporter for our circuit, assigned to Judge Van Pelt, had fallen ill that day with what was reported to have been a massive heart attack. I felt bad for pushing him so hard to get a transcript of that October hearing that he took down, but it was critical that we have it. I hated the thought of going through a jury trial without Joe's insight, cues, and his sharing of his reading of the room.

8

All defendants on the short list for trials had to show up and be on the ready if something happened to the first cases, such as a last-minute plea deal or a witness availability problem, and I was informed that the trial of *State* vs. *Alvin Eugene Ridley* would be next on deck, and we needed to be ready to go. But on Monday, January 4, 1999, I had to be in this first trial, *State* vs. *Canada,* appointed with Mike Giglio for the defendant in a trailer park knife fight that ended in death.

Alvin wasn't happy having to come to answer the calendar call, and he started grumbling again about his interpretation of the U.S. Constitution, but I interrupted him.

"No, Alvin. We must show up, and I'd like for you to stay to watch jury selection and even some of the Joe Canada trial. I'm going to give you a notepad. I want you to get a good look at the jurors, because we'll be drawing from the same list. Write down the ones who smile at you and that you may remember. You may have worked on some of their television sets!"

Begrudgingly, he agreed, but insisted on driving himself.

The entire calendar would be called, including Alvin's case. Anyone not there to answer would get a bench warrant and likely remain in jail until their trial. I mused to myself that if that happened, I would at least rest assured that he would show up.

Judge Van Pelt chose to try all his cases in the smaller courtroom immediately adjacent to his office, in the 1982 courthouse annex. This small, windowless courtroom was not my favorite, as it felt claustrophobic, and I feared that we might have to remain in there for Alvin's trial. I brought it up to the judge and Buzz as we watched the potential jurors file in. "You know, maybe not for this trial, but certainly we should move to the larger old courtroom for Ridley, as there is a lot of public interest. Could we maybe have the Ridley trial in the large old courtroom?" I was close to begging.

"No one comes to watch trials anymore, Poston!" was Judge Van Pelt's blunt response in denying my request. The irony of that is he had just signed an order against CourtTV's request to televise *nationally* the Ridley trial. The bizarre allegations of decades of spousal imprisonment and murder were directly in their wheelhouse. I accepted his ruling, remembering that I could lose the case, and I didn't need to elevate my losing streak to a national level.

I seated Alvin on the long bench immediately behind the defense table, providing him with a legal pad and pen. This courtroom was so small that the defense table and the prosecution table were touching, forming one long table for both sides to share. By law, the state gets to sit on the side closest to the jury. I always thought that was unfair, but I knew that the aroma that radiated from Alvin might make it better in his case to be as far away as possible.

Buzz seemed unusually chipper; he had tasked two of his top assistants to try the first case. He would be fresh for the Ridley trial, and I would be just coming off this murder trial.

Buzz floated in and out of the courtroom during the jury selection process for the first case. While I was trying to concentrate on the case at hand, I knew that this is the same pool that Alvin's jury would come from. I took more notes than ever on each potential juror.

My mind fully focused on the first case, and not facing Alvin, I lost track of time. During a break, we waited for the jury to clear the courthouse so that the defendant in the first case could be discreetly taken downstairs to the holding cell and given lunch.

Buzz followed me into the hall between the small courtroom and Judge Van Pelt's office.

"Mr. Ridley has been arrested at the federal courthouse in Rome," he said. "He's being held by U.S. Marshals."

I had forgotten that I had left Alvin in the courtroom and darted back to see if he was still there. He wasn't.

I called the United States District Courthouse in Rome, Georgia, a forty-five-minute drive. I figured Alvin must have bolted right after I seated him in the small courtroom. After a couple of attempts, I finally got the U.S. Marshal.

"I understand Alvin Ridley is there?" I hoped Buzz was wrong.

"Yes, sir, we recognized him from the news," the U.S. Marshal said. "He seems very upset, and what concerned us was it seemed he had doused himself with gasoline and he ran through our security. He ran into Judge Vining's office and started yelling about his case in Catoosa County, saying that his lawyer hasn't 'knocked his case out' and yelling for Judge Vining to intervene, and we didn't know if he was going to light a match or what he was going to do."

I reasoned with the federal officer that Alvin was harmless and that he was needed back in Ringgold for trial, and I asked him if any laws were broken.

The marshal, who seemed sympathetic to my plight, said, "No, and he's explaining that his car broke down on the way, which would explain the gasoline smell." I thought a gasoline smell might be an improvement. After a few minutes, he said they would release Alvin.

When court was dismissed at the end of the day, still in the prosecution's case in the trial with Mike, I drove directly to Alvin's house. He wasn't there. I just waited, fuming. After about thirty minutes, the familiar Dodge K-car slowly approached the house.

I didn't even wait for Alvin to get out of his car before lighting into him.

"What in the hell did you think you were doing, going to a federal judge?" I was livid. Alvin looked uncomfortable, but got out and calmly said, "My legal advisor told me I should try it."

Then the truth: "Salesman Sam told me to try that."

"Why did they think you doused yourself with gas?"

"My car broke down, and the perfumes of gas got on my body."

I got Alvin into his house and made sure the critical suitcases were also taken in. Oddly enough, the reasoning seemed to fit the history of Alvin and Virginia. While they both felt tortured by local and state governments, they always held the federal government in high esteem, as if it would be their savior. Virginia herself had written to three U.S. presidents, to Congress, and a U.S. senator, all about her and Alvin's 1970 eviction, their plight with the failed business, and, of course, the issue of the "illegal-seized" Chevy van.

But I wasn't going to stand for Ben McGaha, aka Salesman Sam, to interfere with my representation of Alvin Ridley anymore. I drove straight to Tunnel Hill as darkness fell, honking my horn as I saw his familiar bicycle at the mobile home he shared with his mother. He came out, and for the first time, I had seen him without his hat.

"What in the hell are you doing, sending Alvin to the federal judge? Do you realize he was detained?" I didn't tell him that he was released.

And I didn't even let him respond. "And where is your bar card? You can't give legal advice unless you're a member of the Georgia Bar Association!"

He mustered his response. "Son, I've been giving Alvin Ridley legal advice for thirty years!" Realizing my protests were not going to accomplish anything, and that I really needed him as a witness to his interaction with Virginia Ridley during her years of alleged captivity, I stood down.

"Please, from here on, *please* leave the legal advice to me."

I drove through McDonald's to get Alvin some supper and took it back to his house.

Then I went home and told Alison about the bizarre day and stayed up to work on Alvin's case until about midnight, before finally drifting off. The next couple of days I was helping Mike try the Canada case, then taking Alvin supper at night.

On the night of January 6, the Joe Canada jury had been charged and would begin deliberating in the morning. We would start Alvin's jury selection in the morning. But there was one thing on my mind. Alvin had never allowed me access to "Mama's room" even though he had allowed me to see all other parts of the house. The last few visits, I could swear I heard sounds coming from the direction of the room, across from the kitchen. I could not understand he would deny access to the one man trying to save him. I took matters into my own hands, delivering the McDonald's meal to his kitchen. I said loudly, "Alvin, I've got to see this last room!" I put my shoulder to the door and gave it a shove. A flurry of action and sound made my heart race, until I recognized the form of some chickens. Alvin teared up, and started to cry, saying "Some of my chickens froze outside, so I'm letting them live in here." This man was no killer.

The morning of January 7, 1999, was freezing cold and clear. I had barely slept as we were reaching the end of the Joe Canada trial and would certainly start picking jurors for Alvin's trial once the Canada jury started deliberating. I had to have Alvin there, ready to go, and, of course, it was never a given that he would be anywhere I needed him to be.

I drove straight to the house on Inman Street, but the gate was shut and padlocked. The funny thing about that handmade wood-and-wire imposing gate, foreboding and over six feet tall, and featured in all the news stories about this "fortress," is that if you simply walked around the cluster of trees and bushes that bordered its left side, you only had to step over a single strand of electric fence wire, long fallen and without power, to get to the house. And I did just that. It was after 8:00 a.m., and we had to be in court before nine o'clock. I needed Alvin with me because there would be no real break between the trials. In fact, they would overlap. The Canada jury was charged yesterday afternoon, and they would go straight into deliberation. We'd pick Alvin's jury today. If and when the Canada jury reached a verdict, or hung up, we'd stop what we were doing in Alvin's case, and Joe Canada would be brought back in to hear his fate.

There was no answer to my knocks. I turned the knob and, uncharacteristically, the door opened. "Alvin?" I called. "Are you ready?"

A muffled groan came from inside the house. I walked through the covered porch, past the phone that I had tried to call him on earlier to make sure he would be awake. He hadn't bothered to answer. Walking into the room, I immediately saw a form on the bed—Virginia's deathbed—under a big pile of blankets. All that was showing was the top of his head, the rest of him completely covered up.

"Come on, Alvin!" I urged. "We have to get to court!" There was silence. His eyes were closed tight, in either a poor attempt to feign sleep or an outward show of pain.

"Let's go, Alvin!" I nudged where I thought his arm would be.

"I can't go," he mumbled. "The Constitution says you don't have to go to court when you're sick!" He always said this in an explaining way, as if I had never heard it before. Of course, before I met him, I had never heard this bizarre claim, but by then, I'd heard it from him scores of times.

I was ready for him. "Here you go, Alvin!" I threw the paperback pocket-sized U.S. Constitution I'd bought at the bookstore for these very moments. "Find me the provision! If it is in there, I will get this trial continued!"

He reached for, and looked at the pamphlet, flipping through its few pages that comprised our national charter. He was silent.

"Dammit, Alvin!" I said. "Get your ass out of this bed and get ready or I'm walking off this damn case, and I have to report to the court where I last saw you, and I'm going to tell them you're in bed saying you're sick, and do you know what they'll do? They'll send the sheriff for you, Alvin."

I think I probably used a few more words that I am ashamed to write today.

Alvin finally looked at me, gave me the strangest, serene smile, and said, "You're talkin' to me just like my daddy used to . . ."

I immediately felt sorry for him if that's how his daddy talked to him. He pulled off the covers, revealing that he was completely dressed for court, as Alvin would dress for court, with shoes, socks, pants, and a plaid shirt. Completely dressed all while under the covers trying his last-ditch effort to apply the provisions of the Constitution that existed only in his mind.

I had brought an extra tie in my files, and while it wasn't a match for the shirt, I offered it. But in all the haste, we both forgot something very critical to him.

We got into the small courtroom before anyone. Mike came to

wait for the Canada verdict and offered to keep notes as I did the voir dire questioning in the jury selection for Alvin's case. Lori also had covered the other courtroom where the voir dire process was going on for other cases. She had taken great notes that could apply to the jurors today, including whom the state had struck in the other cases, and the revelations that came out during questioning.

Once in the too-small courtroom, Alvin threw open the suitcases and produced a document I hadn't seen.

"I'll need you to file this *emotion* for me," he ordered.

"What is it?" I asked.

He handed me a single page, typed on the familiar typewriter that had been the source of all the missives over the years that were taped on the inside of the front glass of his shuttered television shop.

It was another one of Alvin's classic "emotions."

It was titled "IN STATE OF GEORGIA, CATOOSA CO. SUPERIOR COURT," and as I read it, I thought it was a motion for change of venue, and a motion to dismiss, motions that I had already filed, were heard, and had been denied back in October. It went into the old conspiracies.

Attached to it was a whole page of the offending newspaper that he claimed should get him a change of venue.

The pleading cited that he and his wife could not get a fair trial on September 15, 1970—the eviction trial from almost thirty years ago. It rambled on about the old civil actions, the court dismissing his case against Chief Land, fifteen years ago, and ended, as his posted missives always did, connecting all to his present state of misery and unemployment.

It was signed, in all caps, *SINCERELY, ALVIN RIDLEY, DEFENDANT, PETITIONER.*

"Is that all, Alvin? Do you think that covers everything?" I asked facetiously.

"Uh, yeah, I think so . . . ," he mumbled, seemingly surprised by my calm demeanor. While in October when he first offered "better *emotions*" for his case, I had felt a bit offended by the second-guessing, but once again, I treated it as legitimate pleading.

"Okay, I need to put a certificate of service on this and make Buzz a copy and make us a file copy." I took it across the hall to the clerk, leaving Lori with strict instructions not to let Alvin out of her sight, and had Alvin's pleading stamped and filed. The assistant clerk couldn't suppress a giggle. I made copies and handed one to Buzz in the hallway. "There you go, Buzz, this might knock this case out before it even gets started," I joked. I wasn't going to let him see me flustered.

At 9:00 a.m., Joe Canada's jury started its deliberations. Now new jurors who had been called to serve for just this week were being assembled in the hallway. Today, Thursday, they would soon be informed that this case would certainly go into next week. This would not sit well with people who were thinking their public duty was almost done.

Alvin said, "What about that tie?"

I looked at his plaid flannel shirt and then at the one tie that I had brought for him, a striped mostly blue one, which I never wore, and knew it was not going to match. Still, he was asking for it, so I pulled it out of my accordion file and started to put it on him.

Buzz seemed as professional and together as he always seemed, almost emotionless. Detective Dan Bilbrey was there to "assist" the prosecutor at trial. The prosecutor would always hold that law enforcement witness back to be last, where, having heard all the testimony, they could try to fill gaps or clean up messes of earlier witnesses.

As the potential jurors filed into the small courtroom, I was finishing tying Alvin's mismatched tie. The citizens were asked to sit in the same order as they appeared in the last version of the jury list. This was an important document, ever changing, and the clerk's office did a herculean task to keep it updated for us.

The questionnaires were an attempt to shorten the process. If both sides had the usual disqualifying questions already answered, it stood to reason that the process of elimination by each side's strikes would go more smoothly, and faster. But there were always the wild cards—people who forgot or flatly refused to fill out the questionnaire. The court had to allow us to ask the questions to those who didn't fill one out, and you never knew if it was a mere oversight, clerical error, or if they were antigovernment types who did not want their information out there. Or worse, they harbored some disqualifying characteristic that they didn't want one side or the other to know—and they *wanted* to serve on the jury, and for all the wrong reasons.

As soon as I thought this, James "Cheese" Goins, a courthouse regular from Graysville, marched into the courtroom excitedly, winking at me, while at the same time acting like he didn't know me. I had represented him half-a-dozen times. He was told to go out in the hall and wait by the bailiff. Cheese was well down the list, perhaps too far to reach. I was going to have to disclose that he was a former client, so I was actually relieved. Anyone who had represented Cheese, because he rotated lawyers—always disgusted with and bad-mouthing the last one he had—was familiar with him showing up at the fee-paying time with heavy brown paper bags containing mud-covered mason jars. Inside the jars was moldy U.S. currency that he had dug back up from his property. This was all ready to be paid to the lucky lawyer, who had to dry and flatten it out and get the bank to accept it.

Alvin's only response to my questions about these prospective picks was whether they were "liked" or "not liked" by him. Not surprisingly, he liked Cheese Goins. It had become clear that this very transactional nature of Alvin Ridley was also elevated to the level of interpersonal relations. The ones he had indicated that he liked, I would ask why, and he would say, sometimes with a smile, "Because they *like* me!" And for the ones he didn't like, there was always some fantastic ancient story in his mind that indicated that the prospective juror did not like him. Sometimes there were ancient slights from his school days that Alvin had not forgotten.

Alvin bristled at the activity around the table as we moved the chairs from facing the judge to the other side of the table to face the potential jurors.

"I got to leave!" he loudly groaned. "My head-neck-back-tailbone are hurting, and this is unconstitutional to make me sit here when they are hurting!"

I snapped at him, "Alvin, if you walk out, they'll go on with the trial. It's called a trial in absentia." I continued in the lowest voice that I could muster, yet still get the point across. "The court would make us go on with the trial, and your ass would surely be convicted when the jury sees that you fled the courtroom."

"You made me come here, and you didn't bring my neck brace!" he snapped back. *Damn. Of all things to forget.* Then I had an inspiration. I got Lori's attention and whispered, "Go down the street to Eddie Test's medical supply store and get Alvin a *new* neck brace!" Why didn't I have this idea before? We had suffered for months while Alvin wore what we privately called the "Stench Radiator." Lori was back in record time with the new brace, and I'm sure as I put it on him, I looked quite the shyster to the people who would decide his fate.

One hundred and eleven potential jurors showed up, and I had questionnaires from ninety-two of them. For the remaining mystery jurors, I could ask individually the questions they had neglected to disclose on the form. Determining if that kind of questioning made them angry was good information to have as well.

9

*T*he jury selection process was, ideally, to come up with a jury of one's peers. But none of these people were Alvin's "peers," really, with the exception maybe of Cheese. He ran in the same circles as Alvin did.

Those from the first list who were not eliminated were usually asked to come back to the next trial being queued up. So it was likely that several people we struck from serving on Joe Canada's jury would be back somewhere on the pews to be picked through again in Alvin's case.

Judge Van Pelt entered the small courtroom from his office through the door just behind the bench. He had given the large courtroom to Judge Loggins, the chief judge, and left us in Courtroom B, a windowless box. His voice rose as he said, "Mr. Franklin, have you got a case to sound for this courtroom?" It all seemed so formal.

Buzz, in a most official tone, answered, "Yes, Your Honor. For the purposes of a jury trial, the state sounds case number 98-CR-00836, the *State of Georgia* versus *Alvin Eugene Ridley*, charged with murder, felony murder, and aggravated assault." He lingered with emphasis on the charges. "The state is ready."

The judge looked at us. "What says the defendant?"

I responded slowly, "The defense is ready, Your Honor. We need to have a bench conference about some matters before voir dire begins."

My hesitancy was that there were big issues that Judge Van Pelt had yet to rule on. One of which was if Buzz could go into, and present evidence of, the alleged "captivity" of Virginia Ridley for almost three decades. The others were the state's allegations that he also kept his mother "captive," and finally that he kept his cats cruelly tied up in the house on Inman Street. Ideally, the court should rule on these things before both sides questioned the prospective jurors in the voir dire process. Prejudice and bias were expected, especially in this kind of high-profile case with allegations that had been going around for years about my client. I wanted the judge's ruling *before* we started, as his decisions could change the nature of my opening statement. I might need to know who were "cat people" and who were "dog people"—in case the cat allegation was going to be allowed.

The room full of potential jurors, fifty-six in number, was arranged by the bailiff in rows in the order of their names on the latest version of the juror list. I felt that we would likely be examining only forty or so of them. And Cheese Goins, who had all week been pretending that he didn't know me while stage-whispering and winking at me whenever I drew near, was toward the end of the list. It was unlikely that I would have Cheese, the "ringer" I never asked for. What I was hoping for was to keep him viable just long enough that the state would have to burn one of its strikes to get rid of him. That was the highest and best use for Cheese, I thought.

Juries are constructed by a process of elimination. First the court eliminates a few that patently do not qualify, such as those who have moved away or who are convicted felons without their civil rights restored. After the court's questions, the attorneys get to ask questions, hoping to find other reasons "for cause" that won't count against the limited number of "strikes" that each side is given. At the end of that process, each side whittles down the number with its given number of strikes on who is left. Those still standing after all the dust clears make up the jury.

There were so many people that I knew well and so many more that I remembered from a decade of politics and service. There was a guy who was the nephew of one of our former sheriffs, and a former divorce client. There was a woman who had applied for the job as my secretary, but who after interviews, I hadn't hired—one of a few jurors I had hoped I didn't offend in my past dealings. There was Alvin's next-door neighbor, whom I also knew as a server at a restaurant in town. I saw the familiar face of Kimberly Clark-Barnes, who published and edited the *Catoosa Tribune*. Hell, she'd been *reporting* about this very case.

"No way that isn't a free strike for cause," I mumbled to Mike and Lori. I had even subpoenaed her to our change of venue hearing, for purposes of cross-examination. "No way she is staying on," I said.

And then there was Cheese, "discreetly" winking at me every time I looked his way. I kept scanning the array and noticed a scowl consistently coming from one woman. I scanned the questionnaires to find her. From the Burning Bush community, I couldn't think of a reason for her unpleasant leer.

"I think she must just not like the allegations of this case, or, Alvin, did you have a bad business deal with her?"

Alvin looked up, only briefly. "Naw. I don't know her. *Maybe she don't like you.*"

I dismissed that, moving on to fill out the grid I had created on a legal pad, drawing eight rows of boxes, six across each row, and scribbling the last names of the people in front of me in their order of seating in the order of the boxes on my pad. Then I scrambled to fill in the box around their names with what I knew of them from memory or the questionnaires, and I would continue to do so as we learned more about them. Mike and Lori were doing the same, while Alvin pretended to be helpful. At some point, he started rifling through my files to look busy. I finally had the boxes on my chart filled with last names and scribbled notes reduced from the questionnaires, including plus and minus signs if something indicated from their answers or demeanor that they seemed "good" or "bad" for us, purely from initial gut feelings. As Buzz addressed the panels, I noted a shift in the mood of the room once the indictment was read to the amassed group. Hands started shooting up with concerns about their ability to serve on this very uncomfortable case.

One of the first things each side will ask is if any of the panel

knows the lawyer or their staff on the other side. As Buzz asked if
any prospective jurors knew me, many hands shot up—not surprisingly because of my campaigning over the last decade. But there
was something amiss. Some did not look pleased as they raised
their hands to their familiarity with me. I tried to scribble in each
cube on my sheet which ones were so indicating, so I could follow
up. As Buzz went through each raised hand, asking how they knew
me, the woman whom I had interviewed to be my secretary, but
didn't hire, started revealing that story as Buzz quickly scribbled it
down.

The next one who had raised her hand was the scowling woman
from Burning Bush Road whom we had noticed before. When she
started unloading in front of everyone about how I had totally disappointed her as her state representative, Judge Van Pelt inter-
vened, calling her to the bench. The damage was done, however,
and I had to face the fact that Alvin was right about her. Strangely,
I took it personally, perhaps sensitive that their once-promising
state representative and candidate for the U.S. Congress was now
reduced to this. At the bench, I was pushing her to tell me *one thing*
that I had failed to do for her.

Judge Van Pelt looked at me incredulously, while Buzz silently
watched. "Mr. Poston, she has a right to her feelings, whether you
agree with them or not," Judge Van Pelt cautioned; then the judge
asked questions of her, to see if she could be rehabilitated as a witness who could be fair. Once it was determined that she could not,
Judge Van Pelt said, "Ma'am, you are excused." Except for the collateral damage to my ego, I had dodged a bullet. I wouldn't have to
use one of our twelve precious peremptory strikes on her.

Alvin didn't look as reassured. He actually looked horrified at
what he had overheard. And for once, I couldn't blame him.

The process continued, with other jurors revealing that I might
have to use one or more of my precious strikes to eliminate people
who had problems with me, Alvin's lawyer.

To even things out, Cheese Goins had still not raised his hand
when Buzz asked the panels about me. In fact, he had left most of
his questionnaire blank, other than listing the ages of his seven
children, most of them around my age. On the question "Have you
or a close relative ever been a victim of a violent crime?" Cheese

put, "No." We all knew that was not true, as Cheese was always claiming to be a victim of scrapes that ended up here in court. I fulfilled my ethical obligation when I brought it to the attention of the court and to Buzz at the end of the last bench conference.

"We all know Cheese Goins, and for some reason, he didn't raise his hand when Buzz asked about people knowing me . . ." Buzz just nodded and made a note. He was going to have to burn one of his precious six strikes on Cheese, who continued to wink at me every time I faced the array.

A third from the pews, this time a Ringgold man, indicated that due to some issue with me, he indicated he could not be fair to the defendant. He stuck to his guns and was excused. I didn't go at him, as I had on Scowling Lady.

Alvin whispered to me, "I don't think I can get a fair trial in Catoosa County, Georgia, and I don't think I can get a fair trial with you as my lawyer!" I just tried to calm him.

My interaction with the prospective jurors improved when I asked who knew or remembered the late Dr. Charles Stephenson. This was a nice diversion and a way to warm everyone up from our cold start. Dr. Stephenson had birthed over six thousand citizens in his little office on Tennessee Street, and ten of the impaneled prospective jurors revealed that Dr. Stephenson had assisted their birth, smiling for the first time since they entered the courtroom. I scribbled "Dr. S" in each of their squares on my sheet. He was to be discussed in the case.

When the question went up by the prosecutor as to who was familiar with "the defendant, Alvin Eugene Ridley," a woman whom I recognized raised her hand. She lived on Inman Street and was a server in a restaurant in Ringgold. She was always such a nice person in my dealings with her, but it was obvious that she was terrified of my client.

Alvin whispered loudly, "I don't like that one. Send her home."

Living just up the street with all the years of rumors about what went on in that dilapidated house, it was no wonder. She withstood the efforts of Judge Van Pelt to rehabilitate her as a juror and was excused. But I worried about the effect of others overhearing some of the things she said.

Another important question I had long planned to ask was who among them had done business with Alvin Ridley, or if their family had done business with him, as my father had. Several hands were raised. I asked if anyone with those raised hands had felt he had not done a good job for them in a purchase, delivery, or repair. Not one could criticize his business dealings. This was the legend of Alvin Ridley, even admitted by his detractors, that he was a natural wizard at television repair. Alvin seemed to sit up a little straighter, and he seemed more comfortable in the courtroom during this part of my questions.

I qualified the panels as to reading newspaper articles about the case and acknowledged that one of the writers and publishers of those accounts, Kimberly Clark-Barnes, was among them on jury duty. Both Kimberly and I seemed to know that she would not likely serve, having written about the case, and having been subpoenaed by me about her reporting during our hearing on our motion for a change of venue. Almost everyone acknowledged that they had read or seen accounts of the case in the media, except notably Cheese Goins, who kept his hand down.

Avoiding letting anyone spoil the whole array by blurting out that they believed the stories and accounts, Judge Van Pelt had each person who indicated they could not put the press reports aside come up to the bench. One by one, he successfully rehabilitated them all to say they *could* set aside all of what they had read and seen. *Ugh,* I thought, we had to allocate our uncommitted peremptory strikes.

Regarding relationships with law enforcement, the court excused two more, for cause. But then one man, after first indicating he was not sure he could fairly judge Alvin's guilt or innocence because a relative was murdered, was rehabilitated by the court, meaning he stepped back from saying he could not be fair. I was going to be using up all twelve of our strikes.

On the other hand, I am sure that Buzz was going to use up all of his strikes as well, as he only had six strikes to my twelve. And since he had to announce the state strikes first, there was always a possibility that he would use one of his strikes on one that I had planned to strike, perhaps allowing me to extend my strike list incrementally.

I asked to approach the bench, to discreetly address the issue of Kimberly Clark-Barnes, who wore all hats at the *Catoosa Tribune*— owner, publisher, editor, and, often, reporter. The court called her up to the bench. When asked, she said, not surprisingly, that she *could* set everything she had heard and everything she had written aside and sit as an impartial juror. Everyone would say that, I reasoned, if it was put to them the way the court asked it. Kimberly Clark-Barnes would remain in the jury pool for the selection process.

As each side reviewed notes on both ends of the abutting tables in the small courtroom, we used up all of the fifteen minutes allowed with calculations and recalculations of different scenarios, depending on whom Buzz was going to strike. I could perhaps reach the newspaper publisher/editor/reporter with a strike if I could live with having some earlier questionable ones on the jury. But then again, Kimberly was, as far as I could tell, a fair-minded person. Alvin started to act like he was reaching for his suitcases to leave. "Sit still, Alvin," I ordered.

I knew Buzz would strike Cheese. Lord help us all if he doesn't. Cheese could blow up the case and cause a fight in the jury room. The mayhem that would ensue would mean another trial for Alvin Ridley, and I just didn't know if my practice, or my marriage for that matter, could handle that.

One woman had bought a refrigerator from Alvin when his Zenith and appliance business was open, and she didn't trip any alarms that would make me want to strike her, so that could be another state strike, I reasoned.

At the end of the fifteen minutes of reviewing notes, it was time to pick a jury. But we were interrupted by the Canada jury. Alvin sat back while Joe Canada was brought back in from the jail downstairs. They just had a question, and were sent back to continue deliberations.

We all reassembled, changing out the defendants again, back to Alvin's case. One by one, from the top of the list on down, when a name was called, the prospective jurors were to stand. The state got the first shot and would announce whether they "excuse" the juror or whether they were "content" with the juror. Those were the words used in our tradition.

The first name was a man who worked in the parts department of a Freightliner truck dealership. I couldn't tell if either side had asked him a single question. My notes were empty. Buzz said, "The state is content," and not having a reason to burn a strike, I followed with "We are content." Right off the bat, we had our first juror. He was directed to move to the jury box.

The next name was the woman who had followed the Scowling Lady to the bench. Buzz was naturally content with her and said so. Trying not to offend, I said, "Defense respectfully excuses . . ." *One strike*, I thought.

Next up was a woman who was an assistant in a large insurance firm in Chattanooga that employed a lot of people. Like the first guy, she had flown completely under the radar throughout the voir dire process. Not having any real reason to strike, I followed Buzz in being content with this juror. She joined the first juror in the box.

Next up was an elderly widow, and while Buzz quickly indicated that he was content with her as a juror, I followed my gut and excused her. I had noticed she was one of the ones who would never look at Alvin.

Next came the woman who had bought the refrigerator from Alvin. Buzz quickly said, "The state excuses." She was followed by a young man who was a fitter at a local manufacturer of road-making machinery. As Buzz accepted him, I quickly did the same, realizing that in a system that worked by process of elimination, we knew less about whom we ended up with than the ones we were obsessively striking from serving. Now we had three jurors.

"James C. Goins," the clerk Norman Stone boomed. "James C. Goins." Either Cheese couldn't hear or he didn't recognize his own name, because he had been called Cheese Goins all of my life. Finally he shot up as fast as anyone ever snapped to attention. Buzz didn't waste any time. "The state excuses Mr. Goins." Cheese looked to me as if I could help, for the first time all week without winking.

"You are excused, Mr. Goins," Judge Van Pelt said, because I had nothing to add.

I heard the word *"Shit!"* uttered from the clearly disappointed Cheese, and he stormed out while mumbling additional expletives. Alvin looked clearly disappointed. A few prospective jurors giggled. Judge Van Pelt smiled.

I struck the next two in order, because they both had indicated in voir dire that they were close to my opponent in my last contested state representative race. And then Buzz struck the next two in order, likely because one had said she knew me and she didn't scowl. I don't know why he struck the other one, who worked in the ubiquitous textile industry in our area. It must have been something in their extensive juror files I wasn't privy to.

In turn, I excused the next two names in a row, after Buzz accepted them. One was related to a deputy sheriff, but not close enough to be excused for cause. The other said on her form that she had once been the victim of domestic violence. With charges like these to defend, I couldn't take the chance that she was still overpowered with feelings about her past experience.

At this point, I had used half of my strikes, and Buzz had used two-thirds of his.

We both accepted the next three who were called to stand up, putting on the jury a single woman who worked for a different large insurance company in Chattanooga, and a man in his forties who was the nephew of a former sheriff whom, as it turned out, I planned to discuss in the trial. Also on was the young woman who had applied and interviewed to be my secretary, but whom I had not hired. I figured when she looked at my frazzled state, she might be thanking me.

I struck the next name on the list after he stood up, and Buzz accepted him, because the man had refused to fill out a questionnaire even after being handed a new one by the clerk.

Next came a young man who was an extrusion technician in a textile mill, married with two children. I just had a good feeling about him, but obviously, so did Buzz.

Just as quickly I excused the next name that was called, as he knew too many law enforcement and others whom Alvin didn't trust. This was one of Alvin's few calls, and I obliged.

The next two in order found contentment from both sides and were placed in the box. One was a nice woman in her sixties who was a U.S. bankruptcy court administrator, and the other a very young man who listed his occupation as a "bill poster" for a media company in Chattanooga.

Now we had nine jurors in the box, and I had four more strikes left and Buzz had two more strikes.

But then another interruption. The Canada jury had a verdict. The defendants were switched at the table, Canada having to be brought up from the jail. Alvin sat where he had launched his escape to the federal courthouse from three days before. The jury convicted Canada on all counts. Alvin did not look happy. Canada was taken away for later sentencing.

I had to use three of those last four strikes for the next three names that Buzz had quickly announced he was content with. One was another woman from the Burning Bush community, and I feared she likely knew the Scowling Lady. One was a man who said he knew Alvin, but Alvin did not feel the love and directed that I strike him. The last was a guy who looked very down-to-earth—and with his beard, he appeared as if he was a Mennonite Anabaptist. I thought he was interesting, and likely an independent thinker. He didn't do a questionnaire, however, so I excused him.

Buzz struck the next potential juror, a man, for reasons I did not know. This meant we were both down to our last strike each, and there were nine jurors in the box.

Next up was a distinguished man of seventy-six years, and, apparently, in his working life, he had lived in Kansas City. While I had vowed that I would try to stick to folks who had been in Ringgold for a long time, I felt good about this juror. He described himself as an Adventist. I had a good feeling about him. After Buzz accepted him, I put him on.

I used my last strike on the next name, only because Alvin made me. This put us in the situation of not being able to object to any other jurors, and I didn't see anyone whom I was overly concerned about in the next few names, knowing Buzz had just one strike left. And he used it on the next name.

Both of us being out of strikes meant the next two names were automatically accepted, although by tradition the court allowed us the fiction of both graciously announcing our being content with the next two names coming up. One was Kimberly, the publisher/editor/reporter. The other was a thirty-six-year-old mother of two whom I had very little information on. That's the way it goes when selecting a jury by process of elimination.

Judge Van Pelt announced that we would next pick two alternate jurors. I used two strikes, Buzz used one, and we got a private security officer and a counselor with the nonprofit Easter Seals.

Now we had a jury. Six men and six women, all white, and two alternates, one man and one woman, and both white as well. The county was over 90 percent white, so this wasn't unusual.

I remembered Alvin's late-filed, home-typed motion and signaled to Buzz. "Your Honor, could we approach the bench?" I was waving a copy of the document and pointed to the original, which was now on top of Alvin's official court file on the bench.

The judge snapped, "I haven't ruled on it yet, but the motion, now that you've mentioned that, is denied."

No surprise. I looked at Alvin, who could not have realistically expected to change the court's ruling on something so significant. He looked more dejected than ever.

Judge Van Pelt had released the newly selected jurors, but the rest of us had to remain for the Jackson-Denno hearing to determine the voluntariness of Alvin's statements, and there were many. Even though I started advising Alvin on the street in the first week of the investigation, he had already been blabbing to any officer who would listen, and apparently did not take my earliest advice and spoke to Detective Bilbrey. Now the state wanted to use those statements, and we had to go through this process. Since none of the statements were made while he was in custody, I resolved that they would likely all be admitted, and after a hearing, the court ruled, appropriately, that they would be.

But we were also expecting to have a hearing and get a ruling on Buzz's similar transactions notice, where he was trying to bring evidence before the jury that Alvin had imprisoned his wife for almost three decades *and* that he had also abused, and if you believed the rumors, even murdered his own mother. And, for icing on the creepy cake, we were also fighting against the admission of evidence of the allegation that he kept two cats tied up to a table's legs. This was prompted by Bilbrey's observations, and the two reports in the state discovery packet, one regarding social services checking on his mother in 1993, and the 1997 report of first responders to Virginia's death, both detailing that there were "two cats tied to the table."

At ten minutes after four, a winter evening was falling, and we were still in court without the jury present. Next up was the determination of how much of the prosecution's intended similar transactions evidence could be allowed to be presented to the jury. Judge Van Pelt wanted to continue working. "Let's see how far we can get on trying to get the similar transactions hearings dealt with today, I'd like to do that."

I had plans to meet our star witness, Dr. Braxton Bryant Wannamaker, for dinner, as I had not yet met him personally. I was going to get to call him out of turn to the stand tomorrow, near the beginning of the state's case. This infuriated Buzz, but all thirty cases put on this special trial week calendar were told to be ready for trial this week, and I had to pick a day well in advance to work into Dr. Wannamaker's busy schedule.

We got going in the similar transactions hearing. Georgia was unique in allowing the prosecution to cast a wide net and bring up a defendant's allegedly "similar" behavior that supposedly informs a jury of the defendant's "bent of mind." It was the bane of a criminal defense lawyer's existence, allowing in things that quite often served only to incite the passions of jurors against the defendant. Buzz had given notice of his intention to put up evidence to the jury of the three infamous claims.

Judge Van Pelt started the hearing by saying, "This lists three separate matters. Number one being Ms. Minnie Ridley being kept in violation of her personal liberty. Number two being Virginia Ridley being confined without legal authority. And then number three on or about the fourth day of October, 1997, the defendant did cause unjustifiable physical suffering to living animals, to wit, two cats."

Alvin made a strange, abrupt move, then stood; I pulled his arm back down. "Calm down, don't make any sudden moves in here!" I whispered. While I considered the uniformed courtroom officers as friends, I knew they would not hesitate to immobilize what they perceived to be a threat in the courtroom. Especially one coming from Alvin Ridley.

A similar transactions allegation was an effective tool for a prosecutor to prejudice the jury to support the notion that the defendant was more likely to have committed the crimes, due to the prejudicial effect of the alleged behaviors. We went down the list, as notice had been given.

The first allegation was of Mrs. Minnie Ridley, Alvin's mother, being kept in violation of her personal liberty. Of course, I knew the story quite well, thanks to Alvin's continuing push to have me relitigate matters that one would assume were far in the past. The fact that we were now here arguing the issue of the events of the last years of his mother's life made me think Alvin was prescient to push me so hard on it. Of course, this allegation was present from the early whispers after his arrest, news reports hinting that the body of Minnie Ridley should be exhumed and investigated for abuse.

Virginia had written about the incident where Alvin had rushed his elderly mother to Erlanger Hospital in Chattanooga, strategically across the state line, when trying to evade the court order obtained by the Georgia Department of Human Resources, in the agency's efforts to investigate the elder abuse rumors. This had all happened at a time when the occasional Virginia Ridley searches would still take place as well.

Buzz got right to the issues. Over the next couple of hours, he made his case for the court to allow extraneous matters, which could be quite disturbing to some jurors. He put on the stand, out of the presence of the jury, one of Virginia's sisters, and a lady from the Hickey family's church.

Buzz argued that there was no evidence really of where she was during almost three decades. "And we suddenly find Virginia Ridley dead on October 4, 1997, from what the evidence the state will present shows it to be a case of homicide. Mr. Ridley was the only one who had access to Virginia Ridley, the only one that saw her during all these years. And I think it's evidence that the jury needs to hear to put this case in context."

I cited a few appellate cases—for the first time I remembered ever doing so in court in my thirteen years as a lawyer—to argue that the state had failed in showing how these allegations fit the narrow list of allowed purposes of letting in such potentially incendiary evidence, to wit: bent of mind, course of conduct, intent, or modus operandi.

Judge Van Pelt, obviously exhausted himself, declined to make a ruling yet. "Well, I'll take a look at it. I'm not going to make a final ruling right now." He hinted that he might let the history of Virginia and Alvin's relationship in. All the alleged lies and misdirection as to her whereabouts. That would be damaging, for sure.

The judge continued to speak. "Now, you know, the situation with his mother and the two cats I'm not as sure about and I'll let you know something about that in the morning."

It was nighttime, but I had so much yet to do. I had to put marks on my opening statement to avoid mentioning any issue that the court may rule out, and to preemptively address anything bad that might be allowed in, to take the wind out of their sails, if you will.

I took Alvin through Hardee's drive-thru to get him some supper, then took him home. Alison was to meet me for dinner with Dr. Wannamaker. As the "perfumes" of Alvin lingered in my Jeep for quite a while after he left it, she would drive the Ford Explorer and we would both meet Dr. Braxton Bryant Wannamaker for dinner. He was our most critical witness, and now he was here running up billable hours I could barely afford.

10

*A*s our expert was staying near the big Hamilton Place Mall in Chattanooga, I suggested we meet at the J. Alexander's restaurant near that mall. Alison would meet us there, but after I got Alvin home with supper, I instructed him to stay in the house and call me if anything went awry.

"Alvin, I think we have a good jury. Sleep well tonight."

"What about that newspaper woman?" he reminded me.

"Well, what I know of her is that she's fair-minded. Leave it to me to put up our case. You don't have to do anything but sit there and you can write me notes. Alvin, remember, all you have to do is show up."

"Uh-huh," he muttered.

"Get some sleep. I'll be here early in the morning."

I stumbled through the minefield of obstacles on the crumbling stone steps and through his yard. *He better be here in the morning,* I thought, wondering if I could disable his remaining operable cars. I drove the twenty minutes up I-75, across the Tennessee line to the restaurant.

Having never met Dr. Wannamaker, I didn't know what to expect. He wasn't very conversational over the phone. I had only seen one picture of him, a distinguished, prematurely gray-haired man, with thick glasses. In his picture online, he was in a white lab coat, like straight out of central casting for a medical expert. The familiar-looking Dr. Wannamaker, just like the serious man in the picture, was waiting for me, dressed smartly in coat and tie.

"Dr. Wannamaker, I presume?"

"Yes" was all he said.

"I'm McCracken Poston. It's nice to meet you."

We went ahead and took our seats while we waited for Alison to join us.

"How was your trip down here?"

"Fine" was the answer.

And that's the way it was for what seemed a lifetime until Alison's arrival broke the ice a bit. He was just a serious and very quiet man, I thought. His curriculum vitae spoke for him, I thought. We ordered our supper.

"Well, oh yes, here's a check for you," I gushed, thinking that maybe if I paid him, he would become more gregarious.

He took the envelope and put it in his jacket pocket.

As the food arrived, I couldn't stop talking, just trying to fill the void.

"So we have a jury, and the judge is going to accommodate your schedule tomorrow . . . and I'm going to give you the address of the courthouse in Ringgold, Georgia, just below the state line. Just be there before ten a.m. because we're going to call you out of turn during a break in the state's presentation of its case."

Silence.

I shifted gears. "So . . . this is an unusual case. As I suspected, the state is putting a lot of stock in these things called petechiae."

"I know what that is," the doctor rallied. "My clients have these tiny hemorrhages after seizures. They are quite common to observe in my field."

We continued through dinner, the thirty-nine-year-old former politician trying to carry the conversation with a fifty-eight-year-old neurologist. Alison tried as well to lighten the conversation from our themes of death and dead bodies. He must have thought he was dealing with kids, I thought, a man this smart and accomplished.

As I paid the bill and repeated the instructions for his appearance at trial, the doctor asked what seemed to be one last question.

"Was there anything else that you found unusual about this woman?"

I half-jokingly threw out, "Yeah, she was quite the journalist!"

"What do you mean?"

"I mean she couldn't hiccup without noting everything that was going on around her when it happened," I exaggerated, mostly out of the strangeness of it all.

Dr. Wannamaker perked up. "That's hypergraphia. I see it a lot in mostly temporal lobe epilepsy cases."

I felt my heart start racing. "Hyper-what?"

"Hypergraphia—it literally means a lot of writing that these patients do. Some of my patients have brought in volumes, asking me to look at them to show their daily lives. They can be quite detailed . . ."

What? There was an *explanation* for all of the notes and all of the journals. I had estimated that there were probably close to twenty thousand piled up in Alvin's house. He had made some of them into a shrine to her, I explained to the doctor. I told him more about Alvin's eccentricities, and that I had a theory that Virginia was actually in charge of the conspiracy factory and had written the scripts for Alvin's outcries to and sometimes *at* the community.

Suddenly our conversation flowed, and we spent another hour discussing Virginia's writings and Alvin's behavior. Then we were the only table still occupied in the restaurant.

"So he's an army man, huh? So am I," the doctor responded to my description of Alvin's background. "I'm looking forward to meeting him."

We shook hands and left, just as the chairs were being put on top of the tables for cleaning, and I couldn't believe how productive this meeting had turned out, especially at the end. All along, I had been thinking that Virginia's poems and observations were most useful just to show snapshots from her life and that she seemed relatively happy with her husband. Now I realized the very existence of these writings was evidence of her condition.

All along, there was a reason for her constant writing, I thought as I followed Alison home.

There is a fight here. All we must do is show up, and fight.

I scanned the morning's *Chattanooga Times Free Press,* the week-old product of the merger of the Democratic-leaning *Chattanooga Times* and the Republican-leaning *Chattanooga News-Free Press.* "The case is being hailed as Catoosa County's most bizarre murder trial in history," the article by Beenea Hyatt, a young, aggressive reporter, read. A local man was quoted saying: "He's a little weird . . . I believe he held his wife captive, but he didn't kill her. He just doesn't seem like he has a criminal mind, not in my opinion. He's just weird."

At this point, I'll take it, I thought. *Technically, he isn't charged with holding Virginia captive. Buzz is just trying to get that in to influence the jurors in the murder deliberation.*

"His predominantly blue-plaid shirt and blue-striped necktie didn't match," the article continued. *Damn. That's on me.* I brought him the tie. Even worse: "He was also charged with aggravated assault after allegedly threatening a Catoosa County deputy with a handgun."

What? Is that even true? And now the jury will think it's something that was withheld from them. Sure, they promise not to read the news, but they often do, and their spouses and friends do, and they talk, I thought . . . I had to go get Alvin. I drove to his house.

The first thing I noticed on the foot of Alvin's bed was a copy of the newspaper that I had just read at home.

"I see that you got out this morning and got a paper," I said. "Remember, the judge gave the jury an instruction not to read any articles about the case."

"I've got a better shirt and tie to wear today," he deadpanned.

Of all that was wrong with the news, it was the comment that his shirt and tie didn't match that bothered him.

Alvin lugged the two suitcases from the house to the stone porch. I grabbed them both and put them in the back of the Jeep. I hoped that it was all there. I knew he rifled through it all the time, so I wasn't sure how I could even find a particular exhibit.

Parking back at my office, behind the post office, we walked in the usual pattern, me leading and Alvin casting his eyes downward, behind and to one side of me. We walked through the brisk low forty-degree chill, and into the back of the courthouse annex. "I've got a better match on my shirt and tie," Alvin repeated. "That reporter didn't like the tie *you* put on me." Of course, it was all *my* fault.

I asked Lori to sit on the bench behind us and to signal me if he tried to walk out of court. *I will seriously tackle him,* I thought, probably causing a mistrial, but I wasn't going to let him flee and leave me here without a client. As I had told Alvin, that actually happened once before in a case here, and the trial just continued, and the jury was charged with the law that flight could be considered evidence of guilt. And, of course, they convicted the absent defendant, and eventually he was caught and sent straight to prison. I was determined not to let anything like that happen. I wasn't going to lose again without a fight, even it was with my own client.

Before the jury came in, Judge Van Pelt was supposed to rule on the efforts of the prosecutor to get in the similar transactions testimony that alleged that Alvin held not only his wife captive, but also that he similarly held his mother and two cats captive.

With the jurors and alternates all in the jury room, the court ruled, "I will allow the state to go into aspects of the facts of, the alleged facts that Mrs. Virginia Ridley was not in public view for twenty-plus years, but I'm going to preclude the state from making any inference that somehow or another Minnie Ridley was being held against her will, or not given medical treatment, or neglected, or not given adequate nutrition or anything like that."

So far, so good. We could handle the inference that one woman was being held, but not two.

Judge Van Pelt continued, "I will allow the state to go into the history of the relationship between the defendant and Virginia Ridley . . . I think that is relevant to what they're alleging here."

Alvin leaned in, asking, "And are we going to talk about them illegal seizing my van?" *He's persistent, I'll give him that,* I thought.

"Just let me handle it, Alvin. Remember, this is a murder case."

Judge Van Pelt ordered that Buzz could not mention allegations about Alvin's mother, and as to the cats, he could only mention that there were two twine strings tied to the furniture, and not mention the cats that were attached to them when people were in Alvin's house.

Briefly I panicked. My apparent success in keeping the infrequent restraint of two cats could backfire, giving the jury room to speculate that Virginia had been tied to the table, and not the two cats that witnesses said the twine strings were used for.

The court would allow Buzz to get into the evidence of Alvin and Virginia's relationship, the elusive dodges that he gave her family, and his alleged denial of her existence.

Then the judge stated, "Anything else we need to talk about before opening statements?" The trial of Alvin Ridley was finally about to begin.

The jury filed in, and the court gave them one more oath, to "well and truly try the issues formed on this bill of indictment," and again listed the charges. I saw several jurors look past the tables toward the back door of the courtroom. I looked back over my shoulder and caught the unique appearance of Salesman Sam. I turned and pointed to the door. He shyly withdrew and went back outside the door. He had started off as a state witness, under his real name, Benjamin McGaha. Now he was our witness, and I didn't want him in here.

"Your Honor, I just, before we get into any argument or evidence . . ."

"You want to invoke the rule of sequestration?" Judge Van Pelt had seen me.

I quickly responded, "Yes, I saw one of our witnesses come in and he obviously saw the look on my face and left."

The court said, "The rule of sequestration has been invoked at this point in time. Anyone who is a witness needs to step outside."

A lot of people got up, many I didn't recognize. Salesman Sam finally had served a useful purpose—reminding me to invoke the rule of sequestration to keep all witnesses out of the room.

"Mr. Franklin, do you have an opening statement at this time?" the judge asked.

Buzz gave his opening statement, in his usual calm and professional demeanor, indicating that the science of the case would prove the "defendant, Alvin Ridley" guilty. "Mr. Poston would have you believe" was his usual introduction to any mention of me, as if to prepare them for *these lies from that lawyer over there.* He launched into what he expected the state's evidence would show regarding the rigor mortis of Virginia's body, suggesting that she had been dead longer than Alvin had reported. I made notes while Alvin stared uncomfortably at the back of the prosecutor, who was standing in front of the jury box. Then Buzz went into what he expected the evidence would show, suggesting that Alvin had smothered, or "softly strangled," her to death, then delayed the reporting of her death after untying her and positioning her in the bed to make it look like a natural death.

Alvin was writing something on a pad of yellow sticky notes Lori had brought. I continued jotting down on a legal pad what Buzz was saying so that I could address it either in my opening or closing.

Then I heard Buzz reference the position of Virginia Ridley's left arm. "Her arm was not in the place where it should be." I didn't fully hear it. Alvin was jingling what sounded like a lot of change in his pocket.

"Shh, I have to listen," I whispered. Buzz was again alluding to his theory that Alvin had smothered his wife and then moved her body to the bed.

Finally, on the physical evidence, Buzz telegraphed the state presentation on the presence of petechiae on Virginia's body. He is telling the jury that these tiny pinpoint hemorrhages only occurred due to the asphyxiation or "soft strangulation" of the victim.

Next the prosecutor addressed the oddness of the defendant, in ways that made Alvin seem sinister and conniving. Buzz addressed the "flat" tone the defendant had when he called 911 on October 4, 1997. "He didn't call 911 first," the district attorney told the jury. "He called Erlanger Hospital to come to get his wife," before mentioning the 911 call.

I made note that Buzz didn't share the last two words Alvin Ridley had said in the call to Catoosa's 911 dispatcher: "Please hurry."

He described the "fortress" on Inman Street, where undisputedly Virginia stayed for her last twenty-seven years, with the towering gate and the NO TRESPASSING and KEEP OUT signs.

Buzz carried himself with an air of moral superiority, but from our days together in the DA's office, I had always known him to have a quick and sharp sense of humor. His brother, Jim, was one of my best friends from law school. But in this room, I could tell, Buzz was my enemy. He was not only treating the defendant with disdain, but he was also treating me as if I deserved no respect from the jury. Buzz had smirked when telling me last week that Alvin had fled the courtroom and drove to the federal courthouse in Rome, rushing past the federal marshals and running into a judge's office, seemingly "doused with gasoline." Maybe to him, I couldn't take a joke anymore or laugh along. Or maybe I had actually become invested in defending Alvin Ridley.

The prosecution finished its opening, highlighting its theory that my client was a sinister malcontent and killer, depriving Virginia of her freedom, sustenance, and, ultimately, her life. Buzz was relatively brief in his opening remarks, but he gave me some openings to counterpunch, before the first bit of evidence was even offered to the jury.

Unbeknownst to me, Buzz signaled the court reporter to take down my opening statement. Usually, the arguments are not taken down. This was a pretty good move, because he could read it back to the jury verbatim in his closing argument if something didn't pan out as I said it would.

As I was finishing my notes on the state's opening, the roadmap of what the state indicated it would prove, Alvin thrust the pad of sticky notes into my face. "FALSE" was scribbled in his familiar hand on the top of the pad.

"Thank you, Alvin," I said. "I've got to give our side of it now."

I walked toward the jury. "Ladies and gentlemen," I began, "Mr. Alvin Ridley stands before you on trial for something he did not do . . ." I circled back to some of my voir dire questions, when I got promises from them collectively that they would avoid reaching any conclusions until they had heard all the evidence. *Good Lord, some of them can't even look at me, much less at my client,* I realized.

I confronted it. "Ladies and gentlemen, Mr. Ridley is not the ideal client, and I'll tell you that right now. He is difficult to work with. He's paranoid. It has taken me over a year to develop his trust in me, and he still insists on keeping all the evidence in those suitcases. He doesn't trust a soul, not even the lawyer who is trying to help him."

Buzz looked a bit surprised that I would start off by telling the jury that my client was paranoid, but I had to deal with it. Alvin's history of strange behavior was the elephant in the room.

"Mr. Franklin addressed several things that he said the state is going to prove and I put it to you that the state is not going to prove many of these things that are crucial."

In all, I spoke for half an hour in my opening statement. I covered over three decades, satisfying Alvin that I touched on all his major conspiracies. Couched at the start with "Alvin believes that," I listed them all, from Virginia's family sending law enforcement out to check on her over the administrations of four sheriffs, to what I referred to as the "high-water marks" of Alvin's paranoia that everyone was out to get them. The highest was in the aftermath of Bill Ridley's accident in the company truck, the litigation, and subsequent counterclaims, culminating in the "illegal seize"— as Alvin always put it—of his van.

I ended our opening statement just before 10:30 a.m., and Judge Van Pelt suggested we have our midmorning break. I walked back and sat next to Alvin. He held up a single yellow sticky note, where he had scrawled in big letters: "*RIGHT*," apropos of nothing specific about my opening. Still, I took it as a compliment.

Alvin said, "I'll sit here as long as my head, neck, back, and lower back and tailbone allow me to, because the Constitution says—"

"Stop!" I interrupted him. "We are going to handle this, Alvin. Be confident."

Judge Van Pelt called the court back to order, and the jurors filed into the jury box. "Okay, Mr. Franklin, call your first witness."

Buzz announced, "We call 'Trixie' LeCroy."

Alvin's sister-in-law came to the witness stand, this time in front of the jury. I was glad I had the opportunity out of the presence of the jury to cross-examine her yesterday, in the similar transactions hearing. I handed Alvin his yellow sticky-note pad back.

Patricia Hickey LeCroy took the oath, and Buzz positioned himself so that his witness would answer his questions facing more toward the jury. Asking fairly predictable questions, Buzz got out of her that her given name was Patricia and her nickname was Trixie. She was the younger sister of Virginia. Their father died in 1984— and the fact that Virginia didn't attend his funeral was a major bone of contention already raised in the state's opening. Her mother, Adell, had been living in a nursing home for the past six years. Buzz asked her about her siblings, and she described an older sister Linda, who could not be here due to some surgery, and an older brother, who may or may not have been there, but he wasn't listed as a witness. Linda, who had been the one leading the German film crew around Alvin's home and property, had been very vocal with the press.

Establishing that Virginia was the second child of the four, Trixie testified that she became acquainted with Alvin Ridley when he was dating Virginia.

Buzz asked her about Virginia's social life and their church attendance. "She attended the church up until the time she got married to Alvin Ridley."

She also answered where the newlyweds had first lived. "There was a housing project that was relatively new, built, I'm assuming, by the City of Ringgold, and they lived there."

The prosecutor continued to ask about what happened early in the marriage of Virginia and Alvin. His witness described attending their wedding in 1966.

She described that soon after, Virginia had a severe allergic reaction to her medications and was lethargic. Trixie said Virginia couldn't talk. She returned to her family for care for some time, until Alvin came to take her home.

"He thought they were intervening with their relationship as husband and wife and he himself took it upon himself to come and physically carry her out. And I felt it was against her will, she did not want to go that day—believe me, she did not want to go that day."

I slowly looked at Alvin, who was waiting for my glance, shaking his head, and looking down at his hand, where the top note on the yellow sticky notes now said: "FALSE."

Buzz knew he was scoring points, and asked, "What was her reaction?"

Trixie said, "'I don't want to go,' something to the effect. 'Please don't let him take me.' I believe that was the words. 'Please don't let him take me.'"

I leaned in toward Alvin, whispering, "I thought she said Virginia couldn't talk." Alvin whispered that Virginia wanted to go back to their apartment with him.

Buzz then directed his witness to the subject of the decades-long effort to contact her sister. "Did you ever come down to Ringgold to attempt to visit with your sister?"

It seemed that the young couple became much less available to the Hickey family, and Trixie mentioned Virginia missing several family events. Alvin allegedly told them, "She's visiting a friend. She's gone for the evening. I've told her, but I can't help it if she will not get back with you." Trixie opined that these were "just lame excuses."

When I got the opportunity for cross-examination, I jumped up, grabbing at a few of the large letter-sized envelopes that I had used in an attempt to organize Virginia's writings. As I pulled out three of them, I saw two roaches scramble out, jumping from the envelopes, where they were, to the carpeted floor of the courtroom. I tried not to react.

I approached the small rostrum that lawyers sometimes used, but I positioned it where she would be looking away from the jurors and toward our side of the courtroom, toward her brother-in-law Alvin.

I asked her if they had ever requested law enforcement to check in on Virginia.

"We certainly did," she said, adding, "Well, when they called Sheriff Brown to go down there, and on several occasions, he said he went. On one occasion, Sheriff J.D. Stewart himself said that he went. He took his wife and a member of the church that Mr. Ridley and my sister had gotten married at, and they contacted my parents and said that they felt like everything was okay."

An early gift from a state witness! Lee Roy Brown had beaten Sheriff J.D. Stewart in 1968, but then two terms later, Stewart won the office back in 1976. I asked about Sheriff Brown, because Virginia had written about a conversation that she had with him. In her answer, Trixie had given us the gift of another sheriff, J.D. Stewart, and he apparently took his wife and a church member along with him! I could see Buzz shift uncomfortably in his seat.

"Obviously, this sounds like Virginia wanted to be where she was, doesn't it?"

She snapped, "No."

I continued, "Let me ask you this then. Do you know that Virginia appeared in a courtroom on September 15, 1970, the big courtroom over there in the older building?"

Trixie responded, "I know I was told by my parents she did, yes."

Buzz shot up, "Your Honor, we're getting into more hearsay . . ."

As I didn't solicit the hearsay, but she volunteered it, I kept going.

"After hearing whatever statement she made over there, your parents withdrew for a while, didn't they, in terms of looking for her?"

Trixie became contemplative. "Well, when you make every effort possible, when you go through every avenue you can possibly go through without breaking the law, and you've got to understand they were trying to protect her. They did not want to make her life any more miserable than they felt it already was."

We were on a roll, but I noticed that the jury was neither looking at the witness nor at me. I turned back briefly, and Alvin had been keeping busy during the cross-examination with the yellow sticky-note pad. The problem was, he wrote so loudly; the pen hitting the table made noise, and the animated scratching was clearly distracting them. And he was sticking them on the table, one by one, as he finished each note. I gave him a look and gently shook my head at him, holding my finger to my lips.

I turned back to the witness. "Now, if a woman is telling all these officials that she's all right, and she's writing poems, songs, and recipes, things like that . . . and arguably, if she was doing things like that, does that sound like she was okay?"

Trixie firmly answered, "I've never seen a poem in my sister's writing. I've never seen a song in my sister's writing."

I began to move back toward Alvin at our table, still addressing the witness. "You've never seen anything in your sister's writing?"

"Not since she's been married, and I think that's the issue here," she retorted.

Now, standing in front of the defense table, I saw what Alvin had done, and why the jury seemed to be paying little attention to the testimony. He used up all of the notes in the yellow sticky-note pad. The squares from the sticky pad were all written on, each with one word. He had removed them and laid them all out: "FALSE," "NOT TRUE," "LIES," "NO," and "WRONG."

All these words were repeated, over and over, in no particular order, probably thirty or so times, and now spread out in a grid on the table. I went for the suitcases, but Alvin had moved the envelopes, so it took me longer to collect what I needed for this cross-examination. More roaches scrambled from the envelopes that were once sealed before Alvin kept opening them at night, checking and "reorganizing" them.

"Judge, I'm trying to keep up with all this the best I can."

Judge Van Pelt said, "We've got to be better than the best we can. Just have the court reporter mark them."

Making sure there were no roaches on the five photographs and pamphlet, I handed these to Leigh Ann McBryar for marking. When they were marked, I approached the witness. "Let me show you what's been marked as D-1, D-2, D-3, D-4, and D-5. First, let me ask, do you recognize what's portrayed as D-1?"

Reluctantly the witness said, "That's Alvin Ridley in his, I guess, service uniform."

I jumped on her reluctance. "You don't remember him being in the service while they dated and corresponded?"

"No, I do not."

"Okay. So, do you believe he wasn't in the service?"

"Do I believe he was not? No, I think this settles that."

I handed her D-2, D-3, D-4, and D-5, all photographs from Virginia's belongings.

"Okay, do these photos accurately portray what's depicted in the aftermath of a wedding?"

"Yes."

"Would you turn them over and look on the back? And other than the markings D-2, 3, 4, and 5, there are other writings on the back of these, aren't there?"

"Yes, there's other writing."

"Can you read for the jury, for example, what's on the back of D-2?"

"Sure. 'Mr. and Mrs. Ridley, Shelia Gail Smith, Mr. and Mrs. James P. Hickey.'"

"Do you recognize the handwriting?"

"That's my sister's handwriting."

This was phenomenal. I was getting Virginia's handwriting identified by her own sister, a state witness. I had handwriting expert Brian Carney on call, and he had done excellent work identifying the writings as being "likely" those of Virginia Ridley, but now I had her own sister doing the job, which was good, because I was out of money, completely.

D-6 was a devotional booklet, and Virginia's sister Trixie continued to identify the writing within it as coming from Virginia's hand. I had her read to the jury that this edition of the booklet was 1987.

I wanted to establish different dates that Virginia seemed to be doing normal, happy things that the jurors could identify with. Her writings in the religious booklet printed in 1987 were part of that timeline.

Her sister identified Virginia's handwriting on art and on a handwritten pitch to the popular television show *Unsolved Mysteries* about Alvin's father Bill Ridley's wreck. *As if it would green-light this pitch,* I thought. She obviously loved television and wrote about it extensively.

As Trixie read Virginia's "pitch" to *Unsolved Mysteries* about Bill Ridley's accident with the cement truck, she tried to read into it some meaning, to infer a cry for help from a captive woman. "She's trying to give someone some sort of message, isn't she?"

Now we were entering another realm of the bizarre. I asked, "Oh, you think so? You think she's trying to give a message?" I read aloud, "'Truck driver Bridges, still at large.'" And then I asked, "What kind of message do you think she's sending?"

Trixie's eyes widened, her brows reaching up as she explored the possibilities of Virginia sending coded messages in her writing. "Maybe she is alone."

I tried to put this theory down fast. I was aware, Alvin having insisted that I study the case, that the driver of the cement truck was named Bridges. "Do you know anything about the Polk Brothers Concrete case, what the driver's name was?"

She shook her head side-to-side, and I moved on.

Buzz was not objecting to the admission of all these writings as Trixie LeCroy identified her sister's handwriting, one by one. Admitted, D-9 and D-10, wall calendars: "Okay, it's a diary of sorts, would you say?" She nodded. Then this state witness, realizing that she was helping the defense, tried to back up.

I asked, "And that was just a month before she died, September 1997, when she's talking about someone named Bill Taylor 'messing up' their water?"

Her eyes widened again. "Yes, but do you not agree someone could have written this and maybe those *T*'s? They would have been very easy to have made. I could have if I was accustomed to her writing."

"Well," I said, following up, "you've already testified it looks like her writing."

She shot back, "I testified that it looked like her *G*'s and her *T*'s, sir, anyone could have fabricated those."

"Okay. Let me show you what's been marked as defendant's 11. What does that look like it is?"

"A religious book written by Billy Graham."

"By Billy Graham. Copyright 1984. Look at the back, I guess what they call the back jacket, the back inside cover. Does that look like Virginia's writing?"

"That looks like her writing." It was admitted.

I was getting excited again. "Let me show you D-12, which appears to be part of a box that light bulbs came in, and in Virginia's writing, what did she put?"

She answered softly, "Taking of van is jeopardizing business and family."

I handed her what was marked as defendant's 13,14, and 15, more of Virginia's writings. "Do you recognize that as her handwriting?"

She continued to testify truthfully, but she was trying to read things into her sister's voluminous record. "Yes. Could I please read this to the jury?"

"Okay. You wanted to read that to the jury, D-13?"

She held the document written by the big sister she had not seen in over thirty years, and turned to the jury. "'*Unsolved Mysteries*. Covered up case. We want justice done in his memory.' That kind of gives a message to me that my sister is trying to tell someone something, you know, about the pain and suffering that she has underlined in this book . . ."

I said, "Okay."

She added, "To me, that's still someone trying to cry out for help."

"And what else does it say?" I prodded.

"Oh, well, it has an 800 number, 800-876-5353."

I already knew this was the public call-in number to pitch new episode ideas to the *Unsolved Mysteries* television show. Alvin said it was one of their favorite programs. Virginia had always felt, and he agreed, that their ordeals were worthy of Robert Stack's narration.

"So she's watched, obviously, *Unsolved Mysteries* on TV . . . and that is a TV show, is that correct?" I asked.

"This is correct," she said.

The lunch recess came. We let the jurors and the crowd leave first; then Alvin met me in the hall with our entourage, which by now was Lori and Benita, who had left the law offices, but was so kind to come back to help manage Alvin, along with Elizabeth and Misty Walker, Kevin and Mike's secretary. This group of women reminded me of the story Alvin would tell about having "twenty-one dates" at a high school dance. He went to the dance alone, but the efforts of well-meaning female classmates taking turns dancing with him had left a lasting impression on him.

We walked to lunch. Tommy Eason and another film crew out of Chattanooga followed us to the little restaurant and back. Alvin was quiet and ate very little. Looking down at his plate seemed difficult with the unwieldy new neck brace on. We made our way back to my car and then walked back to the courthouse complex. Alvin hauled the two suitcases of the precious cargo of Virginia's writings, which I insisted we lock in the car and not carry into any restaurant. As long as they are shut, I figured, nothing gets out.

Dr. Wannamaker was waiting in the hallway. This was the only day I subpoenaed him for, and Judge Van Pelt promised he would allow us to call him as our expert witness today, even though Buzz was literally on his first day of the state's case.

I let Alvin and Dr. Wannamaker sit and talk for a while, alone. The doctor was kind, and understanding, offering so much of what Alvin could not get here in his own hometown.

Alvin told him, "Sir, I couldn't get her to leave that house. She could have walked out anytime she wanted to!" Dr. Wannamaker seemed to understand. Alvin told him about her seizures, about her insistence that she stop taking medication twenty years ago, and how they managed. I was a bit jealous, because I could never get this kind of information or cooperation out of Alvin without paying for it.

Once we went back to the small courtroom in the courthouse annex, Trixie LeCroy took the stand again. On redirect examination, District Attorney Buzz Franklin, fully carrying the Hickey family's historical beef with Alvin Ridley, again started trying to make Alvin into a monster.

"Ms. LeCroy, you had mentioned before that your sister, when she was ill at your parents' residence after her marriage to the defendant, that when she left, she didn't want to leave that day?"

Obviously recharged during lunch, Trixie answered in the affirmative.

Buzz pushed further. "Did you also talk to your sister about the time she was getting married? And did she want to get married?"

Trixie started to answer. "No, she did not. She said—"

I shot up from my seat while Alvin was now making his notes on a legal pad that I gave him.

"Your Honor, I object to this hearsay and it doesn't pass any of the exceptions. This is a conversation from before 1966!"

Buzz offered, "Let me back up and ask a few more questions."

The judge said, "All right, go ahead."

Buzz asked more questions, setting up the emotional state of Virginia before the marriage. Nonresponsive to the questions, Trixie blurted out again, "I told her she did not have to do it and she said she did." I wondered if there had been a pregnancy scare.

I renewed my hearsay objection. "Object to what 'she' said, Your Honor."

The judge warned, "Well, we've had all sorts of testimony about what she's been saying, up to this point. I'm reluctant to start weeding, but if you're going to object, I'll sustain it. That will come back to haunt you later, though."

11

My plan for recross was to throw more of Virginia's writings into the case, just as long as Trixie would identify them. Alvin had already opened both old suitcases and had rifled through them. At this point, scores of cockroaches had now escaped the suitcases into the courtroom. One fell on the front of my shirt and tie from one of the papers I pulled out of the envelope. I batted it to the floor and tried stomping on it. Everyone in the room seemed at once repulsed yet delighted to watch me suffer. The jurors were watching it all unfold.

When it was my turn again, I got Alvin's sister-in-law to read D-18 to the jury. It was the proclamation that began: "We citizens of the State of Georgia want U.S. Congress to look into," and, of course, it was all about Bill Ridley's wreck and the ultimate insult of the taking of Alvin's van.

I didn't wait for her to start reading into this anything but what it was. Virginia had obviously shared, and perhaps even inspired, Alvin's paranoid views that the world—or at least local government—was against them.

"Do you recognize that handwriting?" I asked.

"It looks somewhat like her *G*'s and *Y*'s. I will say that," she responded.

I handed her what was marked D-19.

She silently read the document. Buzz objected to this document, by far the most important of all in Virginia's thirty-plus-year journal.

The judge asked, "Any objection to D-19?"

Buzz stood. "Yes, sir. Again, this is testimonial in nature, and I would object to D-19. There's no way to cross-examine that document, as with the earlier document, and we don't know the circumstances under which it was made."

I was going to fight for this one document harder than all others. It was a critical glimpse into the mind of Virginia Ridley. "Your Honor, it squarely places her writing during the administration of Sheriff Lee Roy Brown!"

Buzz objected again. "Your Honor, he's testifying about the document."

Judge Van Pelt looked at the document. "Don't testify, Mr. Poston, I can read it."

And after a moment: "Overruled. D-19 is admitted."

I continued, "Now please read D-19 to the jury."

This is what she read:

> *Earl McDaniels asked me, Virginia Ridley, why don't you and your husband ever go out? He also let himself + the Orkin Man in unexpectedly one day and they frightened me because the Orkin man had allready frightened me because he asked me to go riding with him. I did personal things like changing clothes, taking a bath + when I am doing something personal I feel I should have my privacy so it really would scare me when Mr. Earle McDaniels would come + let himself in and his maintenance man in my house without knocking. From the Fall of 1968 until the Spring of 1970 Sheriff Lee Roy Brown talked to me while I was living at 130 Circle Drive in the Spring of 1970*

McDaniels had headed up the housing authority, administering the new public housing project where Alvin and Virginia started their marital home. Interestingly, before Alvin met Virginia, McDaniels' wife was on the local draft board, and after a series of prank calls by the young Alvin Ridley to the McDaniels' home, he was soon drafted into the U.S. Army. But Alvin forgave all, until the unspeakable happened. As manager of public housing, McDaniels had allegedly let the exterminator into the apartment while Virginia was taking a bath, and she obviously felt the man acted inappropriately. Alvin began taking Virginia elsewhere during maintenance days, and then other days. Slowly the couple spent more time at Alvin's childhood home on Inman Street with his parents than at the apartment. This, along with the constant search for Virginia by the Hickeys, caused the housing authority to initiate eviction proceedings, accusing Alvin of not having two people living in the apartment, in violation of their contract qualifications for an apartment of that size. And the fact that Virginia wrote about talking with Sheriff Lee Roy Brown, who was sheriff of Catoosa County during the eviction controversy, was critical to puncture the state's insinuation that Alvin held Virginia captive.

I quickly got her to identify a total of thirty-four documents bearing her sister's handwriting and had her read each of them to the jury.

"What does D-34 appear to be, a newspaper clipping?"

She answered, "Yes."

I followed, "And it's got Virginia's handwriting underneath?"

"Yes."

Then I asked, "And what did she write under the photograph?"

She read, "'Ron Howard and wife Cheryl.'"

Then I asked, "And do you recognize those people?"

"Yes."

I wanted Trixie to see that her sister seemed to enjoy her life. Of course, I also wanted the jury to see that she enjoyed someone we all recognized and enjoyed from his television shows. What I didn't put in were all the other written references to the actor, now director and producer, which I thought were bordering on obsession. He almost always played wholesome characters. That certainly fit Virginia's profile to make her a superfan.

Buzz briefly examined her once again, but nothing new was established.

Next the state called "The Church Lady," Estella Turner, from the Hickey family church community. I dubbed her that because she reminded me of the Dana Carvey character on *Saturday Night Live*. She had briefly testified yesterday outside the presence of the jury. Now she was before the jury, but the earlier hearing had prepared me for her.

The Church Lady testified that she and another lady were on a church committee to go see people who had missed church, to try to get them back. The newlyweds were on their list, and she described going to visit them in 1967, she was certain, a time when they were still living in the public housing apartments in Ringgold. She thought it was significant that they had stopped coming to church after their wedding. She described some visits with Virginia.

I asked, "She didn't say, 'Take me away, I'm being held captive'?"

Her answer was great: "She just let us in the house, like she was when she came to church, just normal and natural with us, and she welcomed us. She was glad to see us and she was very nice."

I shifted to ask about the other Hickey girls and their post-marriage attendance at the Rossville First Church of the Nazarene. "Trixie kept coming to your church until she got married, and then she quit coming to church?"

She answered, "Well, she went to her husband's church."

I pressed, "And Linda Barber, the other sister, she stopped coming to your church when she got married, is that correct?"

She answered in the affirmative.

I was done, and the prosecutor did not have any further questions.

The third witness for the State of Georgia was Lieutenant John D. Gass, or "Johnny" as he was well known in Ringgold. Johnny was a nice young man, a good officer, and the son of pharmacist Harry Gass, who ran Price Ringgold Drugs, a few doors down from Alvin's shuttered television shop. Harry was also on the state's witness list. Months after the death of Virginia Ridley, the DA had Detective Bilbrey quietly appear before the Catoosa County grand jury with a special presentment of an indictment against Alvin Ridley. Once the special presentment indictment was "true billed," or approved, Alvin Ridley was a wanted man, and Lieutenant Gass was the most likely patrol officer to recognize him in town. Sure enough, at the end of June 1998, he spotted Alvin at Ken Abney's Exxon and tire shop, just minutes before Alison and I limped in with our Ford Explorer on its spare tire. He arrested Alvin Ridley, and I quietly jumped into action, as I had promised Alvin in our earlier talks I would.

What the prosecutor wanted to get from Lieutenant Gass, however, was from before Alvin's arrest. Buzz handed his witness one of our admitted exhibits, D-16. This was one of Virginia's accounts of an incident where Virginia wrote, with her usual mix of misspellings and odd punctuation:

> *Harry Gas' son approached Alvin and John Howard. He said, riding your bike, aren't you? That's a damn shame. Alvin said, yes, it's something your damn government caused. Harry's son said, listen, I don't like you cursing on the street. If you don't stop that I'll have you arrested.*

Buzz asked, "Do you recognize any of the events described here?"

Johnny answered, "No, sir."

Over my objection, Buzz then got out of Officer Gass that Alvin had threatened this young, professional law enforcement officer, without putting one word of it into evidence. I objected because I hadn't been given any notice of this alleged "threat," so I had no idea what he was going to say.

I flew through a brief cross-examination.

"Officer, tell me what happens when a person is arrested in this county?" I jumped in.

I handed the officer the committal form that I had already introduced as D-33. Under "aliases," he admitted writing "Chipmunk" on the form. As in "Alvin the Chipmunk." I sat down.

Buzz got him to state that the nickname on the form was given by the defendant himself. Alvin's flurry of writing "LIES," "FALSE," and "NOT TRUE" feverishly resumed, this time on the legal pad I had given him. "Only the Gass boys called me that," he whispered.

I was assured by the court that we would reach Dr. Wannamaker today, even if we worked into the evening, but I feared jurors would hold it against us if we forced them to be so accommodating.

As we started back, the state called Easton Pyle, a former communications officer who was here to introduce Alvin's flat, so-called "emotionless" 911 call made the morning of October 4, 1997.

I quickly stipulated to the admission of the 911 call, so it was unnecessary to put this witness up.

Finally. I signaled Lori to go get Dr. Wannamaker.

After a moment of transition, the courtroom settled. The judge explained that due to scheduling issues, where I had to secure this busy witness and give him a day to come to court well in advance, a defense witness would be allowed to be called out of turn. I just wanted to get him on the stand before suppertime.

Come on, Judge, they get it, I thought.

"We call Dr. Braxton Bryant Wannamaker," I announced.

The dapper gentleman doctor in the tie and blazer walked up the middle aisle of the small courtroom. As Dr. Wannamaker approached the stand, I noticed two cockroaches scampering from the area of Alvin's suitcases. Alvin kept opening them to ramble through them in what I perceived as an effort to look busy to the jurors and onlookers. He would balance his readers low on his nose as he intently shuffled and rearranged what I had meticulously sorted, and had told him to leave alone. He seemed oblivious to the roaches, I assumed, because he was always around them.

Placing the doctor under oath, I asked his name and where he lived.

"Braxton Bryant Wannamaker . . . I live in Orangeburg, South Carolina."

As I guided him through the particulars of establishing him as an expert witness, the late-middle-aged neurologist described his education, an undergrad at Clemson, just up I-85 from my law school alma mater at the University of Georgia; then he went to medical school at the Medical University of South Carolina in Charleston, and finally an internship and residency at the University of Wisconsin in Madison. After that, he served as a doctor in the U.S. Army for two years. He was perfect.

Buzz was understandably upset that I was dropping this bomb right into the time that was for the presentation of the state's case.

PFC Alvin Ridley, on leave
with his date Virginia Hickey,
in a photo booth at
Lake Winnepesaukah in
Catoosa County, Georgia,
in 1965.

Alvin and Virginia Ridley
were married at Pleasant Valley
Baptist Church, Ringgold, Georgia,
1966.

Parents Seek Married Daughter

Mr. and Mrs. James Hickey of 1119 Wilson Road in Rossville, Georgia, are appealing to the people for help. They report that they haven't seen their daughter, Virginia Hickey Ridley, 21, for three years and have not heard from her in the last 15 months.

She had been a resident of Ringgold where she had resided with her husband. She attended Rossville High School.

Mr. and Mrs. Hickey ask that anyone knowing the whereabouts of Virginia Ridley or if they have any information please phone them at 229-0543.

Culvert Replaced

ent is made by art and Mr. Bert opening of a me in Ringgold. ucture is located ighway number n as Boynton st of Ringgold. ite has approx-square feet of including four nd large Chapel room. It also modern facilities parking space. be 24 hour am-ce available. ar is the director l home. He has ed with the fun-since 1950. W. I. Pritchett, r of Ringgold hurch and Boyn-urch will be the

l home is now ce. The date for ll be announced one number is

t First Church

ain choral drama ity, "Wondrous Eusebia Hunkins esented at First rch, Ringgold.

Donald B Nominee, Scholarsh

McCallie Sc nounced that Ja nett Jr., son of Mrs. J. Donal Carolyn Lane, been selected a the John Motle ward. This is scholarship to of North Caro Hill valued at The nominat bases it's sele

The Catoosa County News, December 18, 1969. One of the articles Virginia's parents put in local newspapers declaring her missing. *(Courtesy of The Catoosa County News.)*

The Ridley house, steeped i mystery and suspicion Virginia Ridley spent mos of three decade within these walls *(Photo by Alex McMahar Chattanooga Times Free Press.*

Alvin was proud of his business, even after it was shuttered in 1984 and fell into ruin. Its demise fueled his conspiracy-laden legal pleadings. *(Photo by Thomas S. England.)*

Alvin holds vigil in his closed and padlocked former Zenith Sales & Service dealership. *(Photo by Thomas S. England.)*

Alvin's yard full of picture tubes and console televisions aggravated neighbors and city officials. *(Photo by Thomas S. England.)*

Alvin shows the truck his father was driving in the 1982 accident with a concrete truck that led to years of litigation *(Photo by Thomas S. England.)*

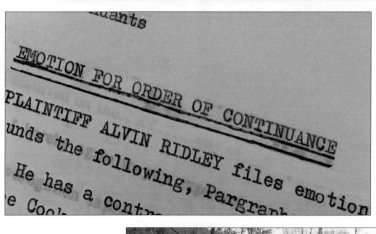

In voluminous civil litigation, Alvin would file "emotions" (motions), and he got the better of a number of high-powered lawyers with his successful appeals.

The three-week seizure of this Chevrolet van fueled years of conspiratorial themes. Although the vehicle was returned to him, Alvin has refused to touch the van for almost forty years. *(Photo by Thomas S. England.)*

The author, left, campaigning
as state representative,
with his sisters and parents.
From left to right: Nancy Poston,
Barbara Poston, Carolyn Poston
Towns, Jan Poston Poole,
McCracken "Mac" Poston,
Katie Poston Stuckey, and
Mary Poston Tanner.
(Photo by Richard L. White.)

In 1996 the author launched his
campaign for the U.S. Congress,
which ended in humiliating defeat.
*(Photo by Robin Rudd,
Chattanooga Times Free Press.)*

McCracken King Poston, Sr.,
known as "Mac," reading the
Sunday Chattanooga newspaper.
This was the best time of day for him.
(Photo by Nancy Poston.)

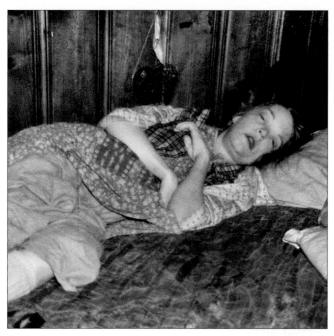

Deathbed photo of Virginia Ridley, after she was turned over by Alvin. *(Photo by Vanita Hullander.)*

Alvin wrote "In loving memor: on the Polaroid photo he too of his wife in her cask at the funeral hom *(Photo by Alvin Ridle;*

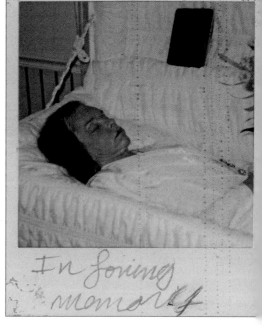

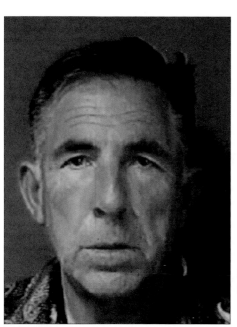

Mugshot of Alvin Eugene Ridley, June 29, 1998. *(Courtesy of Catoosa County Sheriff's Office.)*

Coroner Vanita Hullander at the trial.
The Defense contended that a
frightening confrontation with Alvin Ridley
many years before could not help
but affect her views on him.
*(Photo by John Rawlston,
Chattanooga Times Free Press.)*

etective Sgt. Dan Bilbrey led the investigation
' Virginia Ridley's death after Ringgold Chief
' Police Charles Land recused himself and
s department from investigating the case.
*'hoto by John Rawlston,
'hattanooga Times Free Press.)*

Lt. John Gass, from a beloved
Ringgold family, was just a small boy
when Alvin and Virginia obsessed over
perceived slights from him and his brothers.
The fact he was the arresting officer
added to Alvin's paranoia.
(Photo by Tommy Eason.)

Judge Ralph Van Pelt swears in a par
of potential jurors. Michael Giglio hel
the author manage the juror questionnaire
Court Clerk Norman Stone watches from behir
Alvin Ridley gives his signature glare
the people who will determine his fa
*(Photo by John Rawlstc
Chattanooga Times Free Pres*

Herbert E. "Buzz" Franklin, Jr.,
district attorney for the
Lookout Mountain Judicial Circuit.
*(Photo by John Rawlston,
Chattanooga Times Free Press.)*

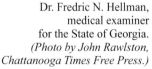

Dr. Fredric N. Hellman,
medical examiner
for the State of Georgia.
*(Photo by John Rawlston,
Chattanooga Times Free Press.)*

The author cross-examines
Patricia "Trixie" LeCroy,
the younger sister of Virginia Ridley.
LeCroy helped identify many of
her sister's writings for the defense.
(Photo by Tommy Eason.)

Virginia wrote of Alvin's interaction
with the children of the local pharmacist
as they hung out near his TV shop.

> Harry, Has Son approached
> Alvin & John Howard,
> He said, riding your
> bike are'nt you, that's
> a dam shame, Alvin said
> yes it's something your
> dam Goverment caused
> Harry Son said listen
> I dont like you cursing
> If you dont stop that
> I'll have you arrested

DEFENDANT'S EXHIBIT 16

> Back in the 1970's I wanted to
> learn more about the Bible &
> as you know the Bible is Gods
> word so I thought to myself
> you could put the Bible & the
> Dictionary together, you & the Bible
> could be the student & the Dictionary
> could be your teacher. I did this
> thing and I began learning so
> much about Gods word, the Bible
> got so interesting I just couldn't
> put it down. And as you know we
> were having troubles with the law & the
> housing project & the Family.

DEFENDANT'S EXHIBIT 15

This document, in Virginia's handwriting,
mentions some of the troubles the couple
were having, including with family.

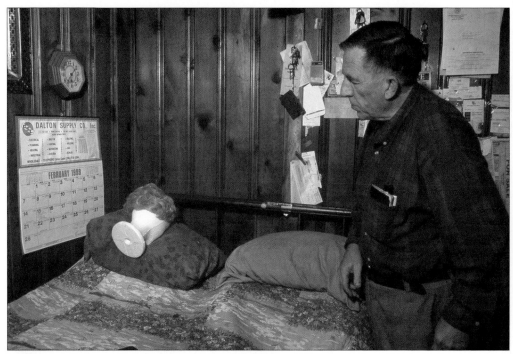

Alvin uses a Styrofoam wig model head
to demonstrate Virginia's position
as he found her.
(Photo by Thomas S. England.)

Alvin with the roach-infested suitcases
that he took to court every day.
(Photo by Thomas S. England.)

Earl McDaniels ask me, Virginia Ridley why dont you and your husband ever go out? He also let himself + the Orkin Man in unexpectedly one day and they frightened me because the Orkin man had already frightened me because he had ask me to go riding with him. I did personal things like changing clothes and taking a bath + when I am doing something personal I feel I should have my privacy so it really would scare me when Mr. Earle McDaniels would come + let himself + his maintance man in my house without knocking ~~in the first few months of 1968539~~ from the fall of 1968 till the spring of 1970, ~~Sheribb~~ Leroy Brown talked to me while I was living at 130 Circle Drive in the Spring of 1970.

DEFENDANT'S EXHIBIT 19

In a key document found in Alvin's house, Virginia explained in her own words
that she shared Alvin's paranoid views.

The author studies during a break in the first days of trial, while "Team Alvin" sits with the defendant. Officer Jeff Brown remains close by. *(Photo by Thomas S. England.)*

Another shift at the defense table. Misty Walker and Lori Duckworth helped keep Alvin in the Courtroom. *(Photo by Alex McMahan, Chattanooga Times Free Press.)*

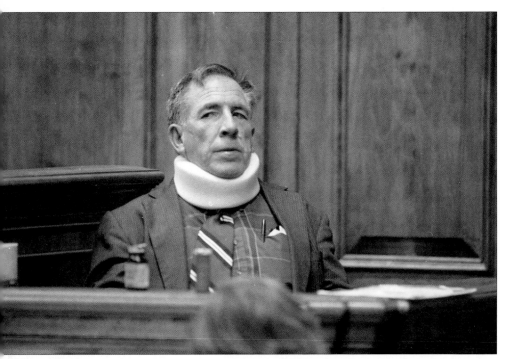

After Alvin's lunchtime vision, when he said that Jesus told him to testify, he revealed a full range of emotion. An observer noted that Alvin had been waiting almost thirty years to get on that stand. *(Photo by John Rawlston, Chattanooga Times Free Press.)*

Judge Van Pelt reacts to the emotion shown by defendant Alvin Ridley. Virginia's epilepsy medicine is on the stand. *(Photo by Phil Farmer, Daily Citizen-News, Dalton, Georgia.)*

Judge Ralph Van Pelt shows the jurors
the form of the verdict and instructs them
on the process of reaching one.
(Photo by Alex McMahan,
Chattanooga Times Free Press.)

Waiting for a verdict with a client
is a hard thing.
(Photos by Alex McMahan,
Chattanooga Times Free Press.)

After the verdict,
Alvin fell back into his chair.
(Photo by Alex McMahan,
Chattanooga Times Free Press.)

Alvin does not remember what my father whispered to him, but I will be forever grateful for the encouragement my father gave me during this time. *(Photo by Alex McMahan, Chattanooga Times Free Press.)*

My father had ten great years of sobriety before his death. Our mother passed a decade later. They were together almost seventy years. *(Photo by Katie Poston Stuckey.)*

Another northwest Georgia man of vision, the late folk artist Rev. Howard Finster featured Alvin Ridley wearing his neck brace in his painting, "The Lost Sheep, Found." *(Artwork © 2023 by Howard FInster/Artists Rights Society [ARS], New York; photoscan by Tracy Knauss, The Photo Doctor, Chattanooga, Tennessee.)*

For years, Alvin Ridley has lunch weekly with his former lawyer, and often with the author's legal secretary, Carlene Renner. *(Photo by Melissa Frisbee.)*

In my defense, the estimation of how long the Canada case would take, and the court's earliest proclamation last month that this case would be tried "the week of January 4" had the most to do with it.

Establishing his impressive résumé, I began to ask him about specific scientific research he was undertaking. He responded, "Mostly clinical pharmacology, certainly epileptology, and I probably put down sudden death in that list, and then I had some basic science interests . . ."

I asked him about SUDEP, or sudden death in epilepsy, one of his research specialties.

He established that the mechanical cause of death in SUDEP was still not clearly understood. I wanted to spoon-feed all of this to the jury, leaving nothing misunderstood.

I wanted to address the presence of the petechiae—the tiny ruptured blood vessels observed on both Virginia and Florence Griffith Joyner, and subsequently mentioned in both autopsies.

I asked, "Have you in your living patients observed a seizure happening?"

He answered, "Yes, yes."

"And have you observed the appearance of some of your patients after a seizure?"

"We can also see in some instances, petechiae, or small hemorrhages, under the skin around the face and eyelids, and some hemorrhage within the conjunctiva of the eye can occur as well, and these also happen on the inside of the lips and inside of the mouth," he answered.

Hallelujah, I thought, *I got it in, and Buzz is still sitting there, watching his precious petechiae being explained away as a natural consequence of a seizure.*

"Dr. Wannamaker, let me ask you if these two items marked defendant's exhibits 36 and 37 look familiar to you?" I handed him the two women's autopsies. One was the Orange County, California, autopsy of one of the most famous and recognizable women in the world, Florence Griffith Joyner. The other was the considerably less comprehensive Georgia autopsy of Virginia Hickey Ridley, perhaps the least-known woman in the world until her death.

"These look familiar," he answered. "Yes, I did review these."

Buzz objected to admission of Florence Griffith Joyner's autopsy, and the court sustained the objection, while admitting Virginia Ridley's autopsy.

I glanced at Alvin, hoping to signal that things were going well. However, I noticed his head was hanging low, and I had seen that expression before. He was sobbing. *Oh yeah,* I thought, *I need to be careful with my questions about his wife's detached brain.*

I shifted to the surprise issue that I only learned about last night after dinner, but it was a big one that explained so much about this mystery woman, Virginia Ridley.

"Can you tell the jury what hypergraphia is?"

He gave a definition, and I followed up. "Do you find hypergraphia to be present in many epilepsy patients?"

The doctor, being precise—which, of course, increased his credibility—answered carefully. "I think there is an undue proportion. I don't know that it's many, but I think that we will see people, particularly with temporal lobe epilepsy, who have certain features such as hypergraphia, writing lots of letters, and making detailed notes. I mean, excessively detailed notes and excessive amounts, reams of paper that they often present to us and to ask us to read so we will know what they were doing, and it's really lots of minutia that's hard to get through."

I was getting excited. We were solving a big mystery about Virginia Ridley.

"And by 'minutia,' you mean tiny details?" I asked.

He answered, "Every detail, and times, et cetera."

I finished my direct of Dr. Wannamaker again, getting from him that hypergraphia is generally associated with temporal lobe epilepsy, and that approximately 97 percent of SUDEP cases occur at home, and half of those are in or around the bed. "Most of the ones who die in the bedroom are in bed, although some roll out on the floor and things of that nature. A minority may be found in the bathroom or living room."

I looked to my opponent at the other end of the conjoined counsel tables. "Okay, you may ask."

Buzz began his cross, gently probing Dr. Wannamaker's experience and accomplishments. Soon he went right to the oldest trick in the book, letting the jury think he was a hired gun, a shill for the opinions of the defense counsel.

"Now you're being compensated, I assume, for your time here today and your time working on this case . . . and what is your rate of compensation?"

Dr. Wannamaker didn't flinch. "That's correct . . . Two hundred fifty dollars an hour."

I fought off the queasiness of calculating what this was going to cost me, but he seemed worth every cent.

"And do you know in dollar terms how high your meter has run to date?"

"About twenty-five hundred to three thousand dollars," he answered.

I was broke. He was going to have to wait on the rest of it. *Hell,* I thought, *I'm sure Alvin will never pay it. But I will, because this witness is saving us, both Alvin and me.*

Buzz rambled on, doing no damage to Dr. Wannamaker at all.

When Buzz sat down, I stood up for redirect. I grabbed Virginia's childhood hospital records, which revealed her history with epilepsy since the age of nine.

Dr. Wannamaker, who had been sent these records, testified that the term "status epilepticus" was mentioned. He said, "Status epilepticus is a life-threatening condition in which one seizure follows another seizure without recovery in between . . . Basically, one seizure after another and it is sometimes very difficult to stop the seizures."

"Doctor, let me ask you one final question. What got you interested in the study of epilepsy?"

He looked at me, knowing that I already knew the answer from our dinner last night, and said, "I have a family history. Two brothers who had epilepsy."

All Buzz could come back with was to correct me and the doctor on referring to D-38 as the "childhood medical records of Virginia Ridley." She was, of course, Virginia Hickey as a child.

This testimony was devastating to the state's case, and he knew it.

Judge Van Pelt released the jurors for the weekend, cautioning them to avoid reading or watching any media on the case, then excused the jury for the weekend, assuring that their notes would be locked up in the jury room.

As the jurors filed out, one of the bailiffs mentioned to the court the roach problem that was emerging from Alvin's suitcases every day. The judge just shook his head and walked out the door behind the bench.

I was upbeat and talked up our successes as I drove Alvin to get some supper.

"I'll call you tomorrow morning, Alvin. Get some sleep. We can win this case."

Alvin was singularly focused. "When is Gold Bird coming?" he asked. He'd become obsessed with the forensic pathologist we'd found online.

"Alvin, we'll still be in the state's case on Monday. We just dropped Dr. Wannamaker like a bomb on the state's case."

As I watched him close the big gate behind him, I backed up and drove home, to explain to my wife that we didn't really have enough money to splurge on this weekend. And I thought, *When I get Dr. Wannamaker's bill, we might not be going out for a while.*

12

Saturday morning, finally. I woke up early, seemingly having inherited my mother's ability to operate on just four or five hours of sleep. Having avoided coffee most of my life, I was just this year in full addiction, having picked up the habit from Alison. I walked to the end of our long driveway to find the morning newspaper.

The headline DEAD WOMAN'S SISTER WARNS OTHERS TO LEARN FROM TRAGEDY screamed of prejudgment in the newly merged *Chattanooga Times Free Press* morning paper. The story, by Gary Petty, an old friend of mine, stated: "Ringgold, GA—The bizarre story of a woman being held captive for more than 30 years before her alleged murder last October is getting national and international attention."

I was furious, telling Alison, "Note that they only put 'alleged' before 'murder'—the part about captivity for more than thirty years is stated as a given fact!" Virginia's sister Linda Barber was quoted throughout the story.

I thought, *So this is the woman too sick or recovering from surgery to come to the trial. But she's running quite a press operation. Damn. I know the jurors are going to read this, even though they've been instructed not to look at the news coverage.*

Linda Barber was also quoted as saying, "When Mom and Dad went down there (looking for Virginia), he got where he would hide behind bushes." Also, "We would go down there and we would ask questions about Virginia, me and my baby sister, and we were told if we didn't stay out of Ringgold, we were as good as dead."

I knew I had two problems. One, the tendency of jurors to read stories they promised not to read. We even had a journalist/editor/publisher on the jury. The second, perhaps more immediate, was what Alvin's reaction to the article would be.

"We were threatened by this man. The man is an idiot," Linda Barber droned on and on; the reporter seemingly was taking dictation from her. "I'll admit, I'm afraid. I'm scared, because I know what the man is. I know what he can do. I would like to see him spend the rest of his life in prison." The vitriol continued.

I got dressed and drove straight to Alvin's house. Sure enough, the paper was spread out on his and Virginia's bed, next to an open Bible.

"I see you're reading Linda's testimony," I said sarcastically.

"Hey!" he shouted. "She wasn't sworn! You need to get this case knocked out!"

I had to explain that I used the term "testimony" loosely. She wasn't a witness, and from what I could tell, that was a good thing. "You know, Alvin, those jurors took an oath that they weren't going to read the paper or watch the news."

"Well, before you got here," he said, "I was fixin' to give it up to the Lord."

Oh no. To Alvin, this was DEFCON 4.

On one of his more talkative days, Alvin had disclosed to me that if someone had been particularly mean to him, he "gave it up to the Lord" and they died in horrible ways. He listed one man who had been mean to him years before and another one who had fired him. The first was electrocuted at work, and the second died in a plane crash. When I asked if he felt bad about condemning these men to their tragic deaths, he replied, "The Lord probably had his own reasons to take them out, not just mine." This process allowed Alvin to forgive those who had offended him, while washing his hands of the way God handled it.

"Alvin," I said, "I don't think you need to condemn people to mysterious and tragic deaths just because they disagree with you."

Then again, I thought those comments in the paper were potentially very harmful. "Let's not quite give it up to the Lord yet, Alvin."

I couldn't believe my own words. Had I fallen so deeply into his world that I thought his spell of "givin' it up to the Lord" would usher tragic ends to those he was "givin' it up" about? Or that God was Virginia and Alvin's ultimate hitman? Was I losing my own hold on reality?

"My head, neck, back, lower back, spine, and tailbone are hurting," rang the familiar refrain. "So, if it gets worser, you're gonna just going to have to continue this trial!" He added, "They won't leave us alone!"

I spent the better part of the day with Alvin, at his house and briefly at the office. I tried my new approach, remembering all my father's dealings with Alvin. I strove to be kinder. I dropped by the drugstore, grabbed some Tylenol, and gave him dosing instructions. After calming Alvin down, I went back to the office for "the books." I'd spoken with several medical school instructors over the past weeks. Specifically, professors and doctors at Eastern Virginia Medical School in Norfolk, all who had instructed the state's chief witness, Dr. Fredric Hellman from the state crime lab. He received Virginia's body, performed the autopsy, and ruled her death a homicide. After looking at the books I borrowed from Bobby Lee Cook, I had bought specific texts that were used by his professors. I wanted to show he was going against his training and education in coming to the findings he'd made in this case.

I'd promised Alison we'd get out of town at the end of this trial and resume our quest to get pregnant. The fact that I often came home those days with the "perfumes" of Alvin's house about me probably didn't set the best mood. She was patient, however.

I worked through Dr. Hellman's med school books all weekend, highlighting the warnings in them about not jumping to conclusions when petechiae were present on the deceased.

In the early evening on Saturday, I drove through the Krystal fast-food restaurant and got a sack of burgers for Alvin. I didn't want him going out. I handed him the bag through the door.

"I don't know if I can come back to court again," he said as the door slowly closed. "I'm hurtin'."

I repeated the same weekend midtrial procedure on Sunday morning. I flipped to the Region section and saw WHO IS ALVIN RIDLEY? I knew the article's reporter, Stump Martin. Like the other article from yesterday that caused Alvin to withdraw back into his fears, they both picked up things I said in opening statements or earlier public statements. Stump didn't even bother to spell my name right. *I'll have to send him a copy of the Dale Carnegie book*, I thought. But as I sat down at the table with newspaper and coffee, my heart plummeted:

> *Here in a small town better known for quickie weddings, one of the most bizarre domestic murder cases to ever hit the Peach State is unfolding. Alvin Ridley, 56, described by some as reclusive and paranoid, is now standing trial on charges he smothered the life from his wife, Virginia Ridley, in October of 1997. The case against Alvin Ridley has drawn attention worldwide, from German and American tabloids to a request from Court TV to air the trial. That request was denied by Judge Ralph Van Pelt, who was uncertain how the accused would react if the cameras were pointed in his direction.*

"Oh, Lord," I muttered, remembering my theory that at least a couple of jurors or their spouses would be reading this article today.

> *Townspeople paint Mr. Ridley as an eccentric with a devilish stare, whose mere presence causes anxiety . . . Townspeople tell of Alvin Ridley, as a teenager, riding around town in his red sports car with a plastic woman in the passenger seat so people would believe he had a girlfriend.*

I thought, *If some of my high school exploits were put in the paper, I would have never gotten elected to anything.*

"This is weird," I told Alison.

She gave a supportive look, with a tinge of *I-told-you-so*, which I guess I deserved. I had put my all into helping the weirdest man in town.

I read on. To the reporter's credit, he fully explored Bill Ridley's accident with the cement truck. Quoting Ringgold Feed & Seed owner Jim Callaway, he wrote:

> *Things began to change for Mr. Ridley after his father was injured when he pulled his car out of the Jackson Chevrolet dealership in Ringgold and was hit by a Polk Brothers cement truck. According to probate Judge Sam Dills, Mr. Ridley later died from cancer, but the younger Ridley believed that his death was the result of the accident. "After Alvin lost his dad, he felt like it was somebody else's fault," said Mr. Callaway. "Something seemed to snap. After that he got in a habit of wanting to sue everybody."*

Also interviewed:

> *Jimmy Cain, who owns Cain Wrecker Service on Nashville Street, (and) went to high school with Mr. Ridley. "I worked the wreck involving Alvin's father and the concrete truck driver could not do anything but hit him."*

This article encapsulated Alvin's whole decline, not that it was going to do any good at this point:

> *Mr. Ridley's disenchantment sparked his desire to run against J.D. Stewart for Sheriff of Catoosa County in 1984, when 210 voters deemed him worthy of the job.*

I mentioned to Alison that it would have saved me a lot of time if these people had come forward with this information. I had been having to learn all of the story through Alvin, and it had taken me over a year to get the information that Stump Martin had collected, knowing how Stump worked, in just a few days. That's because he had people volunteering information, and I had only found a dearth of people willing to talk to me. Despite his misspelling my last name, it was a thorough article. Alvin was fair game, and the court would always rest on the fact that jurors were instructed not to read or watch the news.

The rest of the article focused on Alvin's litigiousness and the contradictions of his self-imposed poverty. It described Alvin's descent into begging. Judge Sam Dills, who was watching the trial every day, told the reporter that he still had two TVs in his house he bought from Alvin, but said, "He has threatened about everybody who has had dealings with him."

Also of note:

> *Judge Dills remembers Mr. Ridley and his mother showing up at the courthouse one Christmas with Mr. Ridley dressed like Santa Claus and asking for money.*

"Well, that sounds familiar," I said. The article ended with accounts of Alvin begging for firewood for his mother and for money to help fix her roof. All were familiar stories to me. The article also went into Alvin's background, including that he once worked for Baxter Roberson, a TV and appliance dealer who tragically died in a plane crash. I remembered that Alvin had interpreted Roberson's death as happening after Alvin had "given up to the Lord" a minor dispute they had once had. When I pressed him one day about it, Alvin was sad about the death, saying, "We had gotten over everything. He trusted me. He trusted me enough to have me give his daughter a ride home, but once you give it up to the Lord, it's out of your hands, really."

"I've got to go see Alvin," I told Alison. "He will be in a fit."

I contemplated my approach, knowing that he got out before daylight to get a newspaper. I called and he answered, "Hello," kind of like he was in a great deal of pain and weakness, simultaneously.

"Alvin, I'm coming to see you." The phone receiver went dead.

His gate was open, his door unlocked. I didn't know what to expect after reading that story, and, predictably, the newspaper was again on the bed, with the opened Bible next to it. Once again, perhaps, I had interrupted a "givin' it up to the Lord" incantation.

"Well, I see that you've seen today's article."

Silence.

"Alvin, we're going to get through this, and I'm starting to think that this plays right into our defense—"

"I got more than two hundred ten votes," he interrupted.

"What?"

"I got more than two hundred ten votes!"

"Oh, well, Alvin, we can *show* the jury how many votes you got. That's something we can prove!"

That was his only problem with the article.

Both Judge Dills and county attorney Clifton "Skip" Patty had told me that Alvin had approached them after that 1984 primary election, complaining about his vote total. He allegedly said, "More people than that told me they were voting for me!" I could relate.

Then I thought a change of subject was in order. "Alvin, the State of Georgia is against you, and they're putting up their strongest witness tomorrow. I need to go get ready for him, but right now let me take you somewhere to get you breakfast or lunch." Alvin never turned down a meal.

"I've already had breakfast," he said, "two pieces of white bread and coffee. That's what I have for breakfast every day since Virginia died."

"Well, let's call it lunch then. We need to show our faces in this community, or we can go to Fort Oglethorpe."

"Let's go to Fort Oglethorpe," he said. I had successfully calmed his soul.

Alvin was putting a great bit of stock in his thoughts that we were going to match the state pathologist with our own internet find, our own *f-o-r-e-n-s-i-c p-a-t-h-o-l-o-g-i-s-t,* whose name Alvin still mangled into Gold Bird.

13

Monday, January 11, 1999, started at a brisk twenty-five degrees. After driving to Alvin's house, I could tell that he had been out already, by doing the detective trick of feeling the hood of his old Dodge K-car and noting it wasn't quite as cold as the sides of the car. He had been out early, likely to get the newspaper. Alvin's door was unlocked and I cracked it open a bit to yell inside for my client.

"Yeah" was the response, so I stepped in and shut the door behind me quickly, to keep any warmth inside. My frozen breath continued showing in the first room, which was the unheated built-in front porch. The next room, the combination living room and bedroom, and the only one with a furnace, was considerably warmer, but the furnace had not worked for some time. The two heaters I had given Alvin were adequately warming the central room in the house.

I had boldly suggested many times that Alvin sell the property on the lake in Tennessee, and invest in his own comfort by getting a newer, better insulated one-level house that he could grow older in. The uncertainty of his future generally stopped these conversations, however.

Alvin was, of course, dressed and ready to go to court, likely because he slept in his clothes, but he was still protesting. He knew better than to push too hard. I was on edge, nervous about the suave and polished Dr. Fredric Hellman imparting his wisdom and experience to the jury.

We drove to my office, got out, and walked together toward the courthouse, Alvin toting his two suitcases like they were handcuffed to his wrists, and me hauling the case files and forensic pathology books. We crossed the spot at the intersection of Nance Lane and LaFayette Street, where just fifteen months ago, the newly widowed Alvin Ridley managed to meet me at the same spot for three days in a row.

In the few minutes we had after settling into the courtroom, I pondered what I was going to face today. I had first met Dr. Fredric Neal Hellman back in December when the newly retained Dr. Goldberg and I went to examine what remained as evidence from Virginia's body. Hellman was the state medical examiner on duty on October 5, 1997, when Catoosa County coroner Vanita Hullander delivered the body of Virginia Ridley to the state crime lab in Atlanta. Hellman was a youthful-looking man, close to my own age, having attained his undergraduate degree from Swarthmore College, one of the Little Ivies, in 1981. Dr. Goldberg, whom I was funding for Alvin after we found him together, dialing up and searching the World Wide Web, got his undergraduate degree in 1976 from North Carolina State University in Raleigh. I was confident enough to put that up against Swarthmore.

Beyond their undergraduate degrees, the paths of the two doctors diverged significantly. Dr. Hellman went straight to Eastern Virginia Medical School in Norfolk, graduating in 1985. However, Dr. Goldberg had gone straight into *law school* at North Carolina Central University, graduating in 1979. According to his curriculum vitae, he then graduated (cum laude, no less) from the World University Dominican Medical School (Universidad Mundial Dominicana, Escuela de Medicina), which was listed as being at "San Juan, Puerto Rico/Dominican Republic." Even from my limited geography knowledge, I believed these were two distinctly separate places, two hundred watery miles apart, but maybe they had two campuses, I reasoned. I really couldn't find much dialing up online about "WUD" or "Medical School at WUD," but, admittedly, I didn't have much time to check it out.

I saw more roaches emerging from Alvin's suitcases. He always opened them right up when he sat down in the courtroom, as if he was directing this show. I felt he was just trying to look busy because it was better than looking out of control of your future, which is exactly where a criminal defendant is situated.

"Alvin, we need to spray those suitcases," I mentioned to him, and I think I did so more than once, but we had not gotten around to it.

"Bring the jury in, Mr. Bailiff," Judge Van Pelt instructed. The jurors and alternates, seven women and seven men, filed into the jury box.

The judge greeted them, "All right. Let court come to order."

Buzz called Dr. Fredric Hellman to the stand. As Hellman was sworn in, it hit me why he looked so familiar. To me, he looked just like David Copperfield, the Las Vegas magician I had seen on television. I decided to keep that notion in my head, as I found that less intimidating than taking on a man with his credentials, which were now being given to the jury.

Hellman swiveled to face the jury before answering his first softball question: "Ladies and gentlemen, a medical examiner is a physician, a forensic pathologist that is a subspecialty of pathology, an area of medicine that studies disease, but basically is a physician, and our task, our responsibility, is to investigate deaths that are either unexpected, unexplained, mysterious, or violent."

Wow, that is a good answer, I thought.

The state witness ticked off his impressive résumé of education and residency and fellowship, including a four-year term in the U.S. Army as a medical examiner. Buzz continued, establishing that his witness was a member of the American Board of Pathology. He went on to describe two years here, two years there, and two years somewhere else, after a minimum of five years of training in anatomical and clinical pathology. I was trying to add up the numbers in my head. He was an extremely well-educated man.

I briefly worried how our forensic pathologist would compare, but hiring Dr. Goldberg was the most excited I had seen Alvin about anything in fifteen months of advising and representing him, and he hadn't even met him yet. Unlike the state's witness, ours was paid by the hour, and I was trying to limit those hours.

Dr. Hellman spoke directly to the jurors, always swiveling and addressing them as "ladies and gentlemen" before launching into an answer. It was almost robotic. He said he had performed over 2,200 autopsies, 516 in Georgia. Finally, after a few more "ladies and gentlemen" dramatically introduced answers, Dr. Hellman got down to business about the autopsy of Virginia Gail Hickey Ridley, performed on October 5, 1997, at the state crime lab in Decatur, Georgia, a suburb of Atlanta.

Alvin was doing a flurry of writing on the legal pad I gave him. His strikes on the paper were so loud, they were again distracting the attention of the jurors. I didn't want him to get into trouble, so I wrote in all caps in the left margin, *DON'T WRITE HARD!* Alvin picked up the pad and held it either on his lap or off the table, creating only slightly less of a distraction.

Buzz asked, "Sir, can you describe the general condition of the body prior to your autopsy?" The swivel, the stare, and then: "Well, ladies and gentlemen, she was clothed in several articles of clothing, some of which had been previously cut. She was approximately five feet two and a half inches in length, and we weighed her at ninety-seven pounds."

The DA offered three pre-autopsy photos of Virginia. Having received them in discovery, I did not object to them. I was concerned about how Alvin would react to them, however, because in them, her body was on the autopsy table, unclothed. Alvin looked down at the table.

"I told them I didn't want no autopsy." Shaking his head, he said to me, not in a whisper, "This hurts me, it hurts my heart. She wouldn't want people seeing this."

"Alvin, she didn't know it, or feel it" was the best I could muster.

The state's theory was that Virginia had died somewhere else, then was moved to the bed, and that a faint red line around her forearm was a ligature mark. Buzz was having Dr. Hellman explain rigor mortis and livor mortis in detail. They were also trying to show that Alvin's statements to law enforcement about turning Virginia over and applying CPR, what Alvin called "re-citation," did not happen.

The DA was trying to finish strong with his witness, the impressively educated and suave Dr. Hellman. "Sir, based upon your experience and your training and your examination in this case, what was the cause of death?"

Hellman wheeled himself to face the jurors, obviously for optimal impact. "Well, ladies and gentlemen, I called the cause of death asphyxia, and I clarified my opinion on the last page to indicate that there was no evidence of resuscitative efforts performed upon the deceased. And the other parameters surrounding this case and the information that I've examined indicate that it doesn't appear to me that—there is no available physical evidence that in this case resuscitative efforts were performed. So those petechiae, in my opinion, did not come from resuscitative efforts. Granted in earlier testimony this morning, I've indicated that where aggressive resuscitative efforts have been performed, like chest compressions, you can get those petechiae. I don't see any evidence with this body that indicates that was the case here, so the cause of death I called asphyxia." Then he added, "A significant contributor was the well-documented seizure dis-order."

I looked to Alvin, whispering, "They're saying you didn't try to resuscitate her."

Alvin looked at me and said, "I did, I did do *re-citation*! Mouth-to-mouth and pressing on her heart!"

Buzz wasn't quite finished. "Now, asphyxia by what means?"

Hellman spun again to the jurors—many impressed, I'm sure, with his profession, his education, and his Las Vegas magician looks—and gave his summary. "Well, remember, ladies and gentlemen, that counsel brought up the term 'positional asphyxia.' In a situation like this, someone's lying horizontal on the bed. I mentioned that how is the head going to get all that pooled blood to give rise to the petechiae? Is it possible there could have been a positional asphyxia with the deceased facedown in a pillow? That's a possibility, but where did all that petechiae come from?"

I dropped my pen and stopped Alvin's scribbling again. *He just said it is a possibility that Virginia could have died from sleeping facedown on her pillow!* Alvin stared ahead.

But then Hellman continued, "So there's an inconsistency here. In my opinion from my examination of the body, those petechiae did not come from resuscitation efforts . . . In order to get those minute hemorrhages, if it was just a straightforward smothering, say someone is smothered in the pillow, how are you going to increase the venous pressure, the pressure of blood in the head, to result in those little minute veins that are called venal popping, okay?"

It was obvious that the casual explanation by Dr. Wannamaker of petechial hemorrhages as being common after seizures had put Buzz on the defensive. Dr. Hellman continued to talk. "You can get a few petechiae from smothering, okay, generally in the whites of the eyes, but to get to the extent of the petechiae that we see, in my opinion based on my experience and my review of the literature, there needs to be some sort of neck compression component cutting off the drainage of blood from the head, ultimately resulting in those minute hemorrhages.

"So, in my opinion, I called it asphyxia, and in my opinion, I stated that I feel that it's likely a combination of perhaps smothering and/or neck compression or some combination thereof. I did not see evidence of a struggle on the body, like scratches, that sort of thing, so that raises other questions of how did this transpire. Perhaps the deceased was in a situation—" Hellman surmised that Alvin killed her during the post-ictal phase of a seizure, explaining "after the ictal phase in this period, folks are characteristically very lethargic, very tired, all they want to do is sleep, and they're confused commonly, characteristically. And so in that type scenario, [they] could very easily be overcome and not put up a fight. That has to be a consideration, in my assessment."

Doing my own quick assessment, I noted that the state's main witness was now acknowledging Virginia had a seizure before she died. This was huge. Alvin told the truth no matter which side you listened to. Alvin had insisted during his interviews that she had a "spell" during the night. Taking Dr. Hellman's theory, the question remained, *Did he then kill her?*

The court then gave the state a gift, a midmorning break just as it seemed Buzz was still fumbling to find the supplemental autopsy report that his witness pointed out was missing.

* * *

Lori, Elizabeth, and Misty from the office, as well as our former shared secretary, Benita, a group I was calling "Team Alvin," went into action, sitting around Alvin at our table to keep him from bolting out of the room. I gathered and organized my notes for the cross-examination. Alvin handed me his notepad, as if it contained a secret formula that only he could concoct. It was mostly indecipherable, except for my own very clear note to him to stop writing so hard.

As we reconvened, I opened up cross-examination to explain to the jury this was not the first time we had met.

"Dr. Hellman, we met before, is that correct? I came down to the crime lab with another pathologist and reviewed what was left, a neck section and the heart, is that correct?"

"Yes," he answered, smiling oddly.

I asked him his age, which was thirty-nine, the same as mine, and I walked him through his education at Swarthmore and Eastern Virginia Medical School. "In the army, you worked with . . . Dr. Freedy, is that correct?"

"Richard Freedy," he answered.

"Richard Freedy, he's well known in terms of pathology, is that correct?"

He answered, "Generally speaking, yes."

I tried to sink the hook. "He has contributed to some texts, has he not?"

"As far as I am aware, yes." He appeared more uncomfortable as I rummaged through my bag of books. He knew what I was up to, and he wasn't going to take the bait easily.

I asked him which texts on the subject of forensic pathology he owned.

"I don't remember all the titles," he answered. "One of the standard textbooks when you go into training of forensic pathology is a book originally by Dr. Spitz and Dr. Fisher. Dr. Fisher has since passed away. Several editions of his book have been edited by Dr. Spitz."

I pulled out the very tome, watching one of Alvin's roaches scamper away from my foot. "Would that be *Medicolegal Investigation of Death* by Dr. Spitz?"

"Yes."

"Okay," I said. "You also own the text *Forensic Pathology* by Bernard Knight?" I pulled out another huge book.

"I believe I own the '91 edition," he answered, adding, "I believe I have a copy of Knight in my car."

I was feeling good now, but there were more books to pull out.

"The fact that you have them, they would be considered standards in the field, is that correct?"

He knew where I was going, responding, "They're standard, but not necessarily authoritative in every way."

"But nevertheless, you own them, and I believe you testified that Dr. Spitz was considered the standard, did you not?"

I was so close, but he wasn't going to be easy, with him hedging, "It's one of the standard textbooks that people who become forensic pathologists read. There are, as I have found with time, a number of errors in them."

He was trying hard to avoid my trap, but he was giving me another gift—the notion that he was coming off as if he thought he knew more than the experts. I continued, trying to physically position myself where the jury would watch the cross-examination, and not be distracted by Alvin as he continued to scribble loudly on his legal pad.

We went back and forth until lunch. I would ask a question, he would wheel toward the jury and start each lecture, "Ladies and gentlemen . . ." I would ask the court to make him answer yes or no first before launching into a speech, and sometimes the court would make him.

I established through cross-examination that he received the body of Virginia Ridley at the state crime lab on October 5, 1997, at 12:30 p.m., over thirty hours after the discovery of the body, and that the body was personally delivered there by Catoosa County coroner Vanita Hullander. I read his own words back to him that he had put in the autopsy:

> *By history, the deceased was allegedly kept captive by husband, with no one in the community in Catoosa County having seen the decedent for 15–20 years.*

Then I pounced. "Do you think it's wise to receive this type of speculative information before you're trying to render a scientific opinion?"

"Ladies and gentlemen, when we do our investigation—"

I wheeled around myself, but to the judge. "Your Honor, I'd like for him to answer my question and then he can make any explanation he wants."

Judge Van Pelt said, "Well, I thought that was what he was doing."

I needed to explain. "He starts off with, 'Ladies and gentlemen, when we do our investigation,' and I asked him a yes or no question. We require it of every other witness that comes in."

The judge looked to Dr. Hellman. "Just, if you would, just answer it with a yes or no and then you may explain your answer."

Dr. Hellman then looked to me. "Okay, counsel, could you please restate the question?"

I was briefly set back by the fact that I had gotten a good ruling about the robotic dodge that had clearly become Dr. Hellman's signature move. I recovered, getting back to the question: "Do you think it was wise to have this speculative information come from Vanita Hullander when you're trying to make a specific discovery of how Virginia Ridley died—that you got this conclusion by the coroner that this woman had been kept in a basement for decades, and . . . do you think that's wise as a doctor to be getting that kind of information, that speculative information, before you're making perhaps what may be a close call on a decision of how she died?"

"We attribute the information that is provided to us as accurate," he said.

The entirety of Dr. Hellman's observation of the faint red line on Virginia's forearm was after-the-fact, having just been shown the photo taken by Coroner Vanita Hullander. He had not even noticed any such mark at the crime lab, nor did he note it on the autopsy report form under "evidences of injury" – yet, he testified to it as being "compelling."

"Let me ask you then, how about photographs? Don't you think that would be the best evidence of such 'evidences of injury,' as you called them?"

"Well, certainly having—"

I turned to the judge. "Your Honor, I have asked him to answer the questions and then explain if he has to."

Judge Van Pelt sighed, looked to Dr. Hellman, and said, "Please just answer yes or no and then you can explain."

"If you forgot the question, let me say it again," I jumped back in, and asked it again.

And then, without any prefaces or wheeling toward the jury, he gave his simple answer. "Yes."

I then got him to concede that he had taken only three photos, S-13, S-14, and S-15, and that he'd gone into great detail about other aspects that he had found significant that did not appear in the three photographs.

"Do you think that it would have been wise to photograph them so that it may have been preserved?" I asked.

A markedly less assured Dr. Hellman replied, "If I had it to do all over again, I would have preferred to take more photographs, yes."

I allowed an extra moment of silence so that it could sink in, but I was a bit scrambled in my thoughts. I started to ask about the post-mortem "artifact" on Virginia's neck created by the assistant coroner trying to draw blood. I hadn't even looked at the clock on the wall. It was 12:05 p.m. I was feeling light-headed, but I thought it was the euphoria of finally getting this witness to agree with me on something. I realized it was my own physiology, my plummeting blood sugar levels.

"Mr. Poston," Judge Van Pelt called out, "why don't we break for lunch." He was aware of my condition. Buzz was as well. It had never really been an issue before, but this was really the longest and most significant case I had ever tried. The judge instructed the jurors to go to lunch and be back at 1:20 p.m., giving them an hour and fifteen minutes.

We went to lunch. When the food came, I guessed as I always did at carbohydrate counting, and put in a number in my pump to counteract the carbs I was now putting in my body. My lunch companions, Alvin and Salesman Sam, stared at me as I punched in my best guess at how much insulin to send into the port on my side. Patrons in the restaurant stared at my company. I tried to concentrate on my insulin pump. If I put in too much, I could end up in a heap on the courtroom floor, covered in flop-sweat and needing an ambulance, if not going into seizures. I thought, *Well, that would be one way to show how petechial hemorrhages can happen!* If I did not give myself enough insulin, my blood sugar would soar in court. I would become sleepy and sluggish. I had made these mistakes before, and I wasn't making such mistakes this week.

As I paid our bill and left a good tip for the brave server, the three of us walked back to the Jeep to retrieve the suitcases and reenter the courthouse annex. As Alvin always did, he fell behind me, no matter if I slowed down or even got back even with him. Oddly, Salesman Sam fell in behind Alvin, so we looked like a small train with me as the conductor, Alvin as the freight car, and Salesman Sam as the caboose. I'm sure we were the talk of the town.

As we were let into the courtroom before the doors were opened to the public, I got to sit and talk with Alvin for a minute. I finally pretended to flip through his legal pad of notes on Dr. Hellman's testimony. As the public walked in, I noticed some friendly faces that were now making eye contact and even nodding. We were making a fight of it. Still, when Alvin suddenly turned around when he heard the door open again, the same faces would cast downward, as if they didn't want to get too friendly with Alvin Ridley quite yet.

"All right, bring the jury back in, please," the judge instructed the bailiffs.

I opened by saying, "Dr. Hellman, if I could get you to refer to the autopsy of Virginia Ridley?"

After warming him up with some simple questions about Virginia's height and weight, I dove into the issues of rigor mortis and livor mortis, which Buzz had spent so much time on.

"In terms of rigor . . . that's full rigor mortis, is that correct?" I asked.

"Yes, sir" was his response.

"She was still in full rigor, would you say?" I continued.

"Yes," he answered.

I asked him about the condition of her hair and teeth. He had reported "a well-developed, thin white female, appearing slightly older than the stated age." I asked about in the report where he said, "'the mucosa of the lips is wet, and there is only mild drying of the lips.'"

"So, on a body that you've seen that's been dead for at least thirty hours, it could have a mild drying of the lips?"

He answered, "Yes, sir."

I queried, "And, of course, you know the significance of drying of the lips in manual suffocation cases, don't you, that it can cause accelerated postmortem drying?"

His response was defensive. "I'm not sure that I would agree with that, counsel."

It didn't matter if he did or not. I had another established opinion that he again had to distance his position from.

She had on fingernail polish, and Dr. Hellman had earlier described her hair was a foot and a half long.

"You weren't trying to give the jury the impression that it was wild and unkempt or anything like that, were you?" This was to counter media reports of how her sister, Linda, had described Virginia's hair, after she had helped identify the body.

"No. I was just trying to describe the hair as it appeared to me," Hellman responded.

"Okay, thank you," I continued, "Now, in terms of lividity or livor mortis, however it's pronounced, is it your testimony that this issue . . . how fast it occurs . . . depends on the individual?"

"Well, ladies and gentlemen"—the familiar opening that he delivered scores of times in not answering my questions—"in my experience . . ."

I called him on it again. "Your Honor, I would like for him to answer my question and then he can explain as long as he wants, but I'm having trouble finding the answer in some of these long explanations."

Judge Van Pelt said, "Well, just answer the question if it's capable of a yes or no, and then you can explain."

Finally Hellman answered, "In general principles in written textbooks, no. In my experience seeing bodies and noting how long it takes for livor mortis to fix, for example, I found that it can be variable, yes."

"Okay," I said, "so it's possible that she could have been turned facedown or at least left arm down under her body at some period of time, is that correct?"

He responded, "And I believe that to be the case."

"So that would be consistent with her lying with the front of her body down below her at some point, postmortem, correct?"

Another rant followed. "As I have already testified, you will note that the right arm is over the abdomen, the left arm is up, so the lividity is over the left arm and not over the right arm. We are in rigor. What that indicates to me is that the body is partly canted over, not so that the entire torso is facedown or at least flush with the bed, but, as I've already testified to, left lateral recumbent position. I believe that the lividity on the face is over the left side of the face, not prominent over the right side of the face, so that indicates to me the left side of the face was down, the right side of the face was somewhat up."

I said, "Not at the time of death, but when lividity began?"

He answered, "Absolutely."

"Exactly," I said, in case the jurors weren't seeing that I scored a point. "And if she's lying in the fashion in which you speculated which would create that suspension, unnatural or whatever you call it, improper rigor?"

"Inappropriate," he corrected me.

"Inappropriate rigor," I accepted. "Then, as you state, then she would be lying in a place where that arm would be extended out from the body somewhat?"

"It actually appears to me, counsel, that arm is pretty well up and against the upper chest," he said.

"So she could have been on that arm?" I posited.

"From the appearance of the photograph, that's what it indicates," he responded.

"Okay, thank you," I said. "Had she been lying on that arm, then it's likely or possible that her face could have been on the pillow, is that correct?"

Back to basics, the spin to the jury, followed by "Ladies and gentlemen, as I've already testified to the position that the decedent was at the time . . ."

I shouted, "Just a moment! Your Honor, every witness that I've

ever experienced in thirteen years has had to answer the question
and then give an answer."

Judge Van Pelt said, "Well, I know that."

Buzz weighed in, "Your Honor, there are some questions you
can't answer with a yes or no, and Mr. Poston cannot insist on a yes
or no when that's not possible."

I felt myself smirk. "What are the odds that every question I've
asked today is one of those questions?"

The judge said, "Well, that last one could have been answered
with a yes or no, so let's try to do that, please."

Dr. Hellman said, "Yes, Your Honor. Counsel, could you repeat
the question?"

I mumbled, "If I can remember it now," then repeated the question as best I could. "It being possible or probable that the arm
was under her body when lividity, postmortem lividity, started setting in—in the way, I guess, human bodies can be configured, it's
very possible that her face was more down toward the pillow or in
a downward fashion than it is portrayed in that photograph, yes
or no?"

After a pause, Dr. Hellman answered, "Yes."

Dr. Hellman had taken the position that the petechiae present
on Virginia's body could not have come from her having a seizure.
This was a different opinion than almost all of the experts who
wrote or were cited in the very books he was trained with.

"In my experience, ladies and gentlemen," he said, "I have not
seen it where CPR has not been applied. I read about petechiae in
a few—petechiae in the whites of the eyes in individuals who have
seizures, but not to the extent in this case."

"Do you receive the *American Journal of Forensic Medicine and
Pathology*?" I asked.

"Yes." I couldn't read his expression at this point.

"Do you agree or disagree with the article by Rao and Wetli titled
'The Forensic Significance of Conjunctival Petechiae'?"

"Actually, counsel, I have a copy of that article right here."

I hoped it impressed the jury that I brought the same article to
court as the state's expert.

I continued my examination. "Excellent! Let me direct your attention to page thirty-three. Conjunctival petechiae were most frequently associated with deaths resulting from natural causes, is that correct?"

"Yes, sir. That's what it states."

After directing his attention to more in the article explaining that seizure disorders can cause petechiae, I asked, "So, do you agree, although you haven't seen it in your experience, do you agree with this article that an epilepsy seizure can cause conjunctival petechiae?"

After a moment, he said, "No, not necessarily. I don't agree with that."

"Okay," I mocked him, "so the parts that don't agree with you are flawed?"

I moved on to his retention of Virginia's neck, throat, and tongue, which he had testified he had kept for additional study.

"The hyoid bone and laryngeal cartridges are intact, the hyoid bone is up under here . . . and is quite fragile on adults, is it not?" I posed.

"Yes, sir," he answered.

We danced the same dance, over and over, me trying to nail him down and him swiveling, saying, "Ladies and gentlemen, as I have already stated . . ." and then not answering my question.

I pointed out to him that his own boss, Dr. Kris Sperry at the state crime lab, had written an article advocating examination of the intramuscular tongue in order to determine mechanical asphyxia death. I had "met" Virginia's tongue with Dr. Goldberg, and it was completely intact, indicating no such examination.

"It appears this article was written by Kris Sperry while he was in Albuquerque, New Mexico," he said, unresponsive to anything that I had asked. He dodged all questions about why he hadn't done this, acting as if he'd never heard of it. I moved on.

"Do you agree with Dr. Knight—the book that you have in your car—on page three hundred forty-eight when he says petechiae can appear almost instantly after a violent sneezing or coughing before hypoxia is even possible? Do you agree with that?"

"It depends on the location of the petechiae," he again stated.

"Do you agree with Dr. Knight or disagree," I asked, "when he says, in summary, 'petechial hemorrhages are highly unreliable indicators of an asphyxia process.' Do you agree with that statement?"

"Counsel," he responded, "I believe you are taking that out of context."

"The beginning of the chapter," I said, "which you apparently didn't read, would you agree with Dr. Knight that says 'a number of factors cause difficulty in the interpretation of petechial hemorrhages? Firstly, there is no doubt that both cutaneous . . .'—and that means skin, correct?"

"Yes, sir," he responded.

I continued, "'. . . and visceral petechiae, especially the latter, can both appear and enlarge as a postmortem phenomenon'—do you agree or disagree?"

I was now so deep in the weeds of forensic pathology that I wasn't even sure where I was going with this. I just knew that while he thought he was so cocksure about what he was testifying about, like everyone else, he had likely jumped to conclusions about Alvin Ridley.

At some point, even Judge Van Pelt was thinking I was belaboring the issue. "Mr. Poston, I think you've been over that text adequately. Let's move on to something else." If he was thinking it, the jury was likely thinking it as well.

"Your Honor," I pleaded, "I've got one more thing in this text."

Looking to Dr. Hellman, I posed one more question. "Do you agree with Dr. Knight when he says, quote, 'It cannot be emphasized too strongly that the mere finding of any of the non-specific features, such as congestion and petechiae, without firm circumstantial or preferably physical evidence of mechanical obstruction of respiration, is quite insufficient to warrant a speculative diagnosis of asphyxia. If such collateral evidence is not forthcoming, then the cause of death must be left undetermined.' Do you agree or disagree with that statement?"

"I think it is all a function of what evidence you have available to make that decision," he said, but he knew that I had him with the books he was taught from, and the book that he carried around in his car.

"That's it, subject to recross."

I turned him back over to Buzz for redirect.

Buzz asked a smattering of questions raised throughout cross-examination, trying to get Dr. Hellman to discount all the issues I had deemed important.

"So it's not necessarily every case you have to take dozens of photographs?"

I had scored points over the three measly blurry photos that the crime lab had taken, and the even blurrier one that the coroner had showing Virginia in the bed. Between that and the other short-cuts by the investigation and by the crime lab, it looked substandard, especially if I could compare the excellent autopsy done on Florence Griffith Joyner.

On recross, I grilled Dr. Hellman on Flo-Jo's autopsy, complete with a body diagram showing loads of petechiae indicated by the doctors in California. If Virginia Ridley were murdered, based on the presence of petechiae, then by that reasoning, it would appear that Florence Griffith Joyner was even more violently murdered. But we all know that was not the case, and there were no shortcuts by the Orange County, California, medical examiner.

Then, after some commotion from the defense table, I had a final series of questions handed to me, questions scribbled out by my client.

"Doctor, I think I know the answers to these questions, but my client has begged me to ask them. Do you know Trixie LeCroy and Linda Barber, the decedent's sisters?"

He answered, "No, sir."

"Do you know Adell Hickey, the decedent's mother?"

"No."

"Do you know Chief Charles Land, the chief of police of Ring-gold?"

"No."

"And you haven't talked to any of these people? I'm not trying to trick you. This is what he asked me to ask you."

Dr. Hellman, without any smugness or any sense of resentment, said, "That's okay. Not that I recall."

Dr. Hellman was excused to go back to Atlanta. After a full day of what seemed like a lot of tooth pulling, he left.

The judge looked to the prosecutor's table. "Do you want to call your next witness?" Buzz called Frank Young. He, EMT Blake Hodge, and first responder Heath Morton were the ones to arrive at the Inman Street house after Alvin's so-called "emotionless" 911 call. I had interviewed them all over the phone a few weeks ago, in October, 1998. After establishing Young's credentials, Buzz guided his witness.

Mr. Young told about getting the call, and since there was a "difficulty breathing" report, the first responder from the fire department went with them, less than half a mile away and a straight shot from the station up Inman Street to Alvin's house.

Buzz asked about Alvin, about his demeanor as all of this was transpiring.

"No emotion," Young testified. "I mean, very matter of fact . . . just no real emotion shown. We always ask a few questions when we come in, to find out what's been going on, and I asked about past history. He told me she was an epileptic or had epileptic seizures. And I asked about if she had had a seizure in a while and he said no, she hadn't. After I did an EKG, which was probably three or four minutes after we had been there, maybe two or three, but my partner went and got the EKG machine, the monitor. After I did that, he asked me if she was going to be okay and I told him, 'Sir, I'm sorry, she's passed away.' And he just looked at me and said, 'I thought so,' but there was no emotion at all."

"He said he found her about six o'clock and he went to the pay phone to call 911. Did he say anything about resuscitation efforts?" Buzz asked.

Young answered, "He said he tried to breathe for her . . . He tried to do some mouth-to-mouth resuscitation."

Buzz passed the witness on to me.

I reintroduced myself to the witness, as we had talked on the phone once, last October. "Do you recall that you heard as you were there working the scene, everyone expressed surprise that she was there?"

He seemed very defensive. "Not everybody. I don't know where you are going with this. I had talked to somebody else after the fact and people had told me that they were surprised she was there."

"If that's the case," I said, "then just say that, and that will be the truth. Do you recall telling me that the body was not warm from body heat, but it wasn't cold, either? Do you recall that?"

"Yeah, I do remember saying that," he said more comfortably.

"Okay, thank you," I said, "Do you remember telling me that Alvin was walking around 'in a daze' as you were hooking up the EKG?"

"Yeah."

"You can explain your answer," I added.

"I say a daze," he replied. "He just had no emotion at all. He wasn't . . . It wasn't a mean demeanor or nice, sad, upset, nothing. Just walked around like this was everyday life."

I countered, "The characterization that you used October 12 was 'a daze,' do you recall?"

"I did tell you that," he responded.

"Okay, thank you," I continued. "Now, you went off shift, but came back in your personal vehicle, is that correct?"

"Yes, sir," he answered.

"And you found Mr. Ridley in a different state at that time, didn't you?"

"Yes," he said, "I did."

"And what was that state?" I pushed.

"Well, he was crying, upset."

"Okay, don't you think that was important after you testified to this jury that he was emotionless? Don't you think it would have been important to follow up with the fact that you came back later and he was crying and upset?"

"Yes, sir."

"You gave an opinion back on October 12 to me that you thought she had been dead for at least an hour, maybe two?" I played with a small microcassette recorder in my hand as I asked him these questions. I had not recorded the call on October 12, but he didn't know that, and by me gingerly holding the recorder, he probably thought I was ready to spring a tape on him, should he deviate from our earlier talk.

"A couple of hours," he answered, looking toward the recorder, "that is my opinion."

On redirect, Buzz asked, "Now, during the time that Mr. Ridley, the defendant, was displaying some emotion, that's when he was talking to Vanita Hullander about the possibility of an autopsy?"

Mr. Young answered, "Yes, sir."

I jumped back in, recrossing. "Mr. Franklin asked you about what was the conversation going on between Vanita Hullander and Mr. Ridley that you heard, not what you've heard since, but what you heard that day."

"I heard bits and pieces," he answered. "I didn't—I was not talking with them in their conversation. I came in to do what I was doing and that was it. I heard him ask her what was it . . . Actually, I really don't recall exactly what, word for word, was said."

"At all?" I asked.

"At all," he answered.

"So, when Mr. Franklin suggested," I pressed, "that [Alvin] was only crying and hysterical when they were talking about an autopsy, then obviously you didn't hear what they were talking about, did you?"

Mr. Young wanted to hedge his testimony. I held my microcassette recorder in one hand, then the other, and asked, "Do you recall telling me on October 12, 1998, that you did not recall the substance of any conversation other than hearing everyone express surprise that she was there?"

He hedged again, but basically stated he had forgotten the content of the conversation he overheard.

"So your answer to Mr. Franklin's question then, under oath, properly should have been, 'I don't remember what they were talking about,' correct?"

He sighed, saying, "Yes, sir," and with no further questions, he was then excused.

Buzz's next witness was the EMT Blake Hodge, a young man who looked like a teenager. He explained that Frank Young was a paramedic, and that he was an EMT, and that the paramedic outranks the EMT, so he went to assist Young. Buzz asked him about the emotional state of Alvin Ridley, whom he had testified he saw at the house that day.

"No emotion" was his brief answer.

Buzz finished with his witness. I jumped in, again fiddling with the microcassette recorder, again, empty of any content, but he didn't know that. "Mr. Hodge, do you remember having a conversation with me back on October 12?"

"Yes, sir" was his answer.

I followed up, "And do you remember telling me on October 12, 1998, that there was nothing funny about the way he acted?"

"He showed no emotion."

"Well," I asked, "how many calls have you been on . . . where people died?"

"Several" was his answer.

"Have you surveyed a range of emotions that family members exhibit when you were there? A lot of times, it's emotional and crying? Sometimes it's a state of shock?"

"Yes, sir," he answered.

"If your partner, Mr. Young, indicated that Mr. Ridley was in 'a daze' would that be a good characterization?"

"Yes, sir," he again answered.

Buzz, obviously frustrated by my "October 12" references, objected that I was asking these witnesses questions about what they had told me on that date. "Your Honor, one point of concern here. Mr. Poston keeps asking witnesses questions about what they told him, and that's fine, but Mr. Poston himself cannot be a witness, and so—"

I interrupted, "Well, Your Honor, as you know, it turned one around a moment ago and we're about to see what this witness says . . ."

The judge said, "Well, he can ask them. Of course, he can't get on the stand to impeach them, so that's just his problem at this point."

I didn't need to; the presence of the microcassette recorder was doing its job as insurance against the pressure to "get in line" with the other prosecution witnesses. So, what they were willing to tell me back in October was preserved, in their own minds, as much as it could be.

Wrapping up, I got Hodge to admit that he had seen petechial hemorrhages in his line of work—on the living, as well as the dead.

Buzz had no redirect for this witness.

After a brief bench conference to discuss scheduling, the judge announced, "All right, ladies and gentlemen, we're going to break for the day now . . . Please remember my prior instructions, be back in the jury room at nine a.m. and we'll pick back up. We're in recess."

Good Lord, I thought when I heard the instruction. One of the jurors, Kimberly Clark-Barnes, was probably on deadline herself to submit an article for her paper. *Surely, she won't report on the trial from inside the trial,* I hoped.

Renzo Wiggins, the lawyer who gave me my first job out of law school, tapped me on the shoulder. He was excitedly wanting to tell me something. He had listened in on the entire direct and cross of Dr. Hellman, because he also had a case where Dr. Hellman was a witness. I walked over to the side, away from Alvin, who was slowly stirring up his suitcases enough to release even more roaches onto the floor.

"You've got him!" Renzo excitedly gushed. "It took all day, but you got Hellman to admit to some possibilities." Renzo offered me his notes from Hellman's direct and cross-examinations, which I gladly accepted, hoping to use them in closing. "You may just have this in the bag, as long as you keep your client off the stand!" he said.

"Absolutely," I told my old friend and former employer. "That's the plan. No way I would put Alvin on the stand!" I had learned a lot from my time working for Renzo and his slightly older brother, Johnny, right after law school. They were excellent lawyers, but did not suffer fools, or Alvin Ridley, for that matter. But their mother, Judy, was Alvin's fourth-grade teacher. "He cried every day of fourth grade," she had told me. Johnny and Renzo were Ringgold born, and had been here their entire lives. Along with that came the prejudices and biases that happen in a small town, but more powerful than that in the Wiggins brothers was their love for the Constitution, and the law. Renzo was "for" Alvin in this case, which pleased Alvin, as he had used their father, a great lawyer himself, to help get Alvin excused from army reserve duty in 1968. I thanked Renzo, then helped Alvin gather up his suitcases and all of my forensic science books. I took Alvin through McDonald's, his preference, and got him a burger meal.

As I arrived home, Alison greeted me with supper, and we talked about the good points from the day. I told her we would get out of town at the end of the trial and resume our attempts to make a family—and since we were trying to predict ovulation, it seemed, per the calendar, that the upcoming weekend would be a good time for it. "If we are finished with this trial, of course," I nervously amended.

14

I woke up on Tuesday with the notion that if the state rested today, I wasn't sure I'd be ready to put on a defense case, beyond putting up Salesman Sam, or Ben McGaha, as I needed to start calling him. And I would put him up only because he'd camped out in the hallway, talking to anyone who would listen to him. He'd hung out there every day, even though I offered to put him on call. "Don't have a phone!" he responded. I would get Lori to touch base with our witnesses and make sure they knew to be on standby, so I didn't have to drag out the testimony of Salesman Sam. I was mainly putting him up only because Alvin wanted it. I didn't think he had much to add, but he did claim to have seen Virginia a couple of times over the years. All witnesses would be put on notice. As I revealed to Renzo, I had no plans to put Alvin up. And Alvin seemed to accept that strategy. At least he hadn't complained about it, as he had everything else.

The morning had started out cold, in the high twenties, but as things go in Northwest Georgia in January, it could be balmy and in the sixties or seventies by afternoon. I felt good for getting Alvin the extra space heater for the chickens in his mother's room.

I grabbed the newspaper, and, of course, yesterday's chief state witness, Dr. Hellman, was featured. EXPERT SAYS MRS. RIDLEY DIDN'T DIE OF SEIZURE, screamed from the Region page of the *Chattanooga*

Times Free Press. The reporter Beenea Hyatt had picked up on much of what I was worried the jurors would focus on. In fact, I told Alison, it's easy to get lost in a case, or in *this* case, trying to manage a difficult client. The article worried me on several fronts. Then again, reporters can miss things entirely.

Virginia Ridley was the alleged victim in the aggravated assault charge in the indictment, and it was the supporting felony to prop up the felony murder count. Hyatt's article, however, reported that Alvin "also faces a charge of aggravated assault, stemming from a threat he allegedly made to a sheriff's deputy who arrested him last June." Worse than that, because Alvin was not charged with anything involving the officer, was the allegation that Alvin asphyxiated Virginia, and, as the Hyatt article stated as fact: "Then, her body was moved." It didn't say "allegedly." It just mentioned it as a fact. At least it wasn't completely bad, as it stated, "Also, Mr. Hellman found a suspicious mark on Mrs. Ridley's left wrist, suggesting she could have been wearing a bracelet, watch—or could have been tied up." I'd take that first speculation and run with it. Besides, Alvin had been asking me from day one to find out who "stole" her ring and her watch.

How could a reporter sitting in the same room as I was perceive this evidence so differently than I do? I thought, but realized that it was my job to make sure everyone listening in a trial understood what was being established. Was this a barometer of how badly I was doing?

I quickly drove to Alvin's house, knowing he would likely have the paper and Virginia's Bible out on the bed, ready to "give it up to the Lord." The last few times, he had seemed fixing to do it, but for some reason, he apparently hadn't pulled the trigger on that for years. All those examples he gave me were from long ago. That made me wonder if Virginia was the one doing the conjuring, I mean, "praying," to "give up to the Lord" all the folks who had crossed Alvin. From her writings, which seemed to be directing Alvin's legal strategies, it certainly appeared to be in her wheelhouse.

Sure enough, when I got to Alvin's house, he had to come open the door for me. He was dressed, but in a mood. Virginia's Bible was not on the foot of the bed.

"I thought you knocked out that charge about Johnny Gass!"

I tried to calm him down, reminding him to put on his neck brace.

"The newspaper flat got it wrong!" I said.

If the universe had been conniving to thwart me, it picked the most effective method: setting me back on the trust I had built with my client.

As we gathered in the small courtroom, I dug into the file and showed the indictment to Alvin. "See . . . there's nothing in this indictment about Officer Johnny Gass."

His response: "You need to refile that *emotion* to move this case out of Catoosa County! I can't get a fair trial here!"

As we bickered back and forth in loud whispers, the courtroom filled up with the same folks who had been there for days—county employees, I guess, having another slow day, Alvin's team of women from my office, and a smattering of new folks. I spotted Salesman Sam just taking a seat like he belonged there. I stood up, pointed toward the door, and he sheepishly walked out of the courtroom. If he violated the rule of sequestration, he couldn't testify.

When Judge Van Pelt slipped through the door from his office, just behind the bench, he asked, "Anything we need to talk about before we get started?"

Alvin stared at me.

"*No!*" I whispered. I knew he wanted me to raise a motion to change venue, for the fourth or fifth time now.

"I can't think of anything!" I announced.

Buzz shook his head, as if eager to get his case back on track.

"Bring the jury in," the judge ordered, and as soon as they were seated, he declared, "Go ahead and call your next witness."

Buzz called Leslie Waycaster to the stand. Waycaster was a Dalton lawyer who had represented the Polk Brothers defendant in the litigation about Alvin's business truck accident, when it was driven by Alvin's father. Waycaster was here to discuss civil litigation from over fifteen years ago, but he seemed to have a chip on his shoulder, as many did, about Alvin Ridley.

In a weird way, Alvin's insistence that I study all of his old civil litigation had prepared me for this, I hated to admit.

Waycaster testified that a key pleading was stolen out of the clerk's file, a situation that allowed Alvin to defeat Waycaster's first motion to dismiss, on the grounds that there was no proof that Alvin had been served with it. Alvin had successfully appealed the dismissal to the Georgia Court of Appeals, representing himself. Waycaster waved around the actual court file, with a jagged tear still hanging out where the missing notice arguably once existed.

"When did you discover that this certificate had been removed?" Buzz concluded.

I jumped up. "Your Honor, that draws . . . He's calling for a conclusion that this witness can't state."

Judge Van Pelt said, "Well . . ."

I continued, "And I object to that question, and I object to any speculation that Mr. Franklin is trying to inject in front of this jury, something that has nothing to do with this case!"

Unartful as I was with my words, I was trying to say that Buzz was accusing Alvin of stealing what turned out to be a critical legal document—a certificate of service—from the court file in the clerk's office, which allowed Alvin, acting as his own counsel, to overturn the Catoosa Superior Court at the Georgia Court of Appeals, and for a time thwart one of the few silk stocking law firms in North Georgia.

Buzz responded smugly, "Your Honor, Mr. Poston in his opening statement made this something to do with this case."

I said, "Well, let's take this up here," indicating that we should be having this discussion at the bench. I argued that while I mentioned all the litigation that Alvin was involved in, thinking that the whole community had turned on him and his family, that shouldn't "open the door" for Buzz to put his character into evidence by calling him a thief.

Judge Van Pelt looked at me and said loudly enough for the jury to hear, "For the record, your objection is overruled. Go ahead, Mr. Franklin."

Buzz led Waycaster through the story of the vanishing document from the court file in the mid-1980s, then turned the subject to a deposition of my client from fifteen years ago.

"Now, during the course of this new litigation that was instituted, did you have the occasion to take the deposition of Mr. Ridley, the defendant in this case?"

Waycaster answered Buzz, "I would say that Mr. Ridley, when I started asking some questions about his family, didn't want to answer those questions."

I knew I could argue that Alvin's general paranoia explained all those deposition answers revolving around people asking about Virginia.

"Well," I started my cross-examination, "let me ask you, in your opinion, do the questions Mr. Franklin asked you have anything to do with October of 1997?"

I thought it was a fair question. The witness was under cross-examination.

Buzz jumped up. "Your Honor, I object to that. This man is merely a witness, he isn't allowed to draw conclusions about what any testimony has to do with the case."

Judge Van Pelt chimed in, "That's for the court, Mr. Poston. Sustained."

I "withdrew" the question, but it was a direct hit. Why was Buzz putting up a witness from fifteen years ago, and what did it have to do with Virginia's death fifteen months ago?

I got back to my cross-examination of Waycaster. "Leslie, you and I have known each other for some time . . . Do you know of a clerk's office to have occasionally lost a pleading, an entire pleading or even an entire file in a case?"

"It happens," he answered.

I took it a step further. "And are you familiar with the court clerk's offices taking apart files, reattaching files, taking apart files, reattaching files, over and over in the course of litigation, with a lot of papers getting frayed?"

"Yes," he answered, "that happens."

Since he was familiar with the old litigation, I utilized the last part of cross-examination to have him interpret the files to tell the jury the story of the second litigation, the one where Alvin sued Ringgold police chief Charles Land, claiming he had "falsified" Bill Ridley's accident report. He described how Chief Land had filed a counterclaim for frivolous litigation and won a judgment against Alvin. Finding the 1977 Chevrolet van as an asset that could be easily liquidated, his lawyer had the matter prematurely executed, before an actual judgment was issued, and Deputy L.C. Cripps was the officer who had the duty of carrying out the levying on the van. This was a watershed moment for Alvin and Virginia, but the van, which Alvin contested and won back within four weeks, still sat on his property, untouched. "If I touch it," he told me more than once, "it'll start up the statute of limitations again."

I got the court to admit the entire case files of the civil litigation, and after reviewing them, Buzz agreed to their admission.

I noticed that there seemed to be even more cockroaches coming out of Alvin's two open suitcases today. While I had tried to ignore them for the first three days, now it was open warfare on them. I'd stepped on three already just during the Waycaster testimony.

Buzz called his next witness.

"Your Honor, I call Vanita Hullander," Buzz announced.

She was the coroner of Catoosa County, and what she lacked in experience when she was elected to the job, she more than made up for in her genuine enthusiasm toward her work. She was one of the first women elected to countywide office, and seemed destined to be there awhile, crusading against drug abuse from the position of the first person who had to deal with the fatal overdose cases.

I had let the cat out of the proverbial bag about the coroner's prior dispute with Alvin in the opening statement. I just wanted the jury to let it sink in that there could be a personal dispute fueling some of the conclusion jumping that formed the basis of our defense. Buzz would try to diminish this by bringing it up with her first.

As Buzz continued to draw out her qualifications, with her history as a first responder, which were impressive for a small-county coroner, she testified that she had won the office in the November 1996 election. *The same ballot that my name last appeared on,* I thought. She was sworn into office on January 1, 1997, when I was lost and drifting.

I did the numbers in my head. She had held the office of

Catoosa County coroner for nine months and three days before being called out to Inman Street to investigate the death of Virginia Ridley.

Buzz showed her S-18, the photo of Virginia Ridley, lifeless on the bed. "And is that the bed you were talking about, being in the living room?" he asked. When he got an affirmative answer, he continued to ask about that bed. He established from the coroner that it was a full-sized bed, pretty old, and then he asked about "visible signs of wear to this bed." I had heard rumor this line of questioning was coming.

"Yes, there was," she answered. "I tried to establish on the picture, on the outside of the bed, opposite of where Mrs. Ridley was lying, there was a sunken area—it was right in here." Pointing to the photograph, she continued to testify. "It looked like somebody had slept there for a long time, but there was nothing on her side of the bed when we moved her."

I understood this as promoting Buzz's theory that Virginia had been kept tied up or locked up elsewhere until her death, and then Alvin moved her lifeless body to "stage" what he hoped others would believe as a death during her sleep—on a bed where she never slept.

The coroner testified that Alvin did not have any documentation, or could not find it, to prove who the dead woman in his bed was.

She testified that he was not consistent in describing how he found his wife and about her most recent medical history; he seemed quite suspicious.

That would be suspicious, I thought, *if he had understood her questions.* I remembered how over the last fifteen months since first meeting Alvin on the street after Virginia's death, he didn't process questions like most folks. I also imagined that this was a very stressful time for him.

My opponent, the district attorney, was going for the jugular. "Now, did the defendant say anything about 'foul play'?"

She looked to the jury and answered, "He kept repeating that there was no foul play, there was nothing wrong, no foul play . . . probably five or six times."

Classic Alvin Ridley paranoia, I thought. Meanwhile, Alvin had resumed his extremely loud scribbling on another legal pad. I put my hand on his arm and he settled. He knew what I was telling him. He stopped writing and looked at the witness.

The coroner went on to describe Alvin's demeanor: "He was very quiet, unattached, just matter-of-fact, then he became really upset, angry. When I was asking him about the chest pain, he said that there was a conspiracy against him, and that people had 'worried' his wife into dying, and that they didn't have any food in the house, and that he couldn't work. He was really upset. He just, you know, said several different things and I was trying to, you know, calm him down."

Now that *sounds like the Alvin I have come to know,* I thought. He definitely subscribed to the prevailing medical knowledge of the connection between stress and health. So many of the stories he had told me repeatedly were about how the authorities had "worried" his mother "to death"; "worried" his wife "to death"; even how the sheriff had "worried" him to "fall off" his house, hurting his "head-neck-spine-tailbone."

When asked on direct about the coroner's efforts to get identification of the dead body, she responded, "He said he didn't have any, that he would have to get with his accountant to try to find out what her social security number was, but he wouldn't give me the name of his accountant."

Alvin suddenly whispered, loudly, in my ear, "His name is H.R. Block, I'm pretty sure." Adding, "I just couldn't think of it then. He's really good. You ought to try him."

The coroner had more to share, and it didn't help our case. She described that when asked if there was anyone else who could provide identification, Alvin gave the name of James Hickey, his late father-in-law. The coroner did not find out that James Hickey was dead until the next day. When she asked Alvin again, on the next day, he gave her the name of Virginia's sister Trixie LeCroy.

She went on to describe that she informed Alvin that she was "required to consult with the state medical examiner, give them the information gathered, and then we have to perform an autopsy to determine a cause of death." She described the defendant's reaction: "He got . . . He became very scared and said there was no foul play, that he opposed it, that he did not want her to have an autopsy. He asked me what I thought I was going to find, and, you know, I just informed him that I didn't know, that she was a relatively young woman without any real medical history, and we needed to find out what had happened to her. He got real pale, looked like he became physically sick, and his legs kind of buckled out from under him."

"What was the defendant saying as the body was being taken out?" Buzz asked.

"He was still opposing an autopsy and saying that there was no foul play on his part," she said.

Buzz then asked the coroner about the ring, and I knew he was trying to get ahead of her earlier denials that she had taken it. It was a smart move. He asked, "Were there any valuables on the body?"

She answered, "The only thing I removed was a ring from her left ring finger."

Alvin stopped scribbling, but he didn't react. Neither did I, because I had not told him yet that the ring was "found." Neither had I told him that I had obtained it a few days ago from the prosecutors. It was in my pocket, attached to my key ring. I wanted to use it in cross, but not admit it, and then I would give it to him. It was the ring he gave Virginia in 1966 at the Pleasant Valley Baptist Church on Ooltewah Ringgold Road. The ring she never took off for thirty-one years. The ring she wasn't allowed to wear to her grave.

15

I could tell Alvin's attention had perked up at the talk of the ring.

The coroner described going back again to see him, on October 5, 1997, after returning from the autopsy with Virginia's body. She took Detective Dan Bilbrey, and two Catoosa County sheriff's deputies, along with her.

She described how Alvin told her he thought he'd figured out what had happened. "When I started walking toward him, he said, 'I think I know what happened. I think I have figured this out.' He said, 'I think she must have suffocated herself in her pillow.' He said, 'She was real bad about sleeping facedown,' and he had to roll her over all the time when she did that. And he said, 'I had to roll her over all the time and tell her not to do that.' And he said, 'I bet that's what happened. She suffocated in her pillow.'"

In quick succession, Buzz then asked his witness several questions that he hoped would close in on Alvin.

"How many different times did the defendant give you about when he got up on the morning of October 4, 1997?"

The coroner answered, "Four different times."

"How many positions did he say he found his wife, upon rising?"

"Two," Hullander replied. "He said he found her on the position that she was in when I arrived, and then he said he found her on her face."

"When did he say she had her last seizure?"

"He said it had been a while," she replied. "He said she had one the morning before the day she died. He said he was not present. Then two p.m. on the day before she died."

Buzz next started asking the coroner about an issue he knew I would seize upon, the past difficulties of his witness and Alvin.

"Now," he asked, "did you at one time have a business located in close proximity to the defendant's business?"

She responded in a curt yes, adding, "I can't remember the accurate address. It was about two stores down from his business."

Buzz pressed on, "And what business was it that the defendant was operating?"

We all knew the answer to that one.

"The defendant? He had a television shop. Some furniture." I looked to Alvin. He seemed to be living in a strange moment where he still had the shop, and he straightened up, looking kind of proud.

"And," Buzz asked his witness, "generally what sort of business was it that you had?"

She answered, "New and used furniture."

"Wait." I looked to Alvin. "You had furniture, too?" Alvin smiled, a rare sight. They had been competitors.

Buzz established that this was around 1981, which would have been in the heyday of Ridley's Zenith TV Sales & Service. Both his parents were alive and living with them in the house, or on occasion when they needed some distance, Alvin and Virginia were living in the shop. Alvin's father's wreck was just about to happen, which would trigger the cascade of ills that, in Alvin's mind, led directly to this trial.

"Now, ma'am," Buzz continued, "have you engaged in any sort of conspiracy to get this defendant?"

She answered curtly, "No, sir."

Buzz introduced the coroner's report, state's exhibit 21.

I guess he had to leave that hanging. The allegation was that there had been an incident on Cleburne Street, behind these businesses, over the future coroner putting her garbage cans behind Alvin's shop. Allegedly, Alvin had gone after her with a broom. If Buzz had brought it up, I would complain that I hadn't been given proper notice of a similar transaction, but in this atmosphere, he likely would have gotten in any evidence of an assault—which does not require actual contact.

I did not object to the admission of S-21, her coroner's report, but then Buzz tried to slip in the official death certificate of Virginia Ridley. "Let me hand you what's been marked as state's exhibit 22."

"It's a copy of the death certificate of Virginia Gail Ridley," she said.

The problem was it had a word that I didn't want them to see. Under "Manner of Death," the word "homicide" was typed.

"Your Honor." I carefully chose my words because this was in front of the jury. "We would allow a redacted copy," I said. "I have no objection to a redacted copy."

The court knew that all I would want redacted was the one word "homicide," because it was an official state form, and some jurors might put too much weight on it. It was up to them to decide that. The judge ruled, "I'll sustain the objection, but the basic death certificate itself is admitted." We would redact that one word.

Buzz was finished with his direct examination of the coroner. I was happy to stand up and get a break from managing Alvin, who it seemed had brought even more cockroaches with him today in his two open suitcases. It was becoming an infestation in the small courtroom.

My first question in the cross-examination of the coroner concerned the notes that I saw her looking at during her direct testimony.

"Ms. Hullander, you prepared some notes as this investigation went on, and are you using them today to refresh your memory?"

She answered, "Yes, I have them."

I wanted to get her to admit that her notes, taken down contemporaneously with her investigation, at a time much closer to the events we were discussing today, would serve as better testimony than just her memory of the events. She agreed to that notion.

"Okay, now," I asked, "would you describe this house for the jury?"

She answered, "It was a white-sided house . . . The windows were blackened out with tar paper."

"All the windows?"

I bantered with her for several questions, finally getting an admission that she didn't see all the windows.

Showing her the photo admitted as S-20, I asked her if when she and others were there responding to Virginia's death, if there was room to move about in that living room/bedroom.

"There was quite a bit," she answered.

Homing in on what I was hoping to establish, I said, "Well, let's say you were in the house and you wanted to talk to Mr. Ridley— you and some investigators—where did y'all sit down?"

"We didn't sit," she curtly responded.

"Okay," I asked, "if you *had* sat down, where would be the opportunities for sitting in the living room?"

Finally she answered, "There was one chair that I recall in the living room. We would have had to sit on the bed."

Bingo! I knew I needed to at least address Buzz's suggestions that the bed appeared sunken in only on the side that was not against the wall, only on "Alvin's side" of the bed.

I continued, "If there's one chair in the whole room, and two or three people in the room, isn't it likely that the bed also served as a chair?"

"It could have," she answered.

"Well, you understand what you are implying when you say to Mr. Franklin one side of the bed was concaved, while the other side was not. What is the significance of that?" I posed.

"The impression that I got of the bed is that only one person had been sleeping on it," she responded.

"But if it's also used as a chair, that might account for an indentation on one side, correct?"

She deadpanned, "If that's what it was used for."

"Thank you," I answered, punctuating the end of that inquiry. "Do you have any strong feelings about this case?"

"As far as guilt or innocence?" she responded.

Crap! I didn't mean to go there, I thought. My pulse quickened. This was an extremely dangerous question, which would allow Hullander, the witness, to blurt out her opinion to the ultimate issue that was for only the jury to determine. I had to steer this question into the narrow lane I should have started out with. "Well, as far as Mr. Ridley, you've known him before. You had an altercation with him outside on the sidewalk one time, didn't you?" I asked. "And he got on to y'all for putting your garbage out in front of his business?"

"No, sir" was her response.

"Well, what was the issue that got him so angry?" I probed.

Then the unexpected happened.

She started to cry.

"I was cleaning up the front of my store, and the garbage can that had been sitting in between the stores had been moved, and he was out there cleaning out his side, and I walked over there with my three-year-old son, and I put some stuff in the garbage can, and he screamed at me and told me I couldn't use the garbage."

I expected a combative coroner, anything but this. I calmed down my tone. "Okay, and that terrified you of him, is that correct?"

"Yes," she answered, sobbing, "it did."

"It kind of made you mad, too, didn't it?" I pushed one last time on the subject.

"No, sir," she sobbed. "I was scared."

I moved on, but felt that from a trial strategy perspective, there was a lot that was just established. Many in town were afraid of Alvin. Had I ever been in such an encounter with him, I wondered, would I even be representing him? But there he was, sitting at the defense table with his two suitcases full of cockroaches, looking childlike as he scribbled feverishly on the second legal pad I had given him.

"Okay." I tried to calm her. "And up to that point of Virginia Ridley's autopsy, how many autopsies had you been a part of?"

She answered, "That was the first one I had taken to the crime lab myself."

I read directly from Dr. Hellman's autopsy report:

By history, the deceased was allegedly kept captive by husband, with no one in the community in Catoosa County having seen the decedent for 15–20 years.

"Is that what you told him?"

"Yes," she said, adding, "I told him that there was a possibility that she had been held captive."

"Okay." I changed direction, asking an easy question. "Do you deal with people who are grieving from losing loved ones?"

She answered, "Yes."

"Have you ever had anyone oppose an autopsy before?"

"No," she said. "I've had one that really didn't want them to— the perception of what an autopsy is, it's hard for the family to deal with sometimes—"

"Why?" I pushed.

She answered bluntly, "They don't want their family members to get cut."

I shifted to address her direct testimony that Alvin had at first stated that Virginia had no medical history, bringing to her attention that her own contemporaneous notes did not state that, instead noting that Alvin answered that she had "spells," which were later determined to be epileptic seizures.

"Okay," I pushed, "is there anywhere in that report before that point saying, 'I asked him if she had any medical problems and he said no'?"

"No."

"You testified he said there was a conspiracy against him?" I asked. "Is that correct?"

"Yes," she answered.

"Now, you are familiar with Alvin—Alvin is very conspiratorially-minded, isn't he?"

"I think so," she responded.

"Was he suspicious about her family?"

"Yes."

"He was somewhat halting about information, as you testified, is that correct?" I asked.

She answered, "Yes."

"But he ultimately did tell you Virginia's father's name—and then her sister's name?"

She answered in the affirmative to both.

I briefly asked about the "artifact" or postmortem damage to the neck of Virginia done by Hullander's assistant. There were two attempts to insert a needle into the neck of the deceased, characterized by Dr. Hellman as creating "postmortem coroner injuries."

"If you had to do it all over again," I asked, "would that have been your procedure?"

She candidly answered, "I would have waited and let them draw blood at the lab, at the crime lab."

I asked, "If Dr. Hellman characterized it as 'postmortem coroner injuries,' then he would be correct?"

Resigned, she testified, "He's the pathologist."

Finally I reached into my pocket, discreetly, and removed Virginia's wedding ring from my key chain. I held it up.

I reminded her of her earlier testimony that Virginia had a wedding band on her left-hand ring finger.

"Did you see it on her left-hand ring finger?" I asked.

"No," she said.

"There was a watch, correct?"

"No, sir."

"Could that have been removed by the EMT operators?" I asked.

"They never told me they removed a watch," she replied.

"But you only got there after one crew had already been there and left, correct?"

She replied, "Uh-huh," nodding.

"Do you recall my earlier requests, repeated requests, for the jewelry that Virginia Ridley was wearing that day?" I asked.

She nodded again. "Yes."

"Matter of fact," I said, "your response was she had none, wasn't it, the first response?"

"Not from me," she replied.

I had a transcript from an earlier hearing where I had asked Dan Bilbrey on the record about Virginia's ring and watch. He said that the coroner said there was no jewelry. I could have hammered her with it, but she was a good person who made an honest mistake and forgot the ring was in her desk drawer for over a year. I was thrilled when she called me to report that she had found it. Not everyone would have done that. But I hadn't told Alvin.

"You ultimately found the ring in the drawer at your office, and I just received this ring from Mr. Franklin recently. Is that your understanding?"

As she answered, "Yes," I slowly walked over and placed Virginia's lost wedding ring into her widowed husband's hand. I had only kept it from him a few days. I knew had I given it to him before, it would have never made it to court. I wasn't introducing it. I was returning it.

"Ms. Hullander, obviously, you could be mistaken if the jewelry had been removed at the scene?"

I often looked at the jury when I asked questions, quickly gauging if they were following and wanting these questions answered along with me. But they were not looking at me, nor were they looking at the coroner. They were looking at Alvin.

I turned around as the coroner was answering, "I recall removing it at the morgue . . ."

Alvin's head was facedown on the table. I went to the side and saw the contorted and frozen expression of silent sobbing. It was just the way he'd looked when I saw him on the street just a few days after Virginia's death when the investigation was focusing on him. It was the way he looked sometimes in my office when I said something that would just overwhelm him, usually unintentionally, like when he misinterpreted my reading of the autopsy, crying and repeating out loud that Virginia had an ovarian *"sisk,"* and thinking it was what had killed her. His frozen expression was like a child's face during that silent moment before the wail begins. But the wail never came in these moments. Alvin's cries were always silent, but the sustained contortions of his face made you know they were real.

A roach crawled out from under the papers where his head was resting, near his lips. I didn't know what to do for him.

Buzz stood. "Your Honor, may we approach the bench for a moment?"

The judge said, "Yes," as if he were expecting it.

The court reporter followed us to a bench conference, where the lawyers are expected to speak in tones low enough for the jury not to hear.

"Your Honor," Buzz began, "the state wants to make an objection to Mr. Poston's orchestration of giving this ring to his client in the courtroom, so as to make a display in front of the jury. He held on to this ring for some period of time, and he's just now giving it to his client, and I certainly object to that."

I tried to keep the emotion from my voice and said, "Your Honor, it is well known how difficult it has been to keep evidence from my client. I got this ring, I'll state in my place, from Mr. Franklin last week, just a matter of days before the trial. I wanted it referred to, but I didn't wish to introduce it as evidence, because Mr. Ridley has been asking for it for a long time. And I was afraid I couldn't have her identify it in court as demonstrative evidence, and that's what it is."

"He didn't have to give it to him in the courtroom," Buzz said snarkily.

"Okay," I said, "I'll take it back!"

Judge Van Pelt injected, "No! That would be worse! Let's just leave it. The objection is noted. Leave it."

"Well," I said to the coroner as I pulled out a tabloid that I had seen at the funeral home and purchased myself at the grocery store, "do you remember talking to the *National Examiner*?"

"No, sir," she said. "I have never talked to them."

I read from the tabloid itself: *"She had apparently been there more than three decades as his captive, says County Coroner Vanita Hullander."*

"Is that you saying that?"

"No, sir," she responded quietly.

I emphasized the quote: *"It appeared that foul play was involved."*

Buzz broke in, "Your Honor, I would object if he intends to keep reading statements she says she did not make."

"Well," I said, "I'll have to read them out to her and ask her, Your Honor!"

Buzz remained standing. "I would object to that. He already knows what her answers are going to be. I don't think that's appropriate!"

"I'm not sure I do know what her answers are going to be," I said.

"Overruled" was all Judge Van Pelt said.

I could continue, and I did: *"It appears that foul play was involved with her suffocation. Someone could have held the nose and mouth shut."*

"Is that you?" I asked.

"No, sir," she said.

"Is there anyone else named Vanita Hullander, coroner of Catoosa County?" I asked the silly question.

She responded, "I wouldn't know."

"Did you tell the *Daily Citizen News* in Dalton some things?"

"I had a conversation with Mr. (reporter Bill) Landauer, but I don't recall what we talked about," she said.

I read from the Dalton paper: *"I had heard stories that he had a wife,"* she said, *"but I'd never seen her and there she was."*

"Do you think you said that to Mr. Landauer?"

"It's possible," she conceded.

"Do you remember saying it appeared that foul play was involved in her suffocation?" I read the newspaper quote again: *"Someone could have held the nose and mouth shut. We don't know."*

"I don't recall," she answered.

I continued: *"He had a temper and used a lot of body language when he talked. He didn't do things that society would consider normal."*

"Mr. Poston," she said, "I don't recall the conversation."

"Do you recall everything being in the media saying that Mr. Ridley called a funeral home first before he called for any help?"

She seemed to warm to this line of questioning. "Yes, I recall that."

"Have you been able in your investigation to find any funeral home that Mr. Ridley called?"

"No," she said, and as I started with the next question, she interrupted me, saying, "I also advised you that I asked the paper to print a retraction on some of these things because it was not accurate—"

"On Mr. Ridley's behalf," I interrupted her sarcastically, "thank you."

Alvin nodded, as if to thank her sincerely for trying to address the false storylines in the news.

"Well, was there anything unusual about the body?"

"No," she said.

This was important to address the picture that Virginia's sisters had painted in the press and in court about the condition of Virginia's body.

Then Hullander qualified her answer. "Just the petechia," she added.

"You didn't make any reference to a left-arm mark, did you?"

"Not at the time," she answered.

"At the autopsy," I said, "the only issue that you and Dr. Hellman found that was significant was the petechia, correct?"

"The petechia," she answered, "and he felt there was hemorrhaging to the soft tissue that may not have been caused by the needle puncture, and he felt like the cerebellum was awfully small." The small cerebellum was implied to be from a lack of nutrition, but there was plenty of food noted in the house, and most of Virginia's writings involved what they were having for supper each day. The "needle puncture" occurred when her assistant jabbed at Virginia's neck trying to draw blood, which caused postmortem artifact. I knew the assistant, and it seemed like an innocent mistake. But I was representing a client.

"Dr. Hellman advised me at the time he was inspecting the neck that he felt like the hemorrhaging in the soft tissue was caused by a soft compression," she insisted.

Dr. Hellman hadn't said that at all. I had the question I asked him in my notes, and I asked him other than the postmortem needle punctures, was there anything else significant about the neck to report, and he had said no.

"Of course, what he testified to under oath is probably his opinion, correct?"

"Yes."

I moved on. "You think—her small cerebellum—that Alvin did that to her?"

"It was from failure to thrive, the cerebellum can—"

I interrupted, saying, "You're also aware she had some allergic reactions in the past to some medications? You're not aware of that?"

"No."

"If she had some allergic reactions to epilepsy medicine in the past," I posed, "you've done a literature search, I'm sure, that explains that this could cause atrophy of the cerebellum?"

She said, "From the research."

That was a victory. The research was relatively new and scant, but she conceded this was a possible cause of Virginia's reduced cerebellum size.

Doubling back to pretrial statements, I asked, "Did you make a statement to the press that she had been dead for twenty-four hours?"

"Not at that time."

I followed up, "Is that one of the statements you asked to be retracted?"

"I asked the statement from the *News-Free Press* to be retracted," she said, "that they had been crossed-over from three different stories." I had no idea what she meant, but the effect was she was distancing herself from the published negative statements about my client.

Shifting again, I started asking another question when the jurors suddenly turned their heads, away from the witness stand where I was closely standing.

I finished the question, "If an EMT that had gotten there before you, said she had been dead for one hour, maybe two, is that possible?"

"I don't think for that amount of lividity . . ."

Just then, something yellow flashed in my right peripheral vision, and Hullander stopped midsentence.

I turned around to see Alvin waving at me with his legal pad, like he was on the tarmac trying to land a jetliner. Judge Van Pelt looked like he was about to say something, so I got ahead of it.

"Just a moment, Your Honor," I said as I stepped quickly to Alvin.

"What's happening? What are you doing?" I demanded.

"You need to ask her *my* questions now," he said.

I had made the mistake of precedent, allowing him to funnel questions through me to Dr. Hellman. It was toward the end, when I thought I saw a bit of compassion from the state pathologist.

He held out the pad as I quickly scanned it. "I'll ask some of them, Alvin, I promise."

That satisfied him for the moment.

Since there was an interruption, and I took the pad from him, the jurors obviously knew what was going on. I figured I might as well ask his questions right then, while it was obvious they were his questions and not mine. And I made sure I was reading the questions, signaling to them that it wasn't really me asking them. I ended up reading some of Alvin's questions.

The first: "'Have you done this investigation as a personal grudge against Alvin Ridley?'"

Hullander predictably answered, "No, sir."

The next question seemed like it was from corporate litigation: "'Did you put up a business next to his in 1982, or somewhere around that, selling the same product that he sold?'"

Her answer, "No, not the same."

"'Did y'all put out garbage cans in front of his place of business?'"

"No," she said. "I thought the city provided them."

"'Did you ever witness a fight in the back of Alvin Ridley's place of business involving Kenneth Petty and his father, Bill Ridley?'"

Please, Buzz, I thought, *please object to relevance!* I needed relief.

Surprisingly, she answered, "No, sir. I know my father-in-law was supposed to have stopped Mr. Petty from striking Mr. Ridley, but that's hearsay."

I looked at Alvin, and he nodded and grinned as if his questions were breaking the case wide open.

I took the pad back to Alvin. He smiled, some gaps from missing teeth revealed, as he always did when he thought he'd done something better than I could have done it.

"That's all at this time, Your Honor." I sat down next to my strange, complicated client, who was still beaming.

Buzz began his redirect examination of Coroner Hullander, trying to mend any damage to his case that I hoped my cross-examination had done. Probing her history with Alvin had left her crying on the stand. That couldn't be a bad thing; however, by bringing it up, I had probably "opened the door," evidence-wise, now to allow Buzz to ask specific questions of the encounter that he couldn't have asked before.

He started asking rapid-fire questions, perhaps knowing lunch was coming, and jurors can be unforgiving to those who go too long. Many of his questions began, "Mr. Poston asked you . . ." I thought that this was good, as he was basically bringing up my questions again when he was trying to ask his.

Then, finally, "Ma'am, Mr. Poston asked you about a time when you had an encounter with this defendant when you were operating a business near his?"

"Yes, sir."

"And he more than just threatened you verbally . . ." Buzz paused, then asked, "How did Mr. Ridley threaten?"

She started crying again. "He had a broom in his hand, and he drew back the broom, and he threatened to kill me."

Buzz pressed, "And did you become afraid of the defendant when that happened?"

"I was very frightened," she said. "He was just furious, out of control, just saying a bunch of stuff that didn't make sense. I'm sorry. I get upset; I'm still upset from this. I had my three-year-old son in my arms when he was threatening to kill me."

Buzz's strategy was hit-and-run, neither savoring nor dwelling on his punches when he connected.

"Now Lieutenant Gass, when he was questioning the defendant or asking this one question that he asked, what was his demeanor?"

"Trying to be helpful," Hullander said. "He was very calm, you know, like he was trying to befriend Mr. Ridley."

Lieutenant Gass had been at Alvin's home with the coroner and other officers in the first days of the investigation, and all were trying to get Alvin talking. He had said to my client, perhaps innocently, "I've known you all my life, and I never knew you had a wife."

"And what was Mr. Ridley's final response to this question that Johnny Gass asked?"

Out of nowhere, quoting Alvin, the coroner stated, "'I plead the Fifth Amendment.'"

This was highly improper. There was a U.S. Supreme Court opinion on point that a prosecutor could not in front of a seated jury refer to the defendant invoking his Fifth Amendment rights, but I could not remember the name of the case.

"And the Fifth Amendment," Buzz continued, "you know what that is, don't you?"

"Choose not to answer due to incrimination," she answered.

Then Buzz followed by saying, "So someone can take that to mean that there was an incriminating response?"

I bolted upright, because I had to object and be overruled to preserve the error for appeal. "Your Honor, I object to what someone could take that to mean, and he knows better than that!"

Judge Van Pelt said simply, "Sustained." But perhaps the damage was already done, I thought. I should have objected earlier.

Buzz then got to what was really nagging him.

"Now, his demeanor on the first day you got there, what was that demeanor?"

"He was just unattached," she said, "really showed no emotion."

Buzz snapped, "When Mr. Poston gave the ring to the defendant here in the courtroom a little while ago, did he show some emotion then?"

"He appeared to," she said.

"And Mr. Poston has had that ring for quite some time, hasn't he?"

"Yes, sir," she replied.

"And he chose today to give it to the defendant?"

She replied, "Yes, sir."

In my brief recross, I added to the bickering about Virginia's wedding ring, asking, "When did you give the ring to Mr. Franklin?"

Hullander replied, "It's been about nine, ten days."

I was following up to note that I had obviously had the ring for a week or less, when I noticed that not one juror was looking at us, or listening to us, as far as I could tell. I turned to follow the direction of their gaze, toward the defense table. Alvin was bent over, trying to humanely scoop up cockroaches with his legal pad and place them back in these suitcases, unsuccessfully.

I ended, having walked a tightrope. While they got some things in that I didn't like, the evidence of the past conflict between Vanita Hullander and Alvin Ridley was clearly established.

Now my blood sugar was plummeting, and I needed to eat.

The judge gave instructions to the jury that we were breaking for lunch, and after the jury left the room, he mentioned to us that the cockroaches had become an issue. Noting that his chambers were in the next room, he informed us, "We are going to pick up this afternoon in the large courtroom. I have to get this courtroom fumigated, thanks to your client, Mr. Poston."

I told him something to the effect that I was sympathetic, having to sit near the source, but inside, I was elated. I took Alvin to lunch, deferring discussing anything because I never knew where jurors were dining.

On the way back, I took Alvin aside and told him, "We're going to be in the big courtroom, Alvin, the old courtroom." He seemed unimpressed at this news. "Alvin, it's the last place that Virginia ever appeared in public. Remember, September 15, 1970?"

Finally Alvin said, "Yeah, Judge Painter and that housing authority case." Then he ordered me to relitigate their wrongful eviction, and do it that afternoon.

"No, Alvin, this is a murder case," I reminded him. "Through her writings, Virginia has been helping you. Now we need to go to where she last appeared in public, so she can really be powerful."

Alvin nodded, but seemed more interested in rehashing all the wrongs done to him. I was used to that by now, but I also felt he probably needed to distance himself from the reality of what he was facing.

16

*T*he grand old courtroom in the Catoosa County Courthouse, built in 1939, was where I was sworn in to start the practice of law in 1985. The first impression going from the windowless box of courtroom B to this spacious old courtroom was that of the sudden expanse of space. The second immediate impression was the craftsmanship of the old oak bench and witness stand, to the right of the bench, left from the perspective of the seated judge.

In the larger room, the defense and state tables were actually several feet apart, and the only negative here was that the jury box was so much farther away from us. The witness stand, like the prosecution table, was closer to the jury box, which was also a greater distance away. I thought that might not be a bad thing, in this case. But I could better communicate with my client here. During breaks, we had more room, so I would not worry that someone was eavesdropping on our conversations. Even though it was a much larger courtroom, with many more seats, the crowd of spectators was growing, so there were not that many available.

The state called Richard Baxter, a deputy coroner who was also a funeral director at the Wilson Funeral Homes/Wallis-Stewart Chapel, where Virginia's arrangements were made. Baxter testified under direct that he first communicated with Alvin by phone, the two in a frustrating game of phone tag about making Virginia's funeral arrangements, finally connecting three days after her death.

"I had just told Mr. Ridley that we needed to go ahead and make funeral arrangements because, obviously, I couldn't proceed without him, because he was the spouse, making him the next of kin, the legal next of kin," Baxter testified.

Buzz got from the witness that the defendant had "volunteered to me a few times on different occasions that she had smothered herself by laying facedown on a pillow."

On cross, I challenged the notion that one could accept my own client's conclusions at that point as to his wife's cause of death. I asked, "Is Mr. Ridley, as far as you know, a doctor?" and then, "As far as you know, is he a forensic pathologist?"

Of course, the answer to both by the witness was "Not that I know of," but I knew the jurors would think that just by talking to or even looking at Alvin, that would be a safe *no*.

"As far as you are concerned, he's a grieving widower, is that correct?" I asked.

"As far as I'm concerned, he's a widower," he answered.

I couldn't resist asking about the *National Examiner* article, because I had seen it on his desk when I went to interview him at the funeral home. He acknowledged knowing about the article.

"And the story indicated that Mr. Ridley had called your funeral home first before he called anyone else about his dead wife. Do you recall reading that?" I asked.

He acknowledged that he had.

"Was that a true statement?" I asked.

"No, sir," he answered. "It was not."

I sat down.

"Call your next witness," the judge directed toward the state's table.

"Your Honor, we'd call Chief Charles Land," Buzz said, and I noticed an immediate tension fall upon Alvin.

I always thought Ringgold chief of police Charles Land had the perfect demeanor for his job. He was smart, and certainly efficient, and he had a laid-back, calm demeanor, like the sheriff played on TV by Andy Griffith, only ten times quieter.

The chief was, of course, the focus of Alvin's ire in the way he handled the traffic report in Bill Ridley's 1981 wreck in Alvin's company truck, when the elder Ridley was hit from behind by the Polk Brothers Concrete truck. But his worst sin was his lawyer jumping the gun on his counterclaim to Alvin's second lawsuit, which included the chief as a defendant and counterclaimant. For a brief period, the executed writ seized the most available asset, Alvin's 1977 Chevy van, and this had become the main symbol of Alvin and Virginia's suffering—even though Alvin got it back after a short period of time. That being said, Alvin still hadn't "accepted" it back, due to his contorted view of statutes of limitations, and for fifteen years, it had sat untouched beside his house.

At the end of the on-the-street investigation, Bill Ridley asked if he could continue driving on his way to the landfill, and he drove away in the rear-damaged truck. The driver of the cement truck also left, with the chief's permission.

He described investigating the skid marks that led to the accident, and came to the conclusion that "the skid marks started in the inside lane, went over into the outside lane, and that's where there was debris indicating that's where the impact had occurred."

Buzz asked, "And so, based on that, what is your opinion as to how this accident came about?"

Buzz established that Alvin Ridley was not at the accident, only his father, and Bill had basically admitted pulling out in front of the cement truck.

"Now," the district attorney asked, "did you write up your accident report in accordance with what you have basically testified to here today?"

"Yes," said the chief, "I did."

The chief described a conversation he had with Alvin Ridley a few days later, in his TV shop, stating, "His exact words I don't remember—something to the effect of, 'it would look a lot better if this truck was here and this truck was here.' And I said, 'Alvin, the way that accident report is written up was exactly the way it happened, and I'm not going to change that report.'"

Chief Land described how Alvin sued him, on behalf of his father, after his father had passed from pancreatic cancer.

Alvin started wildly scribbling until I gave him a stern look, so he stopped.

Buzz asked the chief if he had ever met or even seen Virginia Ridley, and he had not. The chief—wisely, in my opinion—had requested that Detective Dan Bilbrey with the Catoosa County Sheriff's Office take over the investigation of Virginia's death. "I talked to him and asked him if he would take over the whole case due to the conflict between Alvin and myself. You know, years had passed, but I just felt that it would be better to be investigated by someone else."

When it came time for cross-examination, I briefly tried to commiserate with the chief, agreeing that "Mr. Ridley became disproportionately obsessed with the taking of his van, blaming the downfall of everything on your accident report out on Highway 151 . . ."

Chief Land was so nervous that I was trying to trap him, he refused to go along even with my most agreeable questions. I didn't have the heart to grill him. He had acted admirably, and even Alvin noted he ultimately dismissed his efforts to levy on Alvin's van, or anything else.

Buzz next called the pharmacist Harry Gass, the father of Lieutenant Johnny Gass. Harry ran Price Ringgold Drugs, on the end of the historic block where Alvin's building was located.

When Buzz called his name as the state's next witness, Alvin smiled. "He likes me, Harry Gass likes me," he kept saying.

"He's a state witness, Alvin," I reminded him.

I remembered going over the state witness list with Alvin when it first came out, and each time it was supplemented. He sat in my office, smiling, saying, "Harry Gass likes me," as if pleased to see him on the state's witness list.

When I pressed him, he told me two stories. The first, and I took it that Alvin was still young when this happened, described the time Alvin was "sick with the Hong Kong flu." He went on to paint a dire picture, explaining, "With that Hong Kong flu, you *die* on day seven. Daddy went to Harry Gass on day six, and told him about it. Harry Gass sent some medicine and told my daddy he had to give it to me before day seven. He gave it to me on day six, and I was saved, just in time. Harry Gass saved my life."

The other story began with Alvin going to the pharmacy, with a raised bump on his head. "Harry Gass gave me the name of a doctor, and he made me go and get it looked at. That doctor cut it out and sewed it up and said it would have killed me. Harry Gass saved my life, *twiced*."

I remembered Alvin's stories as Buzz began questioning the pharmacist. I had served upon Buzz's office photos of several bottles and labels that were in Alvin's home that came from Price Ringgold Drugs, so I worried that I didn't know what the pharmacist could be here to testify about.

Buzz established that Gass had operated Price Ringgold Drugs since 1963, and was establishing the relatively inexpensive costs of the epilepsy medicines Dilantin, Depakote, Mebaral, and phenobarbital.

"Now, did Detective Bilbrey ask you to check back in your records for anything in this case?"

Gass qualified that his records "don't go back far enough that I can," but ended with "I didn't find anything."

I couldn't believe my ears. In the museum of Alvin's house, and all the bizarre relics of the strange over half-century of his life, I found medicine bottles, several from Price Ringgold Drugs, and the ones dated 1977 and afterward still containing medicines to treat epilepsy. This supported the writing I found in the margin of one of Virginia's Bibles, where September, 1977 was noted as the date when God told her to stop taking her medicine. Alvin continued to pick up the medicines for a few months afterward.

"Mr. Gass, I can call you Harry, can't I?" I asked after Buzz rested.

"That's fine," he answered, smiling. We were both Type-1, insulin-dependent diabetic patients, and I had learned much from him on managing the disease.

"Harry," I continued, "of course, Mr. Bilbrey earlier asked you a little more than if you have any records, did he not? He asked you if you recall filling any prescriptions for Virginia Ridley, is that correct?"

"Yes, sir," he answered.

"And your statement to him in the early part of his investigation was that you had not ever?"

"Not to my knowledge."

I had sent photos of the evidence I was about to introduce to the DA. Even so, he put up this witness, a beloved local pharmacist with an aging memory and a very short record retention policy, and phrased his question precisely to get the answer that he didn't have any *records* of filling prescriptions for Virginia. And Detective Bilbrey had seized on that he didn't remember ever filling *any* prescriptions.

"All right," I said. "Let me show you what's been marked as defendant's exhibit 44. And what does that appear to be?"

Harry Gass looked at the bottle closely, then said, "That's Mebaral and it's a prescription. It's made out to Virginia Ridley from Dr. Stephenson."

I let that linger a moment, and then asked, "And who filled it?"

"I probably did it," he quickly conceded. "It could have been me or John Price or a relief pharmacist, but I did not recall that. I stand corrected."

"I'll show you what's been marked as 45, 46, 47 . . ."

I handed him three medicine bottles.

"Some of the labels appear to be from your store?" I asked.

"Yes," he answered.

"Some of them still have quite a bit of medicine?"

"Yes, sir," he answered. "Some of them have several."

Establishing that he was clearly wrong in his statements to Detective Bilbrey, and his earlier sworn testimony being so narrowly drawn out, he conceded that his pharmacy had filled prescriptions for Virginia Ridley for some time. Additionally, when she stopped going out of the house, Dr. Stephenson switched the name of the prescription for the antiseizure medicines to Alvin's name.

I shifted the subject of the cross-examination to the infamous incident where Alvin allegedly threatened his son, Lieutenant Johnny Gass.

Oddly, Harry answered only, "I think him and some of the boys had some differences. I don't know exactly what they were or when they were or which ones it was, basically." It didn't sound like a father upset that his son's life had been threatened.

I sat down while Buzz tried to rehabilitate his witness.

Beside me, Alvin leaned in and said, "See, I told you, Harry Gass likes me!"

"I think he does, Alvin," I said.

17

Buzz called Detective Dan Bilbrey, the state's main prosecution witness, who had been allowed to remain in the courtroom seated next to Buzz, to "assist the prosecutor with the orderly presentation of evidence."

I told Alvin, "This is their last witness." As a former prosecutor, I knew they usually let their investigator go last, to clean up any evidentiary messes or stray puzzle pieces left lying on the table. Lori knew that meant we needed to tell some of our witnesses that the defense case would likely start tomorrow.

"When is Gold Bird coming to my house?" Alvin kept asking.

I answered in pure economic terms. "Alvin, I have to pay him to be here and for his time here. I have to get him a hotel room. If the state is going to end today or tomorrow, I'll get him up here tomorrow night. Unless you want to pay him to come up and hang out with us . . ."

Alvin said, "Tomorrow night is fine. I want him to see the scene." He had picked up on the idea that I stated during our search, that our expert would be the only one who actually had been to the scene, as opposed to the busy Dr. Hellman.

I watched Bilbrey approach and wondered what the others were thinking. I'm sure it's a powerful signal to the jury to see the person sitting at the right hand of the prosecutor rising from the table and taking the stand. He's a *special* witness, they probably think. He got to stay in the courtroom throughout the case and whisper back and forth with the district attorney. Unlike the stream of other witnesses, passing through like special guest stars on one of Alvin's favorite TV "programs," here was a main player. I'm sure they studied his marine-style haircut, shaved on the sides and back, with a blond flattop. Even his perfect posture suggested a man of rigid training and service. But Buzz didn't draw any of that out in his introduction of his witness, if a military background existed.

Detective Sergeant Dan Bilbrey told the jury that he was invited into the case by Vanita Hullander on the day that Virginia Ridley died, Saturday, October 4, 1997. It wasn't until the next day, Sunday, October 5, after 9:00 p.m., that he first acted. He went to the Ridley residence on Inman Street with Hullander, a deputy from the sheriff's office, and a Ringgold city police officer.

In response to questions from the DA, he said, "We wound up going to Mr. Ridley's house to conduct a welfare check on the fifth of October, 1997."

When Buzz asked him to define "welfare check," Bilbrey, taking a style tip from Dr. Hellman, pivoted to the jury and answered, "Ladies and gentlemen, I had been advised by the coroner that on her visit with Mr. Ridley on the fourth, he had indicated to her that he was suicidal. She had not heard from him up until her contact with myself."

I had been around long enough to know the tricks that law enforcement uses. Suddenly everyone was concerned about Alvin Ridley's welfare? The jurors would certainly remember how the coroner felt about him. This was an opportunity for an interrogation.

Bilbrey continued his testimony. "Again I advised him after we determined his mental status was okay, that he was not suicidal, I advised him I had some questions pertaining to his wife's death."

He went on, "I also asked him if he would show me where she had died, and he replied that he would take us into the residence and show us."

"You let him in on his first visit?" I whispered to Alvin, "and you made me wait a year, and charged me a turkey plate?"

Alvin stared at the detective, not responding to my snarky observation.

I did not object to the admission of state's exhibit 25, the consent form that Alvin signed to allow them to come inside his house. Buzz soon got to the nub of the inquiry, Alvin's allegedly "spontaneous" statement.

"Now, what was the first response that you got from the defendant before anything else?"

"The first response," Bilbrey answered, "was a spontaneous statement. I call it a spontaneous statement. We hadn't even asked Mr. Ridley any questions, and he had blurted out a statement, and his statement was 'I didn't suffocate her, she was bad about sleeping facedown. I constantly had to warn her and roll her over. The bruises on her body were from her falling down all the time. I can't believe this. People are always accusing me of mistreating her.'" Bilbrey added, "And this was in quote." Neither the coroner's report nor the autopsy from the crime lab mentioned any bruising on the body.

Buzz asked about the alleged "indention" on the bed.

"There was one indention in the bed that," Bilbrey answered, "it would be farthest from the wall, and it was—the indention is what I would consider consistent with the outline of a body. That indicated to me somebody had been sleeping there over a period of time."

I envisioned the trope of the white outline of a dead body at a crime scene, and Detective Bilbrey seeing the perfect outline of a body on a bed.

Buzz hit the highlights about Alvin's allegedly inconsistent statements about the time of her last seizure, and Alvin's most certainly awkward attempts at administering CPR.

"Well, later, I had to go back and verify exactly what his definition of CPR was, and in a subsequent statement, he indicated that he wound up breathing for her and giving chest compressions every sixty seconds. He couldn't recall whether the chest compressions were with one hand or two, but stated he gave chest compressions every sixty seconds."

I remembered reviewing the American Heart Association guide on performing cardiopulmonary resuscitation, which instructs "hard and fast chest compressions . . . 100 to 120 per minute." I thought that Alvin's idea of CPR didn't help her much, at the rate of one chest compression every sixty seconds. She was likely already dead, and the feeble effort at CPR seemed sad to me, more than inept. I hoped the jury was thinking that way.

Detective Bilbrey described where Alvin went to find a phone, first turning south on Highway 41, then turning around and coming back to downtown Ringgold, and going to two phones.

Buzz then had Bilbrey inform the jury, "Ladies and gentlemen, the closest medical assistance would be the fire department, station one, here in Ringgold, which also houses the ambulance. It is manned twenty-four hours a day and it is right at three-tenths of a mile from Mr. Ridley's residence." Bilbrey added that he had measured the distance himself, and from the map, the jury knew that Alvin drove right past station one as he turned toward Truck City, only to then turn around in the Battle of Ringgold Gap roadside monument and go to the pay phone near ShopRite.

Of course, now I understood Alvin. Station one was the fire department headed by Fire Chief Chuck Gass, another son of pharmacist Harry Gass, and brother of Lieutenant Johnny Gass. Alvin trusted no one in Ringgold. It all kind of made sense to me, if you just knew the way Alvin thought.

Buzz then asked his witness about the October 6, 1997, visit with Alvin. Accompanying Detective Bilbrey on that visit were two other Catoosa County detectives, Vic Wells and Mike Helton, both of whom I had known for years, and Johnny Bass, the investigator for the district attorney's office. Detective Bilbrey had carried in his pocket a microcassette recorder, which was turned on without informing the others.

The recording of the encounter, which took place in two parts— the first at the Ridley home, and then the second where Alvin let them into his long-shuttered business on Nashville Street—was surprisingly clear and audible. We got copies of the microcassettes as part of our discovery demand. Even though the recording of these encounters existed, Buzz had not offered it in presenting his case, and continued to ask his witness questions from that date as if it didn't exist. I had asked Lori to transcribe it, and to the best of her ability to try to discern who was saying what. Alvin's voice was clear, as was that of Detective Bilbrey. I recognized the voice of Detective Vic Wells. To attribute the other voices, we looked to Detective Bilbrey to help us decipher. He had done that somewhat, and Lori had made his corrections.

Bilbrey testified that Alvin said the last two people to see Virginia alive, other than himself, were his mother, who died in January 1994, and Dr. Stephenson, the beloved town doctor who had died a few years before Alvin's mother. Bilbrey testified that the next day when he talked to the defendant was October 8, 1997, a Wednesday. Alvin came to the detective's office, at Bilbrey's request. On this visit, Bilbrey testified, Alvin's statements were "quite a bit different this time around," stating that "he indicated that his wife did have a seizure the night prior to her death. Further, he indicated that during this seizure that he had grabbed her face, indicating like this to me"—the detective indicated with his own hands on the sides of his own face—"he had grabbed her face, put his hands over her face in order to keep her from hurting herself."

Buzz ticked down a list of inconsistencies, some petty and some curious, with his witness. "Now, going through this residence, did you see any evidence or sign of food in the residence?"

Bilbrey answered, "Yes."

I remembered that Vanita Hullander had also detailed finding food in the home. This was, of course, to counter Alvin's complaining about their needs and his inability to meet them, a practice he had perfected when begging to the local churches. However, these findings also countered the coroner's suggestion that Alvin had somehow caused the cerebellum shrinkage by withholding nourishment. Alvin couldn't win, either way. Thankfully, Virginia had provided us with an almost-daily journal of what they ate.

Finally it was my turn. The state's chief witness, Detective Dan Bilbrey, turned to me to take my questions. On cross-examination,

I got out of him that Alvin was not made aware of being recorded. While perfectly legal, that was important because, to jurors, "fair play" is very often an important matter in the mountains and foothills of North Georgia. His answer of "It's not illegal, counselor" was perfectly defensive.

Then I attacked his written report of the encounter with Alvin on October 6, 1997, because once I finally had the recording, many errors were apparent. Up to this point, he had been testifying only from his written report on direct examination.

Establishing that he had indeed reviewed what Lori Duckworth had transcribed from the tapes, he turned to the jury and said, "Ladies and gentlemen, on my review of this transcript, there were several errors in it. There were also sentences and phrases out of order, so, as far as the contents of this current document, I couldn't say that it was totally accurate."

"Now, your memorialization of this spontaneous quote is different than that of Vanita Hullander, did you recognize that? What Vanita Hullander on that date handwrote, do you recall? You've been in the courtroom the entire time. 'I bet she suffocated herself on her pillow when she had a seizure'—something to that effect, is that correct?"

He answered, "Something to that effect, yes."

"And *your* memorialization of it is, 'I didn't suffocate her'? Which one is correct?"

"I am reporting," he defended. "Ladies and gentlemen, I am reporting what I heard. I can't say that hers is correct, I'm just telling you what I heard."

"You're not telling the jury that both of you are correct, are you?"

"I just answered your question, counselor," he sniped.

"So one of you is wrong, correct?"

"If that's the way you want to put it," he said.

I continued hammering on the faulty information on his report. When a law enforcement officer reads to a jury from an "official" report, it is a powerful tool for that witness.

"Your report indicates Harry Gass said he didn't think he ever filled a prescription for Virginia Ridley, is that correct?"

"That's correct," he conceded.

Moving down his report, I asked, "And your next entry is this, 'Detective advised Dr. Hellman, Alvin Ridley purportedly had done CPR on Virginia Ridley, which could account for petechia found in Virginia Ridley's autopsy.'"

He answered defensively, "It does indicate that, ladies and gentlemen. I would like to expand on that. My opinion is that correct CPR was not administered, by his own statement."

"Was that a fair statement, though?" I pushed.

"You described it accurately. Yes, sir," he said.

"So you concluded," I pushed further, "at least at one time that this could account for the petechia, according to this?"

He again tried to qualify "that CPR was not correctly administered . . ."

"So," I wrapped up, "you don't believe the sentence in your own report that you wrote?"

I then referred him to defendant's exhibits 50 and 51, two near-identical news items from December 1968 and the other from January 1969, one from the *Catoosa County News* and the other from the *Chattanooga News-Free Press*. Both featured a smiling photo of a young Virginia Ridley, with the headline PARENTS SEEK MARRIED DAUGHTER. The brief articles stated her parents were looking for her and ended that she was "last seen with her husband, Alvin Ridley."

I wanted the jury to see that her family was actively and publicly looking for her, which left the conclusion that their claims were likely investigated, and obviously went nowhere.

"Let me show you"—I handed an envelope to Detective Bilbrey—"what's been marked as defendant's exhibit 52. Is that the envelope that you just handed me?"

"Yes," he answered, "it is."

"Contained in the envelope marked D-52 is what?"

"Should be a microcassette tape of the interview of Alvin Ridley on October 6, 1997," he said.

I was trying to utilize the transcript that Lori had created from the tapes, and corrected with Detective Bilbrey's input, but Buzz complained that he had not had the chance to look at the corrections.

Judge Van Pelt seized the lull and said, "Well, let's just go ahead and quit for the day and let him review the transcript, and we'll finish tomorrow."

Seeing Alvin's confusion, I told him, "He means finish with this witness, not the trial. But we'll start putting up our witnesses tomorrow after I finish the cross-examination of Detective Bilbrey."

I could finally promise, without fear of letting him down, that we would likely be meeting with Dr. Goldberg tomorrow evening, and Alvin was all in.

I drove through Kentucky Fried Chicken to get Alvin supper to take home, and then dropped him off after a rapid-fire review of what went well. There was no point in raising any other issues. We were way beyond my pretending that Alvin was someone the jury could relate to. He was just so damned odd, with the two suitcases full of roaches that he tightly clasped or kept a few feet away, under his constant watch.

I hadn't talked to my mother in a few days, so I called her.

"Son, we're reading the articles and watching the news," my sweet mother related. "Your father is really following it closely."

"How's he doing?" I awkwardly asked. "I mean, is he *okay?*"

"Yes!" she replied, as if there had never been any issue in the history of our relationship. "He's reading the papers, and he's turning the TV back and forth to catch the story."

I met Alison to get a bite to eat and discuss our days. I was sure she was getting tired of always hearing about mine, but she was genuinely interested.

"Warming up to Alvin, are you?" I teased.

"Let's just say, I think you're doing him a good job, but he still hasn't paid you, right?"

I told her not to worry. Alvin was good for it. When I had threatened to leave the case, he signed a security deed to the TV shop. Still, the expenses of this case were brutal.

I fell asleep reading the latest version of the transcript of the October 6, 1997, recording of my client.

*   *   *

I woke up Wednesday, feeling on edge because the state's case would likely end today. Then we'd take over running the show, the defense calling the witnesses and putting up evidence. If we fell short of answering all the questions in the minds of the jurors, Alvin and Virginia's strange existence might just be too odd to imagine as a happy relationship. The media still referred to her "captivity" as a given fact.

I thought as I approached, one thing that hadn't changed much in thirty years was Alvin's house, except for the wear of years without maintenance. I pulled up to the gate and was surprised that Alvin was outside, waiting for me, wearing the same clothes he had on yesterday, along with his vital accessory neck brace and the two roach-filled suitcases at his feet.

The courthouse was the one constant, at least the "old" 1939 courthouse was. Those front steps had been a focus since childhood, when I stood with my father, watching candidates speak to the gathered, sometimes rowdy, crowds. When watching the polls, I remembered my father disappearing across the street several times to a gas station, where he joined some of the local men and would emerge each time just a little more drunk as the evening wore on. I remembered as a young man here alone in 1984, watching Alvin Ridley guilt a taunting and disrespectful crowd to stand quietly for the national anthem. I remembered the times I was standing there on those steps myself, in both election night victory and in humiliating defeat.

We went inside, me lugging my trial case and Alvin his two suitcases, but this morning, we were reporting again to the big courtroom in the old courthouse, where, to me, the ghost of Virginia Ridley might still linger.

Detective Bilbrey was already there, ready for me to resume his cross-examination. There's nothing like a criminal trial to put a chill on normally cordial relationships. There was no interaction with Buzz or anyone at the prosecutor's table. We all settled into our seats, and my secretary, Lori, arrived and sat behind us. She had done a great job transcribing the state tapes. A few more observers were walking in, a smattering of county employees and

Judge Dills, and a few more evenly distributed on both prosecution and defense sides of the courtroom.

"Alvin," I told him, "you have people here for you, sitting behind us—on *our* side of the room." He turned around and stared at them, as if not sure whose side they were on.

Unlike most cases, where the families of alleged victims packed the prosecution side, I hadn't noticed any of Virginia's family in the courtroom since her sister testified on the first day.

We started Wednesday, trial day four, January 13, 1999, with the resumption of my cross-examination of Detective Dan Bilbrey. The transcript of the October 6, 1997, interview with Alvin—recorded without his knowledge—had again been reviewed, and the agreed-upon changes, mostly in the attribution of who said what, were complete. The court would allow the jurors to review the transcript as they heard the tape, but they were not allowed to keep the transcript. The tape was admitted into evidence, but the jurors could not listen to it again, even in the jury room.

Judge Van Pelt explained these rules to the jury, and cautioned them, "I instruct you that the evidence in this particular matter is the tape, not the transcript. If you hear something on the tape that varies from the transcript, you go by what's on the tape, not what's on the transcript."

Under cross-examination, Detective Bilbrey revealed that the recording was in two parts, the first at Alvin's house and the last at his shuttered television repair shop. He recorded it discreetly from his front pants pocket, but had not told all of his colleagues that he was recording.

The tape player was turned on, and we all listened while following along on our copies of the transcript. Both Buzz and I feverishly scribbled and highlighted on our copies what we thought would help our cause. Detective Bilbrey listened from the witness stand. Alvin just stared.

It opened with the voice of Detective Bilbrey: "I'm not saying you did anything, okay? Like I said, I know you are going through a trying time here, but I do have some questions and I hope you can answer 'em."

Then the jury heard the voice of Alvin Ridley: "Yeah, I been through it, man, I been through fifteen years of hell! The loss of my mother, loss of my van, loss of my reputation, and business down here, by the sheriff's department, and they's no stoppin' it!"

The officers asked Alvin if they could go inside his house to talk. I'm sure that Detective Bilbrey wanted the best audio conditions to try to catch Alvin saying something incriminating.

Uncharacteristically—to me, anyway—Alvin invited them in.

The familiar voice of Detective Vic Wells dominated the discussion with Alvin for a while. Vic was Ringgold born and raised; his father was Reverend R.V. Wells, the much admired local pastor. He had an easygoing manner about him, one that put suspects at ease. He was often very effective in getting cooperation, as well as incriminating statements, out of them.

Wells tried to steer the conversation back to a more sinister subject: "Do you think that somebody around here caused the death of your mother?"

Alvin stuck to his themes: "Yeah, I know, and it was the sheriff's department that done it! She told them she was okay, and she called them on the phone. She was alright." He described how his mother was "harassed" by social services, accompanied by the sheriff's department, until she fell, broke her hip, and died at age eighty-five.

Wells tried to lighten the mood. "You got a good-looking cat. You got *two* good-looking cats!"

I know now that Kitty and Meowy had likely been leashed to the table, as Alvin had let the four men into his house.

"They're just regular cats, you know," Alvin deadpanned.

I watched the jurors, glad that they were getting to listen to Alvin's voice. It was much more animated in certain moments than the state had tried to portray him. This would be the only time they would hear him tell his story, because I strongly believed that the jurors could only take so much of his conspiracy talk. It could explain his evasiveness, but in cross-examination, if he answered questions about his wife's death with answers about his "illegal-seized" Chevy van, that might be too much. That's why I thought

the jury should hear the tape. Once more, the defense was introducing evidence that originated with the state. This was such a
strange trial.

The tape-recorded Alvin continued, apparently demonstrating
his resuscitation efforts, which he always called "re-citation."

"A little bit harder than that. I kept on hollerin' there awhile,
you know, and then I decided they was something wrong, and then
I started giving her mouth-to-mouth re-citation, you know, how
they tell you to push on the chest some, you know, every sixty seconds, is what I did," Alvin shared.

Detective Wells asked, "But it didn't do any good?"

Alvin answered, for him, poignantly, "No. I wanted her to come
to. I wanted her to come to and say something to me. I didn't want
her like that."

Detective Bilbrey's voice returned. "Alvin, do you recall how
hard you pressed on her chest?"

Alvin responded, "I hope I didn't press too hard, but I just
pressed on it."

Bilbrey asked, "Did you use one hand, or two hands, or—"

Alvin interrupted, "No, I used one hand, I might have used two.
I don't know for sure. About every sixty seconds after I give her
mouth-to-mouth re-citation, blow air in, you know."

They asked him if he changed her clothes before the ambulance
arrived. I had personally seen Alvin wear the same clothes for
weeks, sleeping in them and then wearing them until I would goad
him to go wash them and put something else on. I had even
bought him new clothes, part of our pay-for-cooperation arrange-
ment, only to see the same clothes every day for weeks, looking as if
he had slept in them. I didn't think updating a wardrobe for himself or for others ranked high in his priorities.

"She had her clothes on, already on," Alvin responded, and
then, trying to explain, "Those were her nightclothes."

They asked more about helping them find someone who had
talked to his wife recently; to which, Alvin responded, "She wouldn't
see nobody. She wouldn't go nowhere. I couldn't get her to go to
church or nowhere!"

Wells asked, "Was she scared?"

That opened up the floodgates.

"Yeah," Alvin jumped in. "She was scared because the county took my van in '84, attached it . . . She was scared about that and she didn't really like it, the way her people done her. That's why she didn't go nowhere. I tried to get her to go places. I sure did."

It had to irk Buzz, I thought, that in one transition, one cat clearly "meowed" on the tape. Alvin showed the men pictures of Virginia and told of his two years in the U.S. Army.

When asked what they did for a living, Alvin recited the same mantra he had used for fifteen years. "Well, I had that TV trade down there, TV repairman, then it blowed up when they took my van, and it collapsed! And they advertised the van for sale!"

Vic Wells said that he might be interested in one of Alvin's console televisions, if he would only take them all to the shuttered former Zenith shop.

Alvin was quizzed about his assets, and he, without hesitation, described the wooded property that his late mother's family had in Soddy Daisy, Tennessee, a beautiful area on Lake Chickamauga, north of Chattanooga. Property there was valuable, but Alvin never did anything to it. This was the information that kept him from qualifying for me to be *appointed* as his counsel, where we would have had access to county funds for experts and an investigator.

They convinced Alvin to meet them at the long-shuttered Zenith shop. The franchise long lost, the big sign still jutted out over Nashville Street with the giant ZENITH logo.

In the shop, Vic, applying his folksy charm, again acted as if he was serious about buying one of Alvin's remaining console television sets. All bore the patina of fifteen years in a leaky, powerless building, with no climate control, and the foot-high water marks of a flood from years ago. A refrigerator-sized hole in the ceiling allowed passage directly to the sky above, as well as whatever it let in.

Alvin gave them a tour of that building, as with the house, a privilege that he'd denied his own lawyer for more than a year.

Interspersing discussions about television sets and Virginia's death, their effort to knock Alvin off-balance was going nowhere.

Wells, referring to an old console TV set, said, "Do you not want to sell it? I like the looks of that!"

Detective Mike Helton played along. "That's more your style."

Alvin said, "They go with that table."

Another shift by Wells. "Is there any reason that you would want to hurt your wife?"

"Huh-uh," Alvin said flatly. "I loved her."

I panicked as I read "huh-uh," realizing how easily one could misread it as "uh-huh." But thankfully, the audio was clear.

"Yeah, it cut my heart out," Alvin continued. "I wanted her to live. I tried to give her mouth-to-mouth re-citation—I wanted her to live. It cut my heart out."

"Well," Wells continued, "do you think that unintentionally you did something that hurt her?"

Alvin, unguarded, answered, "Not unless I pressed on her too hard, but I don't think I did."

Then all the warmth, offers to buy old television consoles, and general goodwill finally culminated in the big ask, by Detective Vic Wells: "Okay, have you ever heard of what they call a polygraph test? Do you know what that is?"

Alvin responded, "Yeah."

Wells followed up with, "Tell me what you think that is."

Alvin said, "Check you out to see if you are lying."

Detective Wells went deep into his sales pitch. "That's close. That is about what it is . . . If I wanted you to take one of those tests so we could tell everybody that you didn't hurt your wife, that you didn't do anything to hurt her, would you be willing to do that? Would you be willing to take one of those tests?"

"I might," Alvin answered, qualifying, "if I talk to an attorney first."

I thought, just as I had the first time I nervously listened to this recording, *If only more suspects would take that position.*

Polygraphs are *inadmissible* in Georgia courts, *unless,* however, in-

vestigators can convince, or trick, the suspect into signing a stipulation that it is admissible. There was a long history of this locally.
Getting all chummy with a suspect and convincing him or her that
this test—*just sign this form first*—can set you free. I had seen it play
out many times and heard other defense lawyers complaining
about their clients being lured into signing the form and then the
polygraph of questionable validity becomes a mere extension of
their interrogation, only this time the detective is staring them
down with a "failed" polygraph that they just stipulated gets into evidence.

"Who is he?" Wells asked. "Do you have an attorney that I could
get in touch with for you?"

In that instant, Alvin became the familiar person I had been
dealing with for over a year, guarded, reluctant to speak, and enigmatic.

Detectives Wells and Helton bantered back and forth about
credit cards and interest rates, then asked, "You don't remember
who his name was?"

Wells snapped back on point, "You talking to him because your
wife died or something else?"

"Well," Alvin answered, "I talked to him about my van. Y'all took
my van."

"Still the van deal," a clearly frustrated Wells replied. "Do you
have the name of somebody that took your van?"

Alvin was happy to answer. "Yeah, L.C. Cripps."

"I know L.C.," Wells responded. "He just came over and took
your van for no reason?"

"Well," Alvin waxed accurately, "he explained he had a court
order, and he really didn't have one, so he took it on, uh, no judgment, the judge declared it."

Wells followed him down the rabbit hole. "Somebody sued you?"

"Yeah," Alvin said, "policeman on my daddy's wreck. See, they
never got his side of the story, and the truck was my truck and they
totaled the truck, and it was insured with Georgia Farm Bureau,
and they never did get my side of the story before court and they

took my van. It's really hurt me," adding, "Put a toll on my family. It put a toll on my wife there, too."

Detective Vic Wells then uttered these words—the entire reason I wanted this recording played to the jury. Feigning sympathy, he offered to Alvin, "I understand, but with talking to you, I don't think you had anything to do with hurting your wife. I don't think you did."

Detective Bilbrey had not informed his colleagues that a micro-cassette recorder was on. This was an unvarnished peek, a behind-the-scenes example of how detectives sometimes work, perhaps how some of them have always worked. And the United States Supreme Court has even backed it up, allowing the government to lie to a suspect to trick them into confessing or to warm them up to thinking they had an ally among the investigators.

Applied to this case, I figured these jurors had two choices, to believe either that Detective Wells *really believed in Alvin's innocence*, or that he was lying to a grieving widower, just forty-eight hours after losing his wife.

I looked in the faces of the jurors. A couple of them looked con-fused—an eyebrow raised—but I knew better than to be gauging subtle reactions.

On the tape, Wells continued trying to sell the polygraph, con-vincing Alvin that he would perform the test himself.

"Oh, you do?" Alvin reacted, sounding as if reassured; then in a fashion I had seen played out hundreds of times, Alvin nibbled at the bait when you tried to get him to do something. "Oh, I see what you are doing," he stated, "wanting me just to show every-body—"

Wells interrupted, "Just to show everybody else that you didn't have anything to do with killing her, okay, 'cause it looked like, you know, it looks like to me that she probably died in her sleep. I don't know for sure what happened, but I'd like—"

Alvin interrupted him, "I know I didn't kill her," then added, "I was asleep."

"Right," Wells agreed, "and I believe you, but I'd like to be able to show something on paper so everybody else will know that you didn't have anything to do with it, okay?"

Not responding to that plea, Alvin mused, "I believe that spell was just one too hard for her."

Wells switched to a different tactic he knew could be effective. "From the way it sounds, you've had a lot of problems out of her family . . . and you might have even more now. And I might could help you out there . . . get them off your back, okay?"

"But I tried to bring her back to life . . . it cut my heart out," Alvin continued. "I cried and cried, and I still ain't got over it. I can't eat, my stomach is sick . . ."

Wells was throwing in the kitchen sink. "I understand, I understand. If you need us to help you as far as the funeral goes, if you'll holler at us, you know we'll see what we can do. And as soon as the funeral is over with, I'd appreciate it if you'd give me a call . . . 'cause I'd like to talk to you about the TV, and I'd also like to run that test and get you out of this."

"How long does it take to take the test?" Alvin asked.

"Couple of hours," Wells answered.

"Couple hours?"

"Not long," Wells confirmed.

Then, the most blatant trick, one that I was going to play up in closing.

"Is it one hundred percent accurate?" Alvin inquired.

"Oh yeah," Wells assured.

This was totally false. There are so many variables that could cause a false response, the results are still not admissible without a stipulation—which, of course, they regularly get an unrepresented suspect to sign before they consistently "fail" them. This process often leads to false, coerced confessions.

"It is?" Alvin queried.

"Yeah, the new ones are, the new ones are run by a computer, and they work, they work. So, you know, we can get your name cleared and we can tell the family, 'Hey, you know, he didn't hurt her,' " Wells replied.

"I didn't have any cause to," Alvin affirmed.

"I don't think you did; I don't see where you did," Wells observed.

Alvin told the detective, "I wish she was alive now, I could have her talk—"

"I believe it," Wells interrupted.

Alvin continued his wistful speaking: "Cook some food . . ."

Detective Vic Wells laughed, then said, "Yeah, she could probably help cook food for you. Course I know that is not the only reason you want her around. It is gonna get kinda lonely up there by yourself."

"Yeah, you're right on that. I'm done lonely already back there," Alvin admitted.

The tape ended.

I walked slowly over to resume cross-examination of Detective Bilbrey, allowing time for the bailiff to take up the transcripts from the jurors. I couldn't have directed a better ending to the tape. While I disagreed with the tactics used by Detective Vic Wells, with his folksy manner and expression of sympathy to Alvin, at the same time, I thought these were probably the kindest things anyone said to Alvin after his wife passed.

That tape had been recorded on the Monday after Virginia's Saturday death. By Wednesday, Alvin and I were speaking, and I had finally shut down these little talks, except for his final visit with Detective Bilbrey on October 8, 1997. Thankfully, he did not take up the offer by Detective Wells to take his polygraph test, which would, of course, have resulted in a disastrous "failed" polygraph, tied up with the bow of a stipulation, a binding agreement that it would be admitted in this trial.

The court declared a fifteen-minute break, and I sat down next to my client at the table, Team Alvin having already gathered to keep him occupied.

"Alvin, you did well on that tape," I said. "Don't worry about the minor stuff. You were grieving."

He looked at me, obviously not hearing or paying attention to anything I said. I could not figure him out, for sure. As my father had said a year ago in the hospital, "He just thinks differently."

My cross-examination of Detective Bilbrey resumed, and I started showing photos of the doors of the house, getting Bilbrey to admit that there were no unusual locks on the windows or doors.

After a bench conference, the state's case against Alvin Ridley rested, subject only to the state getting to call witnesses to rebut matters brought up by the defense witnesses.

18

*B*esides Dr. Wannamaker, who was taken out of turn, it was now time to put up a defense case. Who do you put up on behalf of a man who has few friends, whose blank stare has concerned or even frightened people who have encountered it over the past three decades?

We went further back than three decades.

I called Robert L. "Doc" McNew.

When I was growing up, Ringgold had only two drugstores. One, Price Ringgold Drugs, and the other, McNew Pharmacy. Doc McNew operated the latter. I hoped that the jurors remembered him, as his pharmacy closed a decade ago.

I handed him what was marked as D-68, a letter with the McNew Pharmacy letterhead, and he identified it, along with his writing and his signature.

"'To whom it may concern,'" he read aloud the handwritten paper that I had found in Alvin's house. "'Mr. Alvin Ridley has purchased two prescriptions each month from us for the control of epilepsy. These prescriptions are written in the name of Mrs. Alvin Ridley, one being for Dilantin sodium, grams one and a half, and the other for Mebaral, grams one half.' And I've signed it as the pharmacist/owner of McNew Pharmacy."

The witness told the jury the document was dated May 28, 1968.

I did not go into the provenance of this extremely vital document. It had been provided by Doc when Alvin was being called into the U.S. Army Reserve service, and he used the fact that he had to care for Virginia as an excuse not to go. The army agreed, and he was excused from being called up that year for reserve duty.

Buzz didn't do any damage in his cross-examination, which was brief. He likely remembered Doc's former pharmacy and its popular lunch counter as well.

I called Rebecca Smith, an accounts representative of the Ringgold Telephone Company. D-69 was admitted without objection. Ms. Smith testified that the first entry, in 1995, was to convert and move the business telephone from the television shop and convert it to a residential phone, connecting it to the house on Inman Street.

"The next entry," Smith testified, "was on July 2, 1996, where we reconnected for nonpay," or, paying to have his phone turned back on.

Her testimony established that they did a permanent disconnect order on May 29, 1997, just over four months before the death of Virginia Ridley. This was to show why Alvin had to leave the house to call for help the following October 4.

Buzz asked her a few questions on cross-examination, establishing that she had no idea of Virginia's existence.

Panicked, I laid my cards out for the court. "Your Honor, just not knowing exactly when the state was going to close has put us in the position of having several witnesses on call. We're having a particularly difficult time getting them to answer at the phone numbers they gave to us."

I had to kill some time and had a few brief witnesses to present very minor issues, such as Jimmie Nell Spivey, my former English teacher at Ringgold High School, who was now the librarian there. I called her basically to show that Alvin had been a student at Ringgold High School, and I tried to introduce pages from the 1959 and 1960 yearbooks that showed the awkward-looking young Alvin.

Buzz objected, and it was sustained, appropriately.

* * *

I called my next witness, the last one I had available. It was finally time for Salesman Sam.

I announced simply, "Ben McGaha."

Perhaps Alvin's best friend, and my nemesis and competing "legal advisor" to Alvin Ridley, Benjamin Austin McGaha walked into the large courtroom a lot more tentatively than I expected. I needed to kill some time, and with Ms. Spivey's testimony being shut down, I was going to have to really stretch this one out.

Dressed like an extra in an old Western, like the characters always played by Gabby Hayes, Sam's gray beard made him look more like a prospector than a salesman.

"Okay, do you go by any other names?" I asked.

"Yes, sir," he replied, "a lot of people call me Salesman Sam."

I had first seen the name Benjamin McGaha on an early list of state witnesses. In the time since, he apparently had a conversion, and had become a defense witness.

"How long have you known Mr. Alvin Ridley, my client?" I asked.

"Probably since he and his wife entered the courtroom when they got thrown out of the project house," he said. "I didn't know him before then. That's the first time I ever saw either one of them."

"Okay . . ." I slowed down. "How did you get the name Salesman Sam?"

"Well," his response began, "I walked into Kenner Hardware store up here one day and the man that was working there said, 'Salesman Sam,' and ever since then, that's what it's been."

"Now, the first time you saw Virginia Ridley was 1970 . . . ? Do you remember the subject matter that was going on in court when you met them?"

"They had told Mr. Ridley to prove that his wife was alive," he said, "so he brought her into the courtroom."

"Now," I asked, "did you see Mrs. Virginia Ridley on any other occasions since then?"

"I saw her one day," Sam said. "I went into the business. The reason for going into the place of business of Mr. Ridley, I went down there to see if I could sell him some advertising. And his wife was standing over here, closest to the door when I went in."

The detail of such a long-ago meeting was so vivid that I asked, "Do you have the habit of remembering in detail about things in the past?"

"Anything anybody tells me, I remember it," he said, adding, "I don't ever forget it."

"Now you have been—you have advised Alvin in the past on some legal matters, have you not?"

"Well, I've been his advisor for years now."

"At least on one occasion, your advice got crossed up with my advice, didn't it?"

He sheepishly answered, "It did. I didn't mean to do that, but I didn't know what I was supposed to do."

I wrapped up with a final question. "Has everything you've told today been the truth?"

"It sure has!" he said.

The DA went after Ben McGaha/Salesman Sam mercilessly. He went through a review of what the witness had testified; then he sprang previous inconsistent statements on him.

Buzz tried to set him up with a statement that he had made before, about seeing Alvin just after Virginia's passing, but it seemed to confuse him.

"I'm talking about the day after Virginia Ridley's death, October 5, 1997, did you talk to the defendant that day?"

"I did," he responded. "I was walking up the side of the road and he stopped by there."

Buzz seemed to be a bit exasperated, asking, "And at the time, he didn't mention anything to you about Virginia Ridley having passed away, did he?"

"Yeah."

"Do you recall talking to this officer, Detective Bilbrey?" Buzz gestured to Bilbrey.

"I do."

"Do you remember telling him," Buzz probed, "that the defendant didn't say anything about Virginia's death on that occasion?"

"Well," he said, "I might not have understood his question at the time."

Buzz raised his voice. "Well, you say you remember everything that was told you, so do you remember what his question was?"

"Well, sir," he said, "there are some things that everyone forgets."

"So you don't exactly have a photographic memory?"

"Not of everything," he answered.

"Selected things you have a photographic memory of?" Buzz pushed.

"That's right."

Buzz struggled to get a straight answer out of Salesman Sam on cross. "Isn't it somewhat contradictory, Mr. McGaha, that you say you thought it strange that he didn't tell you, and then you say that he did, in fact, tell you?"

"Well, that would be a contradiction," he answered, "but that's what I'm trying to do. I'm trying to clarify this thing for you!"

I thought I heard a chuckling noise from the jury box.

"And the defendant never told you anything about doing chest compressions, did he?"

"Yes," he answered, "he told me about that, too."

Buzz's voice rose again. "Do you deny making that statement?"

"I've never denied making nothing."

"So," Buzz leaped, "it's possible you could have said it?"

"Yeah, I could have."

Ending on the highest note he could find, Buzz sat down.

I jumped up, determined not to look defeated, and pivoted in my redirect. "Did you get a subpoena to be here?"

"Yes, sir," he replied, "I did."

"And who is that subpoena from?" I asked.

"McCracken Poston," he said.

"And you told Detective Bilbrey that you had seen Virginia Ridley, alive and well, on two occasions?"

"Two occasions," he repeated.

"And you never got called by the state to testify?"

"No," he responded, "never."

I let that sink into the jury.

"Nothing further. May he be excused?" I asked the court.

And he was.

Now he could remain in the courtroom and listen, which is really all he wanted to do in the first place.

We had wrangled in a couple more quick witnesses, and the next I called was Alvin's cousin on his father's side, Joan Ridley Harwell, from Rome, Georgia.

"Did you ever, on the occasion of Mr. Alvin Ridley visiting Rome, meet Virginia Ridley?"

She remembered that "they had come to visit," and described it as a social family call. "I recall her to be very pleasant," she said, describing Virginia, "you know, very neat."

I finished quickly, and Buzz announced, "No questions."

Alvin looked interested when I called L.C. Cripps, the chairman of the Catoosa County Board of Commissioners, the governing body of Catoosa County, Georgia. But what I wanted to ask him about went back fifteen years or more, when he was a uniformed officer with the Catoosa County Sheriff's Office.

"I was deputy sheriff of Catoosa County from January of 1977 until sometime in 1986," he answered in my preliminary questions.

The Georgia process on a "fi fa," or a writ of fieri facias, was something that I didn't learn in law school, but it was in the official code of Georgia. A fi fa is the legal instrument by which the sheriff of the county has authority to seize the assets of anyone on behalf of a person who has a judgment against them. Involving the sheriff ensures a peaceful, court-ordered transfer of an asset.

L.C.'s sin, Alvin admitted to me, was merely being the officer picking the document up from a stack of writs to execute. It was part of his job. He secured a wrecker, and Alvin's 1977 Chevy van was seized, on what appeared to be a valid writ.

As it turned out, Chief Land's lawyer in Chattanooga had gotten ahead of himself in the process, and issued the writ before there was an actual order of judgment issued. "The fi fa was handed to me at the sheriff's office, and they said go serve it," Cripps said. "I went to his residence, levied against his van that he had in his possession at the time, had the thing towed in, and took the fi fa back, and it was done as the law said it is to be done."

From earlier conversations, L.C. later knew that something was eventually determined to be faulty in the judgment underlying the seizure. He returned the van, or tried to, on July 23, 1984, just a few weeks after Alvin correctly claimed it was "illegal seized." Alvin got his van back fairly quickly after it was determined that Chief Land's lawyer had made an error. The van was returned, but Alvin wouldn't accept it, refusing to come out of his house to sign for it. It was brought back, under the supervision of Cripps, who left it beside Ridley's house. (To this date, Alvin has still refused to "accept it," or even touch it, almost forty years on, reasoning that touching it would trigger another statute of limitations he would have to worry about.)

Buzz didn't have any questions of L.C. Cripps, either. I wondered if that was the ultimate insult, that my evidence wasn't even strong enough to bother with cross-examination.

I called a few quick witnesses to establish very brief facts or to get a document in.

My last witness for the day, because the others were coming from out of town and couldn't be there yet, was Dr. Robert T. Jones, the president and CEO of Hutcheson Medical Center in Fort Oglethorpe. I called him to the stand to reinforce that seizures and even coughing fits can cause petechial hemorrhages, like the ones found on Florence Griffith Joyner and Virginia Ridley.

"My wife, Sara, at least on three or four occasions, has come to me and said, 'Goodness, look at me,' and there would be little red spots all around her eyes or on her neck or something following a severe coughing spell."

Buzz found Dr. Jones a significant-enough witness, I suppose, to stand up and cross-examine him.

"Your practice hasn't ever been devoted to forensic pathology, has it, sir?"

Alvin leaned in. "Spell that again for me." I hushed him and spelled it out on the margin of his legal pad.

After a bench conference, the judge addressed the jury: "Ladies and gentlemen, the defendant has two witnesses who are coming from out of state that are not here now, so we're going to go ahead and break for the day. Just be back here tomorrow to the jury room at nine. We're in recess."

I left Alvin sitting with Team Alvin while the judge, Buzz, and I went back to have a charge conference to request what the court would tell the jury about the law and what law should be "charged to the jury" during their instructions before deliberation. We were nearing the end of the trial, but I had two more witnesses for tomorrow.

One was Dr. Goldberg, who was costing me an arm and a leg to satisfy Alvin's demand to have his own pathology expert at the trial. Alvin's excitement about "Gold Bird" was very unusual, and I figured it was likely born in years of watching *Unsolved Mysteries* and forensic crime shows with Virginia. The other witness was Dr. Louis Williams, retired and living in the North Carolina mountains. He was a doctor in Ringgold throughout his career, having delivered me, and he was Elizabeth Cheek's grandfather. More important, he had treated Virginia Ridley back in the 1960s.

After the charge conference, I had a better understanding of what the jury would be told. I gathered up Alvin and his suitcases, and we left the courthouse.

"Okay, Alvin, let's go to the office for a while, and then we'll go pick up Dr. Goldberg and take him to dinner. Then we'll end up at your house."

Alvin had not yet met Goldberg, who was potentially the greatest expense in the case. He asked to be taken home first, saying, "I want to get ready for him to come to the house."

I let him off at his gate on Inman Street and went to the office to start a draft of my closing argument, based on the evidence so far.

* * *

Once I determined that Dr. Goldberg had arrived in Ringgold and had checked in to his motel on Alabama Highway, I went to get Alvin. He was uncharacteristically giddy, like he was back in high school headed for the big dance. I had never seen Alvin in such a good mood.

"I've got it all ready for him," he said as he got into the car. "I'm going to sit in the back and give him the front seat," showing rare deference as he shut the front door and jumped into the back of the Ford Explorer, which I had borrowed for the evening from Alison. Getting Alvin, Goldberg, and me into my Jeep Wrangler would have been like a sociology and physics experiment gone wrong. We all needed as much space as possible.

Dr. Goldberg was a big man. The first time I met him, when I picked him up in Atlanta, and we went to the crime lab and to handwriting expert Brian Carney's office, he was wearing the white, classic doctor coat. As I pulled into the motel parking lot, I saw that he was sporting a much more casual look, a very large print shirt with shirttail out. Apparently, this was strategic, as when he sat down in the front seat, he raised up one side of his shirttail, revealing a handgun holstered to his side, while making eye contact with me. He seemed to be signaling, *Don't worry, I'm packing heat!*

I mouthed a silent "That . . . isn't . . . necessary," but I guess he had formed his opinion of Alvin from all the media that had already declared him a dangerous man. Alvin was quiet in the back seat. I figured maybe he was like someone who was starstruck, finally getting to meet someone upon whom he had pinned all of his hopes.

Alvin and I had already started out, months ago, with the premise that Virginia had died from her seizure disorder, and our theory was enhanced when I learned of and obtained the autopsy of Florence Griffith Joyner. Two months later, just a couple of weeks ago, Alvin wanted his own expert, one to counter the state's pathologist. Sitting around the office and showing Alvin the wonders of the World Wide Web, after dialing up a connection, I had searched "forensic pathologist"—triggering months of constantly spelling it

for Alvin. We found a lively website, which included sixteen-bit animation and music. We had just over a week ago given Gold Bird the
whole theory of our defense. All he had to do was give us his
learned opinion on it.

My concerns began when I observed how state pathologist
Dr. Fredric Hellman reacted to Dr. Goldberg when we visited the
crime lab in December, when we were ushered to the bucket that
contained what was left of Virginia Ridley. They were triggered
again as we left the office of our handwriting expert, when Dr. Goldberg suggested that he had picked up enough there to serve as a
handwriting expert for our case. I politely declined.

We decided on Red Lobster, near the Hamilton Place mall in
Chattanooga, Tennessee. It was about twenty minutes of freeway
driving, and Dr. Goldberg and I did most of the talking. His discomfort with Alvin was obvious. I tried to engage Alvin a couple of
times, but he barely answered, seemingly starstruck with Gold Bird.

At dinner, we all ordered, and I made sure Alvin didn't blurt anything out about any testimony in court, trying to keep Dr. Goldberg
pure, as witnesses go. Alvin slowly tried to enter the conversation,
but Dr. Goldberg remained guarded, not speaking directly to him.

Alvin asked if he could take his leftovers home for the cats. I
thought it was a touch of humanity that Dr. Goldberg might pick
up on. He remained guarded. As we walked to the car, I said,
"Okay, Alvin, you're in charge of the tour from here on!"

Alvin perked up and said, "I've got it all ready!" I had no idea
what he was talking about, and what to expect.

Trying to see Alvin's house through Dr. Goldberg's eyes, I should
have remembered that until a couple of months ago, I also found it
to be a very creepy place. There was no exterior lighting. It looked
like a haunted house from a slasher movie, not the classic Victorian
home from *Psycho,* in mild disrepair, but more like something from
The Texas Chain Saw Massacre, and in horrifying disrepair. As we
started climbing the steps, I could tell Dr. Goldberg was very nervous.

Entering the first room, the enclosed front porch, the smell of

Alvin's existence was the immediate thing that the senses picked up. As we turned right, Alvin said, "I've got the scene just like it was!" and pulled the string from the single light bulb in the middle of the room.

On the bed, a female mannequin, which looked circa 1960, was playing the role of Virginia Ridley, sleeping on her face. Another, a model head, made of Styrofoam, was there, apparently, for a closer study of her face.

As Alvin awkwardly fumbled with the mannequin and the head, I could hear Dr. Goldberg surveying the room, mumbling, "Oh, my God . . ."

I quickly pointed out the "depression" in the bed, on the outside edge, which was certainly not in the shape of a human.

I can't remember how long Dr. Goldberg was in the room, but it wasn't long.

"We need to get the hell out of here," he said in a hushed delivery.

Alvin, who saw the handgun that the doctor had on his side, produced one of his own. "Hey, I've got one, too," he said as he brandished perhaps the dirtiest revolver I'd ever seen. One chamber looked like there was mud, or a dirt dauber had put larvae in it. I realized I was the only unarmed man in the room.

Dr. Goldberg was out the door. On my way out, I bade farewell to my client, reminded him to feed the cats his leftovers from Red Lobster, and told him I would come and get him in the morning.

"Do you want this corn bread?" Alvin asked sweetly, offering me the hush puppies.

I declined.

"Good job on the scene you created, Alvin." I tried to cover for any potential hurt feelings. "Is that the mannequin that we read about in the paper last weekend?"

He nodded. "That newspaper article made me mad, but it reminded me I had it in the basement, and so I made the scene that Gold Bird can talk about."

I shook his hand, then said, "Alvin, I'm sure he'll have plenty to talk about. See you in the morning."

Dr. Goldberg was fine, once it was just us in the car. I went over with him that since he was the only defense witness to have observed Virginia's deathbed, I would be asking him questions about what he had observed.

"You don't have to mention the creepy props," I suggested.

I dropped him off at the motel and went home.

19

I drove to Inman Street on Thursday morning to pick up my client. Alvin tried to hand me the two pillows off his bed. He declared, "We have to put these *pillars* into the evidence!"

"What?" I asked, having heard it, but needing the extra time to process it.

He said it again, "We need to let the jury see these *pillars*! They show her *lava*! See?" Alvin pointed to the myriad marks on the pillows, stained dark brown, but with the pattern of, presumptively, dried drool. The pillows were so thoroughly covered in probably decades of saliva, or,"lava," it created an almost paisley-like design covering both sides of the pillows, neither having a pillowcase. They did not smell good. I told him he needed to put them in a trash bag, "so nobody knows what we are about to spring on them." It was really so I could breathe.

He said, "Yeah, you're right," and ran to his kitchen for a bag. I reminded myself to blame Dr. Goldberg for mentioning in his brief appearance last night the "saliva seal" that can happen in facedown seizure cases.

We settled into the courtroom, and were just about to get started when Alvin did one of his episodes of suddenly turning around to see if any of the Hickeys were in the courtroom. Instead, he smiled, and remained turned around, something that I thought odd, as his moves were usually more furtive.

"Your daddy's here," he said while still looking behind.

"What?" I asked.

"Your daddy's here. He likes me, you know."

I wheeled around to see my father, McCracken King Poston Sr., sitting in the courtroom, a couple of rows back. He looked quite sober.

A smile and a nod from him sent my mind racing. As a child, I could detect from yards away if he was even in the very early stages of getting drunk. I looked back again, and he was locked-in with an expression my sisters and I knew well, from after he retired, and, before ever having a drink, he would get into his "programs." These were the soap operas that he and Mama watched together, staring straight at the television with his bright blue-gray eyes, his jaw set and ready to watch the dramas unfold.

This was the first thing I could remember, other than some campaign events, that he had even attended. And, if he was completely sober, this might be the first time for that. I remembered being so concerned during one parade when he was going to drive his antique 1954 Packard Panama Clipper, adorned with my campaign signs, while I walked alongside, occasionally replenishing from an open window whatever I was handing out to the folks lining the street. I was also constantly gauging his level of intoxication. At the start, I had moved the bottle, wrapped in its brown paper bag, and hid it in the trunk. He hadn't noticed yet. When I saw the car weaving, it wasn't from intoxication. It was him trying to reach under the seat to find the bottle.

I snapped back to attention and got up to see him. My mother was sitting beside him as well. Hugging them both, I made sure to breathe in deeply through my nose when I hugged my father. He seemed, well, *sober*! I went back to Alvin and thanked him for letting me know they were there.

"They like me, your folks do," he said.

The Mac Poston who was here today was as clear-eyed and clear-headed as I had ever remembered seeing him, in years. When I was hugging my mother, I gave her that look. Having inherited her ability to communicate volumes through a cocked eyebrow, I looked at her, and she nodded to me with what I understood meant, *He's really okay, son.*

* * *

I called veteran court reporter E. Don Towns to the stand to explain why I couldn't produce a transcript from the 1970 *Ringgold Housing Authority* vs. *Ridley* trial, Virginia's last-known public appearance, in this very courtroom.

He explained that the court reporter at the time was soon discovered to have not been producing any transcripts at all. Don replaced him just weeks after that eviction trial of September 15, 1970, one of Alvin's days of infamy.

Dr. Williams had not arrived from North Carolina yet, so I had to move on.

"Dr. Robert Goldberg," I announced, with a subtle emphasis on the title of *doctor*. Thankfully, my witness was in a dark suit, much better than he looked last night, and I assumed he wasn't packing heat. Goldberg was large, but he looked much thinner in a suit. He was balding, but again utilized a strategic comb-over that covered the top. A scraggly beard gave him a bit of the look of an academic.

After swearing him in, I asked some easy questions to get him comfortable in front of the jury. He did seem nervous for someone who had, as he had professed in the curriculum vitae that I had served on the prosecution, a great deal of experience.

"Do you recall that I requested that you investigate another death in which epilepsy was thought to have played a part?"

He answered in the affirmative. I pressed further. "And you're familiar with the Florence Griffith Joyner case?"

"Yes, sir," he said. He testified about the petechiae in the Joyner autopsy being similar to that in Virginia's autopsy.

I started talking about Dr. Goldberg's observations last night at the Ridley home. "Did you observe the bed?" He affirmed that he had, indeed, observed the bed.

For about 120 seconds, I thought.

I signaled Leigh Ann McBryar, the court reporter, for which number we were up to with the submitted defense exhibits. She mouthed "seventy-nine" as she continued to enter Dr. Goldberg's last answer.

I opened the bag that Alvin brought, holding my breath, and with a Sharpie wrote "D-79, collective" on both pillows. I pulled the incredibly stained, horribly odorous pillows out of the bag.

"I'm not going to ask you to touch these," I stated as the perfumes of Casa Alvin wafted up to our faces, "but I will ask you to look over the bench, if you would, at what I've brought, Dr. Goldberg, and marked as D-79, collective"; and then, "What do they appear to be?"

He looked, and had a look of disgust on his face. "Those are the pillows that I saw on the bed last night." I thought it was a little over-the-top.

Then things took a distinct turn for the worse.

"In your opinion as a forensic pathologist, what would be significant for this investigation to have included?"

Before he could answer, Buzz jumped up. "Your Honor, if I could object to the form of the question. He asked him in his opinion as a forensic pathologist. This man has never said he's a forensic pathologist."

Buzz continued, "He said he's had some training in that, but he's not a forensic pathologist."

Judge Van Pelt, being kind, said, "If you'll run back through, I don't think you've quite completed going through his credentials, Mr. Poston, if you will go back through that."

Bewildered, I looked to my witness. "Let me ask you, have you conducted autopsies before?"

"I have, and participated in them as well."

"In which you were the lead doctor?" I pressed.

He nodded.

"And how many have you done?" I asked.

"Several thousand," he answered.

I tendered D-79, collective, and Buzz had no objection, probably thinking I was out of my mind for doing so. The pillows were now in evidence. I didn't want to overwhelm Leigh Ann with the smell coming out of the bag, so I left it closer to the wooden jury box. Then I thought better of it, grabbed it, and just put it closer to the prosecutor's table.

I was worried about what Buzz had said: ". . . but he's not a forensic pathologist."

"You may ask," I directed to the district attorney.

Buzz led with the usual questions a prosecutor asks a defense expert, trying to reveal them as hacks who were just in it for the money.

"Okay," Buzz said, circling, "when were you first contacted about the case?"

Dr. Goldberg answered, "I guess a month or so ago." He had been in the case one week.

Buzz highlighted the answer, "Only a month ago?"

"Uh-huh," Dr. Goldberg answered.

"Didn't send any reports to Mr. Poston at all?"

"No," he said.

Then came the punch line: "Okay. And so, nothing you saw was of enough significance that you felt you needed to make any notes about it, right?"

Bam.

Buzz masterfully quizzed our witness on his résumé, getting in punch after punch, asking, "Now, do you have any license in this state to go with what you do?"

What? I thought, flipping through my own file, looking for Dr. Goldberg's curriculum vitae.

"No, sir," he answered. "I do not."

I felt the air suck out of the room and the blood rush to my face. *How did I miss this?* I couldn't blame Alvin's enthusiasm for hiring him. This was on me, and my lack of experience was showing.

"Okay." Buzz was relishing this. "Did you have any license in Florida to do what you did down there?"

"No, sir," he answered. "I do not."

Buzz was on a roll. "Are you certified by the American Board of Pathologists?"

His answer: "No, I am not."

The massacre continued. I couldn't decide what was worse, listening to the total disqualification of our "expert" witness, or maintaining a poker face during it.

"Now," Buzz mercilessly continued, "you wouldn't be able to go down and get a job as a forensic pathologist at the state crime lab, would you? You don't meet their qualifications. Is that right?"

Dr. Goldberg answered, "I do not."

"And how many autopsies have you performed in Georgia in the last year?"

"None," he said quietly.

"How many in the last two years?" Buzz probed.

"None."

"The last five years?"

"None."

"How many have you performed in this country in the last year?"

"None," he said again.

"In the last two years?"

"Absolutely none," Dr. Goldberg answered, as if adding "absolutely" helped any.

"The last five years?"

"None."

Buzz then went in for the kill.

"And you're not a licensed medical doctor in this country, are you, sir?"

"No," he said, "I'm not."

I wanted to throw up. I wanted to find Alvin's provision in the U.S. Constitution that says you don't have to sit in court when you're sick.

"And you say you've done how many autopsies, yourself, personally?"

"Two thousand," he answered.

"Two thousand," Buzz repeated so the number would sink in, "and where were these autopsies done, sir?"

"Dominican Republic," he said.

Buzz continued the brutal assault on our witness, who was, of course, fair game for these attacks. I had failed to vet him, having never hired an expert before this case.

The cruelly effective cross-examination by Buzz continued: "Sir, also on your website, you claim to be an expert on firearms?" He asked similar questions about Goldberg's claims to be an expert in accident reconstruction, medical malpractice, economic fraud, explosives, and seventy-seven other areas, all which the witness affirmed.

Goldberg tried to explain that his membership in the Vidocq Society, which he described as "a group of experts, only eighty-two of us," was collectively whom he was including as his own expertise.

My mind went back to just over a week ago, on our trip to Atlanta, when he was asking Brian Carney pointed questions; then on the way back to Marietta, Goldberg offered that he could also be the handwriting expert in our case.

Buzz wasn't finished. I was in agony. Alvin appeared to be looking for an exit strategy. I put my hand on his arm.

"It's going to be okay," I whispered.

"Okay"—the district attorney was enjoying this—"in the 'Honors' section of your résumé, the only honors you claim is a Hardy Boys/Nancy Drew Super Mystery honor of some sort. What is that, sir?"

Jesus, I thought. *Did I not even read his curriculum vitae?*

Goldberg gave it a defense. "There is a book put together with the Vidocq Society as the basis of the story in Nancy Drew and the Hardy Boys. I was asked as an expert to contribute to that book. The author saw fit to dedicate that book to the society, and give special thanks to those people who assisted him in the story."

"I remember the Hardy Boys on TV," Alvin leaned over and whispered. He was the only one in the room impressed with this part of Goldberg's résumé.

Mercifully, the prosecutor sat down, and the court declared a midmorning break. I wasn't mad at Goldberg. But I was extremely mad at myself.

As we resumed, Buzz again asked Goldberg how many autopsies he had done.

Goldberg's response was "roughly two thousand."

Then he systematically went through the various jobs over the years where Goldberg had to admit that he had not actually done autopsies, but had done "forensic review and analysis of pathology cases."

Finally, mercifully, Buzz said, "Nothing further."

I had to give my old friend Buzz his due. He'd destroyed our witness.

Now I had at least a chance to try to rehabilitate our witness in redirect. I avoided revisiting all the weaknesses in Goldberg's résumé.

I asked, "Who creates the laws in the state that lawyers have to deal with?"

"Well," Goldberg answered, "the state does, the legislature."

Then I shifted. "Who creates the laws of nature and physics and the body and tissue and everything else you work with in the Dominican Republic, and that you review there?"

His answer was perfect. "God, sir. The Creator."

"Do people in the Dominican Republic die somehow differently than people in Georgia?"

He answered, "Not that I'm aware of."

That's all I could muster.

Buzz took a few more victory laps around my witness, then sat down, and I jumped back up.

"May this witness be excused and go about his business?"

There was no objection.

I bade farewell to Gold Bird with just a nod.

The court announced our break for lunch, giving the jurors the usual instructions. We were almost to the finish line. I just wanted to put Dr. Williams on, hoping that some of the jurors would remember him. I looked at Alvin as we left the courthouse. Today he had an entourage, a young family from his latest church, over in Murray County. I didn't necessarily want to entertain this group, but they seemed joined at the hip with Alvin.

"Alvin," I said, "let's all go to the same restaurant, but I'm going to let you dine with your new friends," adding that I would treat them all.

As we walked into the Trackside restaurant, trying to avoid jurors, I saw to it that Alvin and the church family were seated first, and I kept them within eyesight, but not earshot. But, Lord, as it turned out, I really missed something.

After lunch, I paid for everyone and walked with Alvin, the church family following us back to the courthouse. "Nice folks," I said to Alvin, who seemed troubled, as if he needed to tell me something.

"What's wrong, Alvin?" I asked.

"Jesus appeared to me at lunch and told me to testify. He said the truth would set me free."

This was a shock. We had long discussed the issue of Alvin testifying or not, and I thought that I had convinced him that if he took the stand and launched into talking about eviction, or his van, it would not sit well with the jury.

"Well, Alvin, that's your right to testify, or not to testify, but you need to know something first," I cautioned. "Everybody talks about themselves a certain way, and that is fine in normal conversation, but if you say something a certain way on the stand, it will unleash a load of stuff that I have fought hard to keep out."

In the courthouse, I asked the judge for a few extra minutes to talk to my client in a private area, without the glazed-over entourage or media following us. We went into the recently fumigated small courtroom, where we had started the trial. I told Alvin to take the stand, just as he would do if he testified.

"Alvin, tell me again how Jesus gave you this message?" I needed to know.

"I was eating lunch," he said, "and Jesus came in and filled my heart and told me, 'Alvin, you need to get on that stand and tell the truth.'"

"He came into the restaurant?" I asked. "I was in the same restaurant, remember? Did your friends see Jesus?"

"He came into my heart"—Alvin shook his head—"and he told me to take the stand."

I put Alvin on the stand there in the small courtroom, where we were alone, hoping that being in the unfamiliar setting of facing the room would change his perspective. "Let's practice a few questions, Alvin," I said. He was up for it. "I'll be the district attorney," I said, then pelted him with some questions to prove a point.

I became a menacing inquisitor, grilling, "Mr. Ridley, you kept your wife tied up for years, and you killed her, didn't you!"

"Naw, I loved her. She could have walked right out the door. I would never do anything like that."

"Wham!" I yelled. "See how you just put your own character into evidence, Alvin?"

I briefly switched back to the role of his counsel. "Now the DA can bring your mama and the cats back into the case. Everything I fought so hard to keep out will come crashing back in!" I told him.

"But I love my cats," he pleaded.

I yelled, again assuming the role of prosecutor. "And you tied up those cats, just like you tied up your wife, didn't you, Mr. Ridley? And you kept your mama in the house, and the state thinks you abused that poor woman, too, didn't you, Mr. Ridley?" I pushed. I was doing my best impersonation of Buzz tearing him a new one.

"I wouldn't do that," he pleaded. "People trusted me. Benny Jackson at the Ford place asked me to take a satchel to the bank. They gave me a receipt to take back. It was sixteen thousand dollars cash he trusted me with. And Walter Lee—his brother, Walter Lee Jackson at the Chevrolet place—he trusted me and sent me to LaFayette to fix his TV, and the only one home there was his wife. He trusted me with his wife! I'm a good person!"

I calmed down. "Alvin, just saying 'I'm a good person' opens the door to all the things that I kept out for you," I cautioned, explaining, "Mama, Kitty, and Meowy—all that stuff comes rushing back in, and if it does, I'm not sure I'm prepared to counter it."

I explained, in ways I hoped he could understand, that we all have the tendency to defend our own character, but that it would be a disaster if he did it on the stand.

I looked at his face and saw a sincerity that was a rare thing in my history with Alvin. I finally resigned to his request. "But if Jesus insists, who am I to try to out-advise Jesus? Just promise me this isn't Salesman Sam telling you to do this."

"It wasn't Salesman Sam," Alvin assured me. "It was really Jesus—He's taller." His eyes were wide and full of wonder, as if a modern miracle had indeed occurred.

"He just showed up," Alvin insisted. "I didn't expect Jesus to show up at lunch, or I would have had you sit with us. Jesus makes His own plans and arrangements." Strangely, I was sort of touched by the sentiment that Alvin would have included me, had he known Jesus was going to drop in.

20

We walked back from the small courtroom to the old grand courtroom, and I tried to quickly outline a direct examination of my client, all while reminding Alvin, "Don't say one damn good word about yourself!"

It was January 14, and a week after we selected jurors for this trial. I now called Dr. Louis Williams to the stand. Describing the Ridley family of Ringgold, Dr. Williams said, "I could say they were kind of withdrawn, and possibly use the word 'eccentric.'"

I wrapped up with my new favorite subject, petechiae, showing the universal view of the experience of the scientific community—with the lone exception of Dr. Fredric Hellman.

I asked, "Have you ever seen it in the eyes and face of patients? Were those patients living?"

He answered yes to both.

Buzz briefly cross-examined him, establishing only that he was not a forensic pathologist.

I gathered up what I had left in me and stood. "Your Honor, we have a matter to address the court with, a matter we need to bring up at this time, outside the presence of the jury."

The jurors filed out. I put Alvin on the stand just to certify to the court that I had advised him of his right not to testify, as well as his right to testify, even though I had advised him not to take the stand.

The court called for the jury to be brought back in. I let them settle into their seats, keeping my eyes on them as I called our next witness. "Your Honor, we call as our next witness, Alvin Eugene Ridley."

I almost stumbled as I included his middle name. *Why did I include his middle name? Only infamous killers get their names expanded to include their middle name in the public parlance—John Wilkes Booth, Lee Harvey Oswald, James Earl Ray—why did I do this?* I cringed on the inside.

As I placed him under oath, my mind was electric with all the ways this could go off the rails.

Alvin raised his weathered right hand to take the oath. I also had him place his left hand on the Bible, something that wasn't necessary, but we needed all the help we could get. *Who knows, maybe Jesus will pop in, since He's in town,* I mused.

"All right," I began, "tell the jury your name."

"Alvin Eugene Ridley," he said clearly. *Three names, but this one is on him,* I thought.

He told the jury that he was fifty-six, and that he had grown up in Ringgold, in his parents' home, where he still lived.

He answered my questions, revealing that he graduated Ringgold High in 1960, and served in the U.S. Army. While in the army, on leave, he met Virginia Hickey from Walker County.

He wasn't going to volunteer anything beyond the most specific limitations of the question asked. *This is good, actually,* I thought. *He's doing just as I coached him after lunch.*

I added, "And did y'all fall in love, or what?"

"Yes, sir," he replied. "We fell in love."

"How did you propose to her?" I asked another question I didn't know the answer to, hoping for an anecdote that would stir the romantic side of the jurors.

"Well," he said, "I just asked her. I really just gave her a wedding band and engagement ring and she accepted."

I had a sudden memory that this was not very far off from the way I proposed to my first wife, in her Atlanta apartment, in the kitchen, by her refrigerator.

"Okay, where did y'all get married?" Easy enough question, just bringing him along.

"Pleasant Valley Grove Church, up at Pleasant Valley Grove."

Over the years, Alvin had gone to so many churches, staying with each one until he wore them out asking for funds to "fix his mother's roof" or some other grift, and he was compounding the names of two well-known local churches. I thought it best just to leave this alone.

"Where did you live after you got married?"

"In the Ringgold Housing Project."

I got out of him that the Ringgold Housing Project was brand new and that they were among the first residents of the subsidized housing program.

Answering my questions in his characteristically brief, literal style, we established that Virginia had indeed gotten sick not long after the marriage, confirming his sister-in-law Trixie's testimony that Virginia had suffered a reaction to her epilepsy medicine.

"Trixie also testified that you went and took Virginia away from the Hickeys' home, saying something like 'a wife belongs with her husband' and took her against her will, is that correct?"

Alvin's demeanor saddened as he answered awkwardly, "I took her on her own will."

"What was the relationship like with the Hickeys at this time?" I asked.

"Well," he said, looking at the jurors, perhaps for a sympathetic ear, "we wasn't getting along very good, and they were trying to break up our family."

Alvin was describing a major event in his and Virginia's saga. The Hickeys had seized upon, or had even caused, the housing authority eviction action in 1970. Alvin had, of course, fought the eviction to the point of having a jury trial. I was frustrated in my search for the files or notes or transcripts from the former court reporter John Aunan. Alvin described the trial, and how it was abruptly stopped by Judge Paul Painter, who ordered Alvin's father to go get Virginia and bring her to court.

"Well," Alvin testified, supplying details that I did not know, "the judge called her, but it didn't go before the jury, but he called her back there, somewhere back in that room." He pointed behind the jurors, to the door behind, where the jury room and a judge's chambers still existed. "In a back room, on the side there, and talked to her in the presence of my daddy, and her mother and daddy."

Wow, I thought. Judge Painter had obviously not allowed Alvin to go with Virginia into his chambers, but he did allow her family—in an *eviction* case. Whatever she said in those chambers, or in the courtroom, led to her parents leaving the courthouse without her, and led to her going back home with her husband. Everything Alvin had told me before about what she had said was obviously reported to Alvin by his father. Virginia told Judge Painter something to the effect that she was where she belonged, and where she wanted to be, with her husband.

"Whatever was said that day," I asked Alvin, who was making a surprisingly good witness for himself, "did that end the newspaper articles?"

The newspaper articles, the only ones regarding Virginia Ridley until she was dead, were the ones her family got put in the Chattanooga, Tennessee, and Catoosa County, Georgia, newspapers, with headlines such as PARENTS SEEK MARRIED DAUGHTER.

"Yes, sir!" Alvin again reared back in the seat, smiled, and then pronounced in the double negative, "There wasn't no more newspaper articles after that!"

I asked him about some times Virginia did leave his parents' house with him. "Well," he answered, "she kept going out with me to different places, until around July 1984, when my van was seized by the county. Then she quit from then on."

"Let's go ahead and clear the air," I said. "Where has Virginia been for the last twenty-seven, twenty-eight years since that court appearance?"

"Here in the community," he answered without hesitation. "Catoosa County."

"All right." I tried to pivot, asking about Coroner Vanita Hullander. "You heard her testifying about you getting after her with a broom?"

"I wouldn't have threatened her, no," Alvin said. "Well, you know it was so long ago, you know, but I know I wouldn't have threatened her."

But then, he added, "If I had a broom, she might have made me mad and I might have threatened to hit her with a broom, but I wouldn't have done any harm to her."

He spoke lovingly of pharmacist Harry Gass.

"How about his boys, how have y'all gotten along?"

"We didn't get along." Alvin's voice fell.

Next I asked him about his last hours with Virginia. He described a seizure she had "about two o'clock in the morning, a real bad one, jerking real bad." He said that he didn't recall telling what the state witness had testified—that she hadn't had a seizure in a while. "I don't recall telling no witnesses that."

When I asked if he had done anything for her, he answered, "Oh, I always, every time she has a seizure, you know, I try to put my hands up here to keep her from biting her tongue and mouth. She hated me doing that because it would leave her hurting all day the next day or two."

I asked, "What happened next, did you stay up, or did you go back to sleep?"

"Well," he said, "I asked her if she was all right and I stayed up awhile, you know, and she said, 'Yeah, I'm all right, I love you,' and smiled."

"All right," I continued, wishing that I could have prepared him better to give his testimony. "What's the next thing you remember happening?"

"I fell off to sleep and I woke up that morning, and she was laying on her mouth facedown. I hollered at her and shook her, and she didn't respond."

In my right peripheral vision, I noticed that the jurors were listening intently. I asked, "Did you move her?"

"Yes, sir. She was laying down, facedown, where her mouth and nose were down on the pillar."

"And, Alvin"—I moved over to the dark garbage bag, removing D-79, collective—"you've been toting some of those pillows to court this week, haven't you?"

"Yes, sir."

"Alvin"—the smell was overwhelming—"those pillows are not very clean."

"Well, they've been sitting around there, you know," Alvin explained, "and I haven't washed them because of this case. Because I didn't want to wash any evidence off the pillars. I'm saving them as evidence."

"Alvin," I said, "what did you do next, after you turned her over?"

"Well," he said, "I tried to give her CPR and breathe in her mouth."

I asked if he was trained in CPR. He answered, "No, sir."

"So, what made you think that you could do CPR?"

"Well," he said, "I was in shock."

"Alvin, what does CPR stand for?"

He lowered his head. "I don't know." He said that he had "heard people call it that, on TV."

I asked, "Did y'all watch a lot of TV when you were together?"

He answered, "Yes, sir," then added, "She loved TV and reading the Bible."

I asked, "How long did you try to give her CPR and blow in her mouth?"

"Awhile," he said. "I don't know how long, but I didn't take no time limit on it or anything," adding, "I didn't time myself."

He described how he got into his truck, and "went down toward Truck City by the old Sweetwater plant," turning away from Ringgold. Thinking better of it, in less than a hundred yards, he turned around and came back into downtown Ringgold, driving to a pay phone at the ShopRite, one of the first addresses on LaFayette Street. He testified that this phone, mounted to the side of the outer wall, "didn't work." He then went farther up LaFayette Street to a pay phone stand just behind the courthouse complex and the 911 office.

I asked, "Did you realize where you were going to call?"

"Well," he said, "the only place I knew to call at that time was Erlanger Hospital."

Erlanger Hospital, in downtown Chattanooga, Tennessee, was almost a half-hour drive away, but it was a place Alvin trusted. First, he was born there. Second, it was where he took his mother, Minnie, as the Georgia authorities were getting a court order to check on her, and where he and his mother successfully defied their efforts. It made all the sense in the world to me, but would these jurors understand? I was relieved that the rumored first call to a funeral home never materialized in the state's case.

"So," I continued, "after you call Erlanger Hospital, what did you do?"

"They told me to call 911," he said.

I reminded him about the 911 tape that was played in the courtroom. "Alvin, you heard what you said to the 911 operator? Some folks have characterized, and Mr. Franklin has characterized, that your voice was funny that day."

"Well," he said, "I always talk all the time like that, you know, that's the way I talk."

It was the perfect answer, in the exact tone of his so-called "emotionless" 911 call.

Referring to the first responders' testimonies, I asked, "Did you hear them testify that you were, well, first they said 'without emotion,' then later they said, 'dazed.' Is that true?"

"Well," he said, "I was in shock and upset, but, yeah, I got *in emotion* and cried after that, at some time."

"Did you see Vanita Hullander there? Did you know she was the coroner?"

"I didn't know at that time, until she told me."

"When was the last time you voted, Alvin?"

"I haven't voted since they seized my van," he said.

I asked, "Why not?"

His voice lowered. "I've just lost confidence in the system."

"Alvin," I asked, "Ms. Hullander, when she got there, what happened next? What did you tell her, if anything?"

"Well, I know I told her about my wife laying there."

Jesus, please help me remember how literal this guy is, I silently thought.

"Well, I'm sure that was obvious," I said, in frustration, "but let me ask you this, what did you tell her about her condition, about her past history, her medical history?"

"I told her she was an *epi-letic.*"

"And you pronounce it 'epi-letic,'" I softly clarified, "but, of

course, you meant—and I don't pronounce all the words right—
she had epilepsy?"

He answered, "Seizures."

"She had seizures," I repeated. "Okay. Did you tell anybody that
she hadn't had a seizure in a while?"

"No," he said with conviction, "I know I wouldn't have said that,
because she had a seizure."

I asked him about the young men who were paramedics and
EMTs. He summed up their testimony: "They didn't cause me no
trouble."

I asked two simple questions: Had he kept Virginia's family from
Virginia? Had he kept Virginia from her family?

He answered, "No, sir."

"How did Virginia feel about seeing these people, her people?"

He answered without hesitation. "She didn't like it, because they
helped get her evicted out of the Ringgold Housing Project, and
she wanted that house back."

"A lot has been said about this bed having a dip on one side of it,
and not a dip on the other side," I asked. "How old is that bed,
Alvin?"

"Oh, it's several years," he said, "probably was, probably thirty,
forty years."

He said that his daddy had gotten the bed, and admitted it was
not in the best condition.

I switched to ask Alvin about Virginia's ring, knowing that it
would likely gall my worthy opponent. "Alvin, let me mention
something. You've been requesting something since day one that
belonged to your wife?"

"My wife's ring that she wore for about thirty-one years and
never did take it off."

I pressed, "Did she have any other jewelry on?"

"Well," he said, "she could have had a watch on at that time, you
know. She did have a watch like that, but I haven't been able to find
it. I found some of the other watches she wore."

"You're more concerned about the ring than the watch, right?"

"Right."

"And who have you been trying to get to help you get that ring?"

"You."

"Now, Alvin," I asked, "you haven't been real good to bring me evidence when I demanded you bring it to me, have you?"

"Right," he said, "I've been a little slow."

"The other day when I pulled that ring out of my pocket and had the coroner, Ms. Hullander, identify it, did you know I had it in my pocket?"

"Not at that time, no," he said. "You surprised me."

"Where does that ring belong?"

"It belongs on my wife's finger."

"Is she buried without it?"

"Yes."

I looked at the jury, asking him, "Did she ever take it off during the marriage?"

"Not one time. She wouldn't let me take it off."

There were true looks of compassion on some of their faces. One female juror was touching the ring on her ring finger.

"Did you kill your wife?"

"No, sir."

"Did you do anything to your wife that led to her death?"

"No, sir."

"You told the investigators and we heard on that tape that y'all had arguments sometimes."

Alvin answered perfectly: "Well, I reckon all married couples has arguments, you know."

I asked, "What did y'all argue about . . . something about the garbage, was that it?"

"Well, I wouldn't take the garbage can out and she said I needed to take the garbage can out, and arguing about it."

"Did that cause you to suddenly decide to kill her?"

"No, sir."

I asked him about the little red spots that he would see on his wife after one of her "spells," the petechiae.

"Have you seen Virginia develop these spots before?"

"Yeah," he answered, "when she was having a *epi-letic* spell. Seizure."

I asked, "What were y'all planning on doing involving the *Unsolved Mysteries* television program?"

Alvin perked up a bit. "That was my wife's idea, you know. She wanted that case resolved about my daddy and them seizing the van."

I asked, "Was she helpful to you?"

"Oh, yes, sir," he answered, "very helpful."

"In what way?" I asked, holding my breath.

He looked proud. "Cleaning the house, cooking, and talking to me about the Bible."

"And how long were y'all married?"

"Around thirty-one years," he answered.

"Did you have any insurance, Alvin?"

"No, sir."

"Did you gain anything from Virginia dying?"

"Naw."

"What did you lose, Alvin?" This was a long, slow, underhanded softball pitch.

He thought, and answered, "I lost . . . a funeral bill."

When will I learn? I thought. *I can't ask this guy any question that isn't direct. Buzz is going to have a field day with that answer.*

"Did you lose anything else?" I asked, hoping to get "my best friend" or something sentimental.

"Yeah," he answered, "about all my business and everything."

I needed to move on, and quickly.

It was like an exorcism, I hoped, for Alvin to finally get all of this out, all that he had been pushing me to investigate and spend my time preparing for. All of this I had pushed back against and resented him for bringing up. He was getting it all out today. *Thank you, Jesus.*

"You heard Harry Gass testify, right? He admitted that he sold you and Virginia that medicine, didn't he?"

Alvin nodded. "Yes, sir, he admitted it."

"So you don't think everybody is out to get you, do you?"

"No."

"Is there anybody in this whole group of detectives that you like and you trust?" I asked.

"I trusted Vic Wells," Alvin said wistfully. "He seemed like a nice guy."

"What made you trust Vic Wells?"

"Well," Alvin said, "he seemed to be truthful in all his speeches and stuff."

The way I had figured it, Alvin lacked the capacity to recognize the classic "good cop/bad cop" strategy they had tried to use on him, and Vic didn't have the knowledge that he was being tape-recorded while playing the role of the sympathetic inquisitor. Buzz did not call Detective Wells to the stand during the state's case.

"Okay, Alvin. Did anything happen, or not happen, at the housing authority that scared her?"

"Yeah," he chimed in, "the Orkin man went in there, you know, and insulted her and tried to get a date with her, and she was scared, and she'd have me take her out of there every time he was supposed to run."

Trying to bolster his testimony, I asked, "She wrote that down, didn't she?"

"Yes, sir," he said.

I questioned him about all the lawsuits he had filed, and all the lawyers who had started out representing him, but who all had withdrawn, or been fired, before the end of the litigation.

"Have you ever kept a lawyer from one end of a matter to the other end of it?"

"Nobody but you," he answered, and as I turned toward the jury, he added ominously, "So far."

It caused an audible chuckle from more than one juror. They were enjoying my torture. *He's keeping his options open to drop me before the end of this trial,* I thought.

I barked back, "Have you ever been told that you are difficult to work with?"

"Yeah," he said, "you've told me that."

Another suppressed laugh from a juror. Buzz looked dismayed. How could there be laughter in a murder trial? In a sinister wife-imprisoning murderer's trial?

"Alvin," I took a risk and asked, "what else is missing from your life right now?"

He gave the perfect answer: "My wife."

I asked, "Are you blaming anyone for her death?"

"Yeah," he answered without hesitation, "I'm blaming some-body."

"Well," I asked, "who?"

He looked at the jury as if he had solved the mystery. "People who took my van."

"Back in 1984?" I asked, not even trying to mask the quizzical tone.

"Yes, sir."

"Alvin, you know that sometimes bad things happen to people?"

"Yes, sir."

"And do you know that . . . Do they or do they not usually re-cover and move on?"

"Yeah, some people do," he answered, "yeah."

I was asking questions I had never asked him before. "Well, why didn't you?"

He drew a breath, and said, "Well, I didn't have no place to go, my wife was sick and she wanted to live here. She wanted that busi-ness opened back up." He started to sob.

I asked, "Your Honor, if I could have about thirty seconds to as-sess . . ."

Judge Van Pelt interjected, "Well, let's take a fifteen-minute re-cess."

This allowed me ample time to assess if I had gotten everything in that I needed to get in from this "surprise" witness, Alvin Ridley.

"You know, Alvin, you did okay," I whispered as we sat back at the defense table, "but remember what I told you about cross-examination."

I rifled through the rest of Virginia's writings, scattering roaches again in the courthouse. Team Alvin set up around him, but he wasn't going anywhere.

I looked back at my parents, and some of my sisters were there as well. My father gave me a lit-up look on his face, a flash of his eye-brows raised, and his teeth bared in a smile. *That's a good sign,* I thought. *He's definitely sober. That's a morning look, in the afternoon.*

* * *

We started back, with Alvin again taking the witness chair as I tried to wrap up any loose ends that I thought could help him.

"Mr. Ridley, have a seat," I said. "Let me show you what has been marked as defendant's exhibit 88, collective." I handed him a pile of Virginia's writings that had not yet been entered into evidence. "Now, who wrote all of these things?"

"That would have been my wife, who wrote them," he answered. "Virginia Ridley."

"And were you familiar with her handwriting?"

"Yes, sir."

"And all the exhibits," I asked, "that Trixie identified as her handwriting the other day, those were also Virginia's handwriting?"

He answered, "They looked the same."

"Well," I clarified, "you provided these to me, didn't you?"

"Yes, sir."

"Answer up," I said, meaning to speak more loudly.

"Yeah, them are my wife's, Virginia Ridley."

"Do you recall Trixie saying that she never knew Virginia to write poems?"

"Yeah, seems like she did."

"Did Virginia write these poems?"

"Yes, sir."

"Finally the jury is going to have a lot of handwriting to look at, and I am tendering to you these two things that are both considered defendant's exhibit 91," I said as I handed Alvin two letters from Private Alvin Ridley addressed to Virginia Hickey, which she had saved.

"That would have been wrote from me when I was in the army to my girlfriend, at the time we weren't married," he answered.

I went no further. Buzz knew what was in them and would certainly accuse me of triggering another emotional outburst from the defendant. In fact, the letters made me tear up when I first read them. I knew the jury would open them and read them, and they would be very effective. In one, Alvin professes that he misses Virginia "every second, every minute and every hour of the day," and then, plaintively, "Virginia, you are the only girl in the whole world that ever treated me with kindness and understanding, and you know I can never forget you." I was dropping a love bomb on the jury, timed to go off when the first one opened it up and read it.

I dipped back into the pile of Virginia's writings marked D-88, collective. Alvin described the document as Virginia's listing of the cast of TV's *The Waltons,* a popular, wholesome show in its day.

"Is that one of her favorite shows?" I asked.

"Yes, sir."

"She just wrote down the cast of it?"

"Yes, sir."

"Did you have any friends in the world that supported you as much as Virginia?"

"No, sir, I didn't."

I handed him a torn-off cardstock cover from a red spiral notebook. Virginia was industrious in using any medium that would accept pencil or pen.

"And do you . . . Did Virginia pray, or not?"

"Yes." He looked at her writing on the back of the cover. "She prayed every night that I'd get my business opened back up and help her, and she always prayed this prayer every night."

I asked, "Is that her handwriting?"

"Yes, sir," he said, "that's her handwriting."

"Where did it come off of? It looks like . . . What is it written on?"

He answered, "Come off of one of her notebooks. Do you want me to read it?"

"You may read it."

Alvin read:

> *When I lay me down to sleep,*
> *I pray the Lord my soul to keep;*
> *If I should die before I wake,*
> *I pray the Lord my soul to take.*
> *Amen.*

I let that sink in. *"If I should die before I wake . . ."* That was the line that horrified me as a young child, and from the realization that I seemed to be assenting to be taken out that way, I changed my prayers from then on.

"Alvin," I finished, "do you have any idea what caused Virginia to die?"

He answered, "No, sir."

I looked to the district attorney's table as I started toward my seat. "You may ask."

As I turned Alvin over to District Attorney Buzz Franklin for cross-examination, I felt like parents probably feel when they are dropping off their kids on the first day of kindergarten.

"Mr. Ridley," he began, "you say you don't know what caused Virginia Ridley to die?"

"Well," Alvin replied, "I'm no doctor."

"Do you remember telling Dan Bilbrey the day after her death that she had suffocated facedown on her pillow?"

Alvin said, "I wouldn't have told him that."

Buzz continued to badger him.

"Well," Alvin replied, "she *was* laying on the pillar, you know, with her mouth down and nose, and I guess that's where I got that from, if I said it."

"So you *did* make that statement? Are you saying you *did* make that statement then?" Buzz fired.

"Well . . ." Alvin looked to the ceiling as if trying to recall. "I could have."

He asked about Alvin opposing an autopsy, and Alvin answered, "Well, I didn't want my wife cut on."

"When you were making this statement, you knew they were investigating the cause of death, didn't you?"

"Yes, sir."

"Yes?" Buzz reacted like he was surprised at the answer.

"Yes," Alvin said again.

Buzz shifted to the dispossessory, or eviction, trial in 1970. I knew the longer the state would be bogged down in the past, the better things were for us.

"Now," the prosecutor posed, "you say y'all were removed from the housing projects here in Ringgold back in September of 1970, is that right?"

Alvin, without missing a beat, said, "September 15, 1970."

It was one of several dates that would live in infamy for Alvin Ridley. That one, and the dates of Daddy's wreck, the dates of Daddy's and Mama's deaths, the date he was chased across the state line with his aging mother to evade a Georgia adult protection order, are just a few of the dates that are etched into his brain just like those important dates of history we learn as schoolchildren.

"What was the problem, Mr. Ridley?"

"There was people all the time getting the law, causing problems . . ."

"What did the housing authority allege was the problem?" he asked.

Oh, this is starting to be fun. It was a huge undertaking to get Alvin Ridley to stay on track, and then not to pivot to one of his favorite diversions, to wit: police misconduct, state agency misconduct, Hickey family misconduct, etc.

"Well"—Alvin looked at the ceiling as if he were really trying to remember, to help the prosecutor—"the Orkin man insulted my wife."

Buzz argued with Alvin, back and forth, about whether they were occupying the apartment.

Well, that ate up a lot of time, I thought.

Frustrated, Buzz finally moved on to another topic.

He cross-examined Alvin on how he didn't get along with Virginia's parents. Alvin countered that Virginia's father had taken out a warrant on him. Buzz got him to admit that it was a "peace warrant," then asked him to tell the jury what a peace warrant was.

"That's somebody saying they're scared of you," he answered accurately, adding, "Well, I never did threaten nobody."

I got lost calculating how to parse a double-negative answer: *Does that make it an admission?*

Buzz taunted him. "You didn't threaten Vanita Hullander, either, did you?"

"No, sir."

"Didn't threaten Johnny Gass, either, did you?"

"No, sir."

"Didn't threaten the mailman, did you?"

Wait, what? I tried to remain poker-faced. *This is the first time I've heard anything about a mailman.* I made a note in my file to object if it got any deeper. If I objected now, it might draw more attention to it than was warranted.

"Well, they were harassing me," Alvin said.

Oh, great.

Buzz went through Alvin's history with lawyers and all the various civil cases that started out with lawyers, but ended up with Alvin representing himself, his wife, his mother, or his late father.

Bizarrely, Buzz started accusing Alvin of plagiarism. He read out two of the pleadings from the 1980s civil cases about Bill Ridley's wreck, chock-full of legalese, and challenged that Alvin didn't write them by himself. Alvin was resolute. He was the author. I knew he was stretching, but at this point, it was a matter of pride.

I thought, maybe I should point out the "emotions" that Alvin had filed in some of those cases, to distinguish his work from the "motions" that other lawyers filed.

Alvin seemed to frustrate Buzz at every turn, much as he had done with me, whenever I slipped, forgot, and asked a question that had any abstract aspect. The problem is, in normal conversation, we often speak in the abstract. The way Alvin needed the questions was a lot more precise, more literal.

Buzz asked about trouble with Virginia's father, James Hickey.

"Well, he's all the time causing us problems over there, you know, trying to break up the home," Alvin said, seemingly oblivious to the fact that Mr. Hickey had long passed on. "There was people, and her mama and daddy going through the house and looking through the refrigerator all the time, causing me trouble."

"So," Buzz asked, "they were down there visiting you all the time during this period?"

"Yeah," Alvin said, "they was looking in the refrigerator for beer."

"Okay, this van shown in state's exhibit 8, is that the van that you had complained about?"

Alvin lit up, because here was the subject he came to talk about. "That's the van the county and sheriff's department seized, yeah, and it's up there. The tires are rotting off of it."

"How long has it been sitting there?" Buzz asked.

"Since they seized it in '84!"

"You got it back fairly quick, didn't you?" Buzz asked the same questions I had asked him for months.

Alvin countered, "They didn't return the van back like they took it."

Classic Alvin response.

Buzz asked if he had ever attempted to get another vehicle. Alvin answered in classic hyperbole, "Yeah, but I had problems with them. Somebody *victimized* it and put sand in the motor and it blowed up, an '81 Chevrolet van. And I had another '77 Chevrolet van and somebody put the transmission in wrong on it and blowed it up. The motor is blowed up in it."

"But your daddy had a truck, too, didn't he?" Buzz asked the fair question, since he was in his daddy's '65 Chevy pickup when he was arrested.

"Yeah," Alvin answered, "but the motor blowed up . . ."

Buzz rocked back and forth, to and from the various highlights of Alvin's history and the night that Virginia died, as if trying to keep him off-balance. Alvin was being Alvin, and if anyone was kept off-balance, it was the Lookout Mountain Circuit DA. Even I had not completely learned the best way to ask Alvin questions in order to get an answer.

I noticed the subtle signs that the jurors were getting tired of this. They were looking at their watches, looking at the clock on the wall across the room, and I even heard a sigh that was converted at the end to a small cough, I believe, out of embarrassment.

He took Alvin through Virginia's last hours, over and over, looking for a crack in Alvin's strange armor.

"And, Mr. Ridley, you've shown a lot of different ranges of emotions while you've been here in the courtroom, haven't you?"

"Yes, sir," Alvin answered automatically.

"And you've grinned, and you've laughed, and you've carried on all throughout this trial?"

"Yes, sir," Alvin again answered just as Buzz wished.

I stood and stopped them. "I object to the characterization of 'carrying on.'"

Buzz defended himself: "He's on cross-examination."

"That's an editorial judgment by Mr. Franklin," I offered.

The judge didn't buy it. "Overruled. Go ahead."

Alvin, hopefully sensing something wrong, interrupted, "Can you repeat the question?"

Good, a reset, I thought.

Buzz asked again, "Through this trial, you've shown a whole range of emotions, haven't you?"

"Yeah," Alvin again admitted.

"You've laughed?"

"Yeah." Alvin was in control. "Something 'Ken' said got me laughing. I forget now what he said." He was referring to me by my childhood nickname, the last syllable of McCracken.

Dammit, Alvin, I wanted to say, *don't drag me into this!*

"And you just grinned right then, just a little bit?" Buzz continued to twist the knife.

"Yes, sir," Alvin again agreed with him.

I didn't remember being particularly jovial during this trial, and did not at all remember saying anything that made Alvin laugh, but he did smile and engaged the jury on a couple of questions that made me, his lawyer, look foolish. I was happy to play the foil to a warm and smiling Alvin Ridley.

Another humorous moment came when Buzz again pivoted to the morning of Virginia's death and Alvin's response.

"Now," the prosecutor asked, "you say you called Erlanger first?"

"Yes, sir."

Buzz said, "I take that back. You called directory assistance first?"

"Yes, sir."

"Okay," Buzz said, "so you had a quarter for directory assistance?"

Alvin paused, put on his glasses, even though there was nothing to read, then slowly answered, "It was thirty-five cents at that time."

It seemed putting on his glasses and taking them off again was an affectation, or a nervous tic. *Maybe he thought it makes him look smarter,* I thought.

"That's right," Buzz agreed. "So you used thirty-five cents to call directory assistance?"

"Yes, sir."

"Then you used another thirty-five cents to call Erlanger?"

"Yeah."

"Does it require any change to call 911?"

"No, sir."

"Now, the change that you had on you, where did it come from?"

Alvin mulled the question over and finally answered, "Out of my pocket."

Another abrupt cough from the jury box, and I thought perhaps a snicker.

If Buzz had been paying any attention at arraignment, or at the motions hearings, or in six days of this trial, he would know that Alvin *always* carried what sounded like $27.50 in change in his right front pocket, and jingled it constantly.

"Were you dressed?" Buzz asked, genuinely surprised. He lacked my advantage of inside knowledge, having literally gotten Alvin out of bed, fully dressed, this week. Lori and I had long figured out that he wore the same clothes until we either shamed him into going to the coin-operated washers or bought him new clothes, which were worn for weeks and months on end.

"You didn't have any money in your pocket when you were in bed, did you?"

Of course he did!

"I could have," Alvin answered honestly. "Sometimes I sleep with my pants on, sometimes it drops out."

"Okay," but Buzz couldn't let it go. "But before you left to go to the ShopRite, did you have to pick your money out of a dish on the table?"

"No," Alvin answered. "I'd say it was probably already in my pocket."

"Did you check and make sure you had enough money before you left home?" Buzz asked.

"I always have change in my pocket."

So does my father, I thought.

I gave the jurors a look. They knew I had been silencing the jinglejangle of change throughout the trial. One smiled at me. A good sign.

* * *

Judge Van Pelt declared an afternoon break, and I accompanied Alvin to the restroom to assure no false claims of encounters with jurors, or real claims; and second, to make sure he came back.

While he was in the stall, I said, "Alvin, don't say anything in response to this. You are doing very well!"

He immediately started talking loudly, of course, but I successfully *hushed* him. We went back to the courtroom to our table, and I hovered around him like a manager over a prizefighter. There was nothing with which to cloud his head. He was doing just fine, being himself, the very literal Alvin Ridley.

Back on the stand, Buzz peppered Alvin with the same questions, over and over, about what he had said to the coroner, and to Detective Bilbrey.

"Your Honor," I interjected, "he's asked and answered, and he's asked and answered, and he's asked and answered it."

Buzz got a lick in with his response, "Well, I get a different answer each time."

The judge said, "Well, he's on cross. Overruled."

The prosecutor started asking about the 1980s litigation. He got nowhere.

Surprisingly, Buzz said, "All right, Judge, I think that's all."

I redirected for two minutes on one minor issue, to introduce a 1986 article where Alvin had gone to the newspaper in Chattanooga to appeal for funds for his "mother's roof."

With that, I got to say the words that I had been praying for: "The defense rests, Your Honor."

The judge, with a bit of pep in his voice, instructed the jury, "Please remember my prior instructions . . . We're in recess until nine in the morning."

I hugged my parents and sisters and hustled Alvin and his suitcases out of the building. At least I got Alvin's pillows (his "pillars") admitted. I didn't know what he would lay his head on tonight, but he was hellbent to get them into evidence, although everyone kept trying to retie the garbage bag or move it away from the jury box, the court reporter, and the prosecutor's table. I stuffed it under our table for the night, with the court reporter's thankful approval. *If we lose, she's going to have to take them home with her,* I thought.

"Where can I get you some supper, Alvin?" I asked as we loaded up the Jeep with the roach cases and my files. "You've earned it."

He chose McDonald's.

He was silent after we drove through the line and got his supper. I got him into his house. He promised to stay in, and on the way out, for the first time I ever heard it from him, he said in a low but clear voice, "Thank you, Ken."

It had been quite a day. The disaster of Gold Bird, the surprise appearance of Jesus at lunch, and Alvin's testimony, which was very good, considering all. Between seeing my father in court at trial, sober, and hearing that from Alvin, I was elated.

21

*T*he morning of January 15, 1999, RIDLEY SAYS HE AND WIFE SHARED FEARS was the front-page article by Beenea A. Hyatt in the *Chattanooga Times Free Press. This should be the last day of trial. Way to go, Alvin,* I thought. *Way to go, Jesus!* Even in the half-assed law practice I maintained while being obsessed with elected office, I always wanted my clients to take my advice. But Alvin had been hiding his light under a bushel. He *could* communicate, very well, even though it was the strangest, conspiracy-filled sort of communication. I was just hoping that the jurors would remember their oaths—that the *state* bears the burden of proof, beyond a reasonable doubt.

Alvin would like this one. The article made it clear that he took the stand against my advice, but I really thought he did well. Maybe I had helped drive expectations so low, so all he had to do was exceed them. But there was more to it. I could tell that he had *charmed* some of them. You know, sitting second chair to Jesus' advice is nothing to complain about—that is, unless we lose. If, however, I learned that Salesman Sam had had anything to do with that move, I might just find another career.

I had not slept well. Not out of worry, just that I was exhausted, but could not let up now. I did want to go over my trial notes for closing argument today. I even pretended to go through Alvin's almost unintelligible scribble, looking for inspiration, and stuffed them back in the file.

I took the newspaper, as promised, to Alvin's house. Naturally, he had gone out against my advice and gotten his own newspapers, including the *Atlanta Journal-Constitution*. Jack Warner's *AJC* article, DEFENDANT TAKES THE STAND, begins: "To the dismay of his attorney, Alvin Ridley insisted Thursday on taking the witness stand he has been trying to occupy for 30 years."

I never thought of it that way, but it made sense. Alvin had been frustrated since the Ringgold Housing Authority eviction trial in 1970. Judge Paul Painter had stopped the trial and ordered Virginia Ridley to be brought in, where he took her into his chambers with her parents and Alvin's father. Judge Painter simply ended the trial once Virginia told him she wished to be left with her husband. Neither of the two cases involving Bill Ridley's accident made it to trial, denying Alvin a chance to air his grievances there, either. The subsequent counterclaim, which took his van—for less than a month—was the last straw that sent Alvin and Virginia over the edge. Ridley's Zenith TV Sales & Service was shuttered. Zenith pulled the franchise—and I'm sure they had legitimate reasons. I had no doubt there were meddlers whispering information to corporate headquarters, just as there were whispers to the housing authority, and also to Leslie Waycaster before he deposed Alvin. To someone already loaded and cocked with paranoia, it was the perfect storm that drove the couple even deeper into seclusion.

"You know, Alvin," I told him, "considering all the cases you've had, going back to 1970, and your court of appeals victory in the early 1980s, I think one could argue that you have more actual legal experience than your lawyer does."

That made him smile, baring his suffering teeth. He must have felt good, because I didn't have to threaten him to come with me to court. Also, he forgot the neck brace. I didn't think of it until we were almost to the courthouse. I worried that the district attorney would make a big deal of its absence in closing, though. Apparently, Alvin now had sufficient confidence to go without it.

We walked into the courthouse, and I could detect that Alvin was being treated with just a little bit more respect by the bailiffs than before, certainly better than last September at arraignment, after

running half a lap around the courthouse, away from Tommy
Eason. As we walked into the main courtroom, we were both taken
aback by the crowd, mostly sitting on the defense side of the room,
behind the defense table.

"There's your daddy again," Alvin leaned in to say, adding, "He
really likes me!"

My father was again clear-eyed and sober. Next to him was my
mother, along with some of my sisters, Alison's parents and grandmother, and half a courtroom full of local folks who were curious
or probably knew Alvin, but just weren't comfortable about him
until reading about his performance yesterday. I could tell that the
mere presence of these people lifted Alvin's spirits. He was a different man, although still guarded.

No one wanted to be here any longer. The jurors had served two
weeks, having come in and out for one week until being selected
on Thursday of last week for this trial. The state had rested, and the
defense had rested. Nevertheless, the DA wanted to bring in some
rebuttal witnesses. I told Alvin that this meant the State of Georgia
was worried that he might just win this trial.

All settled into their seats, the signal that the jurors had all arrived in the jury room would send Judge Van Pelt out to get us
started.

Judge Van Pelt seemed a bit surprised by the almost-full courtroom. He had told me at the start of the trial that nobody came to
watch trials anymore.

He greeted the gallery and said, "Anything we need to take up
before we bring the jury in?"

No one responded.

"Bring the jury in," the court ordered.

"Good morning, ladies and gentlemen," the judge said. "All
right. I understand the state has some witnesses to call here in rebuttal. Call your first witness, Mr. Franklin."

Buzz stood. "Yes, sir," he said with a renewed tone. "We'd call
Dr. Fredric Hellman."

Great, I thought, *he's going to parade his actual certified pathologist doctor around for a victory lap around the ruins of Dr. Goldberg.* And that's exactly what he did. Later, he asked his witness about petechiae again.

On cross-examination, I asked the difference between the coroner's photo and the crime lab photo as to the tiny red hemorrhages. He blamed the lack of resolution on the coroner's camera. I thought that was funny, as he seemed not to understand camera resolution earlier in the trial.

"Call your next witness, please," the court directed to the prosecutor.

"Call Frank Young," Buzz directed to the bailiff.

This was one of the first responders. Buzz led him through testimony that he had attached EKG pads to Virginia's body, insisting that he didn't remove any of Virginia's clothing. "I didn't remove it, I arranged it."

I hadn't even made an issue of this, so Buzz was reacting to scant evidence of how upset Alvin was about Virginia's shirt being opened up for the EKG leads. Then Buzz raised the issue of Alvin's testimony about Virginia's missing watch.

"Sir, did you steal anything off this body?"

"No," he answered.

No one had accused him of stealing anything. The confusion about the ring was enough to establish that inventory and clear chain-of-custody protocols had not been in place. Buzz was overreacting.

I asked a few questions, until I noticed Alvin was crying again due to talk about the witness moving her shirt to put on the leads. I ended quickly.

"Redirect?" the court asked.

Buzz quickly approached the witness, addressing his trip report. Then Buzz said, "Okay, nothing further."

I sat down, saying, "That's all."

God, I was hoping Buzz would rest.

Buzz looked to the bailiff. "Call Vanita Hullander."

Alvin stiffened, looking straight ahead. Buzz went through the obligatory "You understand you are still under oath in this case?"

and other unnecessary reminders to the jury of her position as the coroner of Catoosa County.

Buzz asked a series of questions that were just basically rehashing her earlier testimony about her discussions with Alvin about the funeral bill, his alleged first statement that it had been a while since Virginia had a seizure; he was doing a quick review of her entire earlier testimony.

There was no way any of this was "rebuttal," but I was tired, and I wanted to pick my battles, not just react to everything. The jury was worn out. The apparent false lead for a contact in Virginia's family came up again, reminding the jury that Alvin gave her the name of his dead father-in-law, James Hickey. I was not worried about this and told Alvin as much.

"And, ma'am," Buzz asked, "did you steal anything from the body at the scene?" Buzz must still be butt hurt about Alvin's reaction to Virginia's ring, and the missing watch.

"No, sir," she answered in an understandably indignant tone.

I hoped the jury remembered I accused no one of stealing anything, just misplacing. If anything, I had thought that the coroner had been quite kind to let me know that she had found the ring in her desk drawer. It was an honest reaction to an oversight.

"Now," Buzz said, marching on, "there's been an issue about a ring. Are you familiar with Virginia Ridley's ring? And were you contacted about the ring by Mr. Poston?"

"Yes," she said. "I asked him to provide me with a written, authorized statement from Mr. Ridley to release personal property to him." She said this happened "shortly after he became his attorney."

"What did she say?" I whispered aloud to Alvin, not really wanting an answer from him. He stared ahead.

I scrambled for the transcript of the rescheduled motion hearings in October, when I was on the record *still* asking where the ring was. I had begged Joe Randles to transcribe it, and he just got it done before falling severely ill. I knew I had asked Richard Baxter, her assistant, and that I had been asking her privately for the ring and watch for weeks.

Court reporter Joe Randles was still in the hospital from a massive heart attack, and apparently was not doing well. I believe this was the last transcription he had done before suffering his heart attack, and he had just gotten it to me. As much as I liked Leigh Ann, I missed the cues that Joe would send when I had gone too far or too long. Scrambling for the transcript, I knew that as recently as October, Assistant Coroner Richard Baxter had clearly denied, under oath, any knowledge of a ring or a watch. Then, too, there was what the coroner said herself in her earlier testimony in this trial, that she "found" the ring in her desk drawer and gave it to the district attorney's office to give to me just nine days before trial.

Buzz stopped on that high note, which basically accused me of orchestrating the ring drama. He'd been at the hearing in October. I was disappointed, but at the same time, this rebuttal had given me an opening to correct the record.

But then I remembered Joe Randles, still in the hospital. He'd be giving me the quick finger across the throat sign, telling me to let the issue go. At the same time, I also remembered Joe's past suggestions, which he shared during breaks late in trials, telling me that I needed to close strong.

"Okay," I asked. "Now, why isn't that ring on Virginia Ridley's finger right now in the Gordy Cemetery?"

I saw Alvin's face start to tune up for another cry.

The coroner's last answer came: "I kept the personal property."

"Thank you," I said as I rushed over to calm my client.

The judge asked, "Anything further?"

I'm sure he was tired of all of this.

Buzz confirmed, "Nothing further."

But he meant nothing further for the coroner.

"Call your next witness," the judge directed.

"One moment, Your Honor," Buzz said as he conferred with Detective Bilbrey at the prosecutor's table. I was hoping it was over. But then, "Your Honor, we'd call Dan Bilbrey."

Batting cleanup, again, I thought. *This must be the last witness in this trial.*

* * *

Detective Bilbrey went back on the stand, and Buzz hurried through establishing his witness was still under oath, still the investigating officer on behalf of the Catoosa County Sheriff's Office, etc.

Then he sprang, "Did the defendant tell you the first time you met him on October 5, 1997, around nine o'clock p.m., that he did not suffocate his wife?"

I objected, to no avail, to leading his own witness.

"Overruled."

"Yes, he did," Detective Bilbrey answered.

"Sir," Buzz continued, "were you permitted to search the entire residence of Mr. Ridley's after you got consent to search?"

"No," the detective answered, "we were not."

Buzz established through his so-called "rebuttal" witness that Alvin had given consent, but later limited it, asking them not to go into certain rooms. That did not surprise me one bit, having experienced that myself until I, without permission, put my shoulder to the door just a week or so ago, and uncovered an indoor chicken rescue mission.

"And without probable cause"—Buzz was wrapping up—"you can't get a warrant and go in and search someone's residence?"

"And seize property also," Bilbrey answered. "Correct."

Poor, poor State of Georgia, I thought as I considered all the other times officers had found numerous reasons for warrantless searches or simply got easy search warrants from willing magistrates.

Then Buzz, surprisingly, rested. "That's all."

"Cross?"

I was tired, and a bit punch-drunk from the battle. I should have listened to my inner Joe Randles. I stood, then snarked, "Is an officer totally impotent when it comes to a person saying, 'Oh, I don't want you to look here'? I mean, do you just have to say, 'Oh, man, I wish we could go in there!' If you have suspicion, what can you do?"

"Sir?" Bilbrey asked, understandably confused as to my raving, rambling question.

"If you have probable cause, what can you do?" I barked.

"Ladies and gentlemen," he did a Hellman-esque turn toward

the jurors, not having picked up on how tiring and robotic that act had become, so much that even the master of it had abandoned it. "If you have probable cause, you can seek a search warrant. As the district attorney indicated, that as to the manner of death we had no probable cause, as counselor is leading up to, at that particular time, there was no suspicion to announce probable cause to get a search warrant."

"Did you feel Virginia Ridley's death was suspicious?" I asked.

"On that particular date?"

"Yes."

"I don't believe I had enough information to make that determination," he very appropriately answered, as if he were teaching a class. And that is what was driving me crazy. This was the first interrogation that was thinly disguised as a "welfare check." I had to figure out another angle.

"So you were with Vanita Hullander?" I asked. "And that was in the evening of October 5, right?"

"On October 5, yes, I was," and he answered yes to it being in the evening.

"If in the morning of October 5," I asked, "Vanita Hullander told Fredric Hellman, 'This woman has been locked in a basement for thirty years,' do you think she had some suspicions while she was with you?"

Buzz jumped up, objecting, "This is outside the scope of rebuttal!"

I refocused, wanting to show that the poor State of Georgia was not "tied up" by Alvin Ridley's quirky selection of where they could look in his house. Besides, Alvin told me they looked everywhere, against his protestations, but I would not put him back on the stand.

"Did Vanita Hullander express to you anything throughout the whole day that she personally told Dr. Hellman that this woman had been locked in a basement for thirty years? Did she express that to you?" I asked.

"I don't recall," he said.

It was really the perfect answer, for the jurors were smart enough to know that a hot subject like keeping his wife locked in the basement for thirty years was going to be at the top of conversation among those investigating.

"Okay." I focused. "And did Vanita Hullander express to you any suspicion that she might have had about the circumstances surrounding the death of Virginia Ridley, before you went into that house?"

"I don't recall," and then he did a mini-civics lecture about it being his job, not the coroner's, to determine probable cause to get a warrant.

"You got Dr. Hellman's report when, last April, March? You could have gone at that point with reasonable suspicion and gotten a search warrant, couldn't you?"

"I could have gone . . ." He stalled, looking at Buzz.

"Do you want to wait for him to object?" I said as I pointed to Buzz.

Buzz did stand, as I predicted, and not-so-subtly tucked his help to the witness into his objection. "We've been through a lot of the legal questions. There is an issue of staleness after that many months have passed. If there's going to be probable cause for issuance of a search warrant, it has to be done within some proximity of time."

The judge, surprisingly, said, "Well, I'm going to let this witness answer that."

Of course, he regurgitated just what Buzz had stated in his objection, about the "staleness" from the length of time that had passed.

"And so," I continued, "you had no information that there was a suggestion that Virginia Ridley had been held for decades, at that point?"

"No," he said, which surprised me. "I will not say that, no."

"Maybe I've gotten a little tripped up here." I did the verbal version of a double take. "You will not say you didn't. That means you think you might have—"

"Yeah," he interrupted.

I finished, "Had some suspicion there?"

"Yes," he answered.

Surprised at the suggestion that had been adopted by the witness to explain why they had let Alvin Ridley boss them around, I finished by physically acting out my next questions.

"A man is suspected of holding his wife for thirty years, and you're testifying today on rebuttal that he said"—and I acted out what an extremely suspicious Alvin would look like, jumping over to the side, keeping my back to an imaginary door—"'Don't go into this room'?"

"I believe my belief is," he started to say, twice, as I was acting out Alvin telling them not to look into one room, "I believe my belief is that she hadn't been seen over thirty years, twenty-five, thirty years, not that she was being held captive."

"Well, whatever"—I was really pouring it on—"you had some suspicions and the guy's in there talking to you, and you're walking around his house, and then he goes"—I jumped again, to block an imaginary door—"'Don't go in here!' Y'all go ahead and look around, but"—I jumped again, to block another imaginary door—"'Don't go in here!' And you're saying that that is not reasonable grounds for suspicion to go get a search warrant to search that room, to search that entire house, to search his suitcases that he's brought to court, to search his cars, to search his van?"

"No." He then pulled another Hellman. "Ladies and gentlemen, it wasn't as dramatic as defense counsel just demonstrated for you, and I've already testified several times—"

I interrupted him. "That's all, Your Honor."

Buzz did not try to rehabilitate anything that just happened. "Your Honor, the state rests in rebuttal at this time."

The evidentiary portion of the trial was finally over.

As I sat down, Alvin leaned in and said, "You're funny! You had me and the jury laughing together. I think they like me!"

"They were laughing?" I asked.

Alvin came back with, "Well, I was laughing. Two of them smiled, though, because I think they really like me."

If they don't, it will destroy him, his spirit, his life, I thought, knowing in my heart that all we needed was to highlight the reasonable doubt.

* * *

I snapped back to the present as the court announced the plans for the lawyers going over the exhibits with Leigh Ann, to see if we could agree and not have to involve the court in what evidence was admitted, and what stayed out. The court announced a twenty-minute break for everyone but me, Buzz, and Leigh Ann. And whatever time was left we could use to prepare for our closing arguments.

I couldn't believe we were here. During the few jury trials where I had been involved, I began to mark on the outside of the file some key moments. Jury selection began a week and a day ago, on January 7, as we awaited the Joe Canada verdict. A week ago this morning, January 8, we started this trial, and I had successfully wrangled Alvin into coming to court every day of the trial, which wasn't easy.

I stopped reminiscing and worked with Buzz and Leigh Ann on which exhibits actually got admitted, and which we both may have tried, but failed, or simply forgotten to tender.

Team Alvin gathered around the man of the hour. They deserved much of the credit for keeping him in the courtroom.

I walked quickly over to my family, and gave my parents each a hug, breathing in slowly my father's breath. He was still good. This was a remarkable thing. I could not remember anything from my youth that he had ever attended, or had shown up and stayed in good shape like this, and for the entire time, to the end.

Buzz and I stood around the pile of admitted and not admitted documentary evidence and went over the court reporter's list of what was admitted and went into the jury room, and what stayed out. After about thirty minutes, the court came to order, and the crowd in the courtroom was addressed.

"Ladies and gentlemen, let me tell you, we're about to begin opening statements and charge. The practice in this circuit is that the doors will be locked during argument and charge . . . so if you don't think you can sit still for at least an hour, maybe two hours, you need to leave now."

Not a soul stirred.

The court directed, "All right, bring the jury in."

As the jury came in, applying the old rules that Joe Randles and

E. Don Towns taught me from their years of court reporting, I could tell either juror Kurt Pulver or Kim Clark-Barnes was going to be the foreperson. This was based on what order they reentered the room, who was opening the door for others, etc. While the jury hadn't even been told to select a foreperson yet, it was an eerily accurate study of human nature and leadership, just watching how the potential foreperson revealed these leadership traits in the group, well before being elected.

"All right. Ladies and gentlemen, we're ready," the judge said to the seated twelve jurors and two alternates. "The state has the opening and concluding argument to the jury in this case. Mr. Franklin?"

"Your Honor," Buzz announced, "we'd make a very brief opening and then reserve the remainder of the time for concluding." So the state would get the first and last word, a right we lost under Georgia rules the moment we put up evidence.

Buzz spent only two minutes in the opening part of his two-part closing, basically stating to the jury that the evidence was all in, and that "death by epilepsy didn't happen." He went so far as to say that "Virginia Ridley's destiny was to be killed by the defendant."

I watched the jurors as they watched him or did not watch him. A lot of lawyers have placed a lot of bets on their gut feelings after closing arguments. I think it's too hard to tell. Some folks just don't like you looking at them while you are trying to convince them about your case. Buzz finished his dramatic prelude.

That left him fifty-eight minutes he could use after my hour. I figured I would need every second of that hour, but I took a deep breath before starting.

I first thanked the jurors for their service and for listening closely to this case. In a move mimicking the prosecutor at the start of the case, I read the indictment to them, all three counts: Count One, Murder, which I described as, basically, murder with malice aforethought; Count Two, Felony Murder, a death that happens during the commission of a felony, with no requirement of intention to kill; and Count Three, Aggravated Assault—the state's suggestion for the underlying felony to prop up the felony murder count. I knew that the court would read the indictment to them during the charge process, but I wanted to do it as well, to give the first spin on it.

I tried to establish eye contact as I spoke to the jurors, not lingering too long on any one of them, at least not long enough to make them feel uncomfortable. I'll dart around in a random manner and try to hold eye contact with at least one of them during the big points.

At the end of reading out the charges, I asked a simple question: Why did the state spend so much time on the issue of whether Virginia Ridley was held captive? There was no charge, nor any count in the indictment regarding false imprisonment, so I argued there was apparently not enough evidence for the state to charge it, yet the allegation loomed ever present throughout this trial. I suggested that the state wanted them to believe Alvin was capable of such a bizarre thing to help push them into accepting that he had just woken up one morning and decided to kill his partner for life, his only true friend in the world.

From my notes, I mentioned, "A man who talks to few, and few talk to him, is suddenly thrust into this?" Multiple questions by the authorities. Old grudge holders finding an opening to take down the most litigious gadfly around. Outright false allegations in news reports, with everyone quoted in the articles denying they said it, once they were put on the stand. The chance of a rush to judgment was extremely high, and it happened. It had been a colossal rush to judgment about Alvin Ridley.

I went through many of the witnesses whom they had all heard in the trial, hopefully helping them interpret what these witnesses had said, if helpful, and trying to discredit what was not helpful. I wanted to start strong, so I started with Dr. Braxton Bryant Wannamaker, the neurologist and epilepsy expert, who just so happened to be an expert on sudden death by epilepsy, or SUDEP.

I candidly admitted that even as the trial was starting, I knew nothing about hypergraphia, Virginia's compulsion to write things down constantly. She had produced a loose-leaf journal of tens of thousands of pages, cardboard, notebook liners and Bibles, spanning three decades. I admitted how dumb luck had played a role in it, with Dr. Wannamaker asking the off-the-cuff question the night before taking the stand, "Is there anything else unusual about this woman?"

I told about my opening up in response to his question, and about how I learned about hypergraphia, an affliction that often affects temporal lobe epilepsy patients. I publicly apologized to Buzz for scheduling him to appear in the middle of the state's case, but reminded everyone that we had heard the first part of Detective Bilbrey's rebuttal out of turn as well.

It was hard to get a good read on these jurors. Some would not establish eye contact. Perhaps it was a personal issue, as if they didn't like my politics, or perhaps they just didn't like how manic I was during the last witness, jumping around out of sheer punch-drunkenness.

I went down the list of witnesses, giving the defense perspective. Mrs. Estella Turner, the nice little Church Lady who came, trying to goad the Ridleys back to church. I reminded the jurors that *all* of the Hickey girls left the Church of the Nazarene after getting married.

That 911 guy, Easton Pyle. In his opening, I reminded them, Buzz failed to tell them the last two words Alvin said to the operator Pyle on the tape, "Please hurry." But they heard it, and they heard Alvin. He just talked that way.

Alvin's sister-in-law Trixie LeCroy testified, I reminded them, that she clearly identified so many of Virginia's handwritten notes as from the hand of her sister, sparing them from another expert witness.

I expressed empathy for this witness. She was very young when Virginia became estranged from her family. I expressed that anyone who was young and not sure what happened between Virginia and their parents would be uncertain and even suspicious. As I spoke of her, I began to look out in the gallery of observers. I wanted the jury to know I was willing to look right at her and say these things. But I already knew that she wasn't there, nor were any recognizable members of the Hickey family.

I hoped that the jury would see that as well.

Trixie was just there long enough to take the stand, and then she left. She was there to honor her parents, to continue to wage the war they had started while searching for beer in the housing authority apartment. She left after her testimony, and, to my knowledge, none of the rest of the family had shown up at all.

"Where is she now?" I continued to look around the courtroom, hoping to acknowledge her, but really to help the jurors who hadn't picked up on the subtlety to realize that she was not there.

"Dr. Fredric Hellman." I announced my next witness to review in closing. "The smartest man in the room!" I mocked. "He's smarter than his medical school instructors. He's smarter than *five* learned treatises."

I quoted the Knight text, a standard in forensic pathology: "'It cannot be emphasized too strongly that the mere finding of any of the non-specific features, such as . . . *petechiae,* without firm circumstantial or preferably physical evidence of mechanical obstruction of respiration, is quite insufficient to warrant a speculative diagnosis of asphyxia. If such collateral evidence is not forthcoming, then the cause of death must be left *undetermined.*"

I emphasized the key words to wake up any of them who weren't listening.

I tried to remind the jury how they could tell that his opinion went against that of the scientific community, and that it was likely influenced by the information that was given to him with the body, and I read them exactly what he was told, as he reported it on Virginia's autopsy:

> By history, the deceased was allegedly kept captive by husband, with no one in the community in Catoosa County having seen the decedent for 15–20 years. Allegedly, the husband of the deceased had kept the deceased locked in a basement, only letting her come upstairs inside the residence when he was home.

I spoke of the local attorney Leslie Waycaster. I acknowledged that while Alvin was pretty astute to win in the Georgia Court of Appeals over the big Dalton firm, filing his "emotions," Alvin never simply substituted the deceased party, his father, properly. The notice was quickly reissued, and the case was finally dismissed, even if Alvin thought that not touching his long-returned Chevrolet van kept open the statute of limitations to that day.

Beloved local pharmacist Harry Gass, father of "the Gass boys" Virginia wrote about, was put up to testify that in all his years as a pharmacist, he had never filled prescriptions for Virginia. I reminded the jury of the years of bottles of medicine, some after 1977 still filled with pills, that were filled by his pharmacy. He was a good man and apologetic for the mistake.

As for Lieutenant Johnny Gass, Alvin had clearly had many encounters with him, dating back to when the young deputy sheriff was a mere boy, along with his brothers, boys running around on the narrow street behind their father's pharmacy and Alvin's business, one of them dubbing him "Alvin the Chipmunk." This name stuck with them when the officer, who also arrested Alvin over eight months after Virginia's death, filled out the "alias" portion of the arrest report. Lieutenant Gass was a good young officer, and he had seemed a reluctant witness, once he was on the stand, to the great frustration of the prosecutor. It was clear, I told the jury, that his earlier report of Alvin's response to questioning had been contorted in Detective Bilbrey's report to sound more incriminating. He testified just as I had hoped.

Chief of Police Charles Land once had a legitimate grudge with Alvin, having failed in seizing his van to cover his expenses for the frivolous lawsuit that Alvin had drawn him into. To the jury, I made it clear that while Alvin's conspiracies and fears were indeed baseless, they were very real to him. But, as I quoted Joseph Heller, in *Catch-22*, "Just because you're paranoid doesn't mean they aren't after you." It was clear that years of being a litigious nuisance had made Alvin lots of enemies.

Detective Dan Bilbrey, who got to bat cleanup for the state, was clearly not expecting having to account for the secret recording he hadn't let his colleagues in on. While I could have regaled the jury with the unfairness of the tactics revealed by the tape—Detective Vic Wells playing "good cop," and even going so far to tell Alvin that he believed him and believed he had nothing to do with his wife's death—I decided to play it straight.

I asked the jury, "If the Catoosa County Sheriff's Office is conflicted as to his guilt, how can you find him guilty?"

Last, as to the state witnesses, I talked about Coroner Vanita Hullander. It was unfortunate that she had gotten so upset in cross-examination, reduced to tears. Whatever encounter they had so many years ago over where she put her garbage cans had obviously really frightened her. But that meant she likely went into this investigation completely biased, and unlike Chief Land, who had recused himself from a death investigation in his city jurisdiction due to his historic troubles with Alvin, she had delivered the body to Atlanta with this now-infamous "history," which was received and included by Dr. Hellman in his autopsy report.

She was a popular and well-liked public servant, and I didn't need to beat her up in closing any more than she had beat herself up by her testimony. She was a good person and a good public servant, in a bad situation influenced by the past.

I sped through the defense witnesses as well, because each one was there for such limited testimony. Benjamin McGaha, aka Salesman Sam, was one of the Band-Aids that I just had to rip off, so I played it straight with the jury. He testified that he had seen Virginia, I reminded the jury, "but who among us can give fine details about someone we only met a couple of times, almost thirty years ago, and with great accuracy?" I humored them with acknowledgment of his competing with me as Alvin's legal advisor.

The other defense "problem," Robert Goldberg, I had to play straight, too. Only at trial did I realize, after witnessing the prosecutor's blistering cross-examination of him, that Goldberg, trained in the Caribbean, was not licensed to do what I had put him up to testify about. He did go to the scene, however, and with me to the crime lab to examine the scant preserved remains of Virginia Ridley. Not even Detective Bilbrey had seen the body, I reminded the jurors, and one didn't have to have a medical license to describe the bed that the state was obsessed over, I reasoned.

* * *

Finally I talked to the jury about our, albeit unexpected, surprise "star" witness, Mr. Alvin Ridley. I fully disclosed to the jury that it was not in my plan for Alvin to testify, but that I was nevertheless very pleased with his testimony. I took the jurors back through the testimony of my client. He obviously suffered from some paranoid condition. As I looked at Alvin, he didn't seem to mind these un-flattering descriptions, nodding at me each time I looked at him, no matter how offensively I described him.

It was hard to fathom that the disastrous Goldberg testimony and Alvin's Jesus-encouraged surprise testimony happened on the same day of the trial. While I had glossed over the former, I was going over Alvin's testimony—Alvin's world—point by point.

A veteran of the U.S. Army, Alvin fell in love with Virginia, I re-minded the jurors, as evidenced by the love letters they had to re-view in the jury room. I led them through the marriage ceremony, attended by the Hickey family, and then the moment the honey-moon was over—when Virginia's religious parents began searching for beer in the newlyweds' public housing apartment. That, and the advances of an exterminator who barged in on Virginia in the bath, drove the couple to leave the housing projects whenever they feared such visits would recur. This led, I reminded the jurors, to the two articles (PARENTS SEEK MARRIED DAUGHTER) that appeared in the local papers in 1968 and 1969.

This led to the first act of Alvin's fabled hyper-litigiousness, the housing authority eviction trial, where the judge ordered Virginia into the court. On September 15, 1970, "right here, in this room, and back there next to the jury room," I reminded them. There, in front of her parents and Alvin's father, she told the judge some-thing that caused the search for Virginia to stop, for a while.

Alvin cared for Virginia as best as he could, holding her during seizures so she would not bite or "swallow" her tongue, getting her to the doctor, picking up her medicine. All while opening and op-erating his own Zenith TV sales and repair franchise in the 1970s, with the help of his father.

I pointed to the doctor's notes and evidence that Virginia went for treatment, until her apparent agoraphobia caused her to withdraw from even that. Alvin continued, however, getting her medicine, the prescription for the antiseizure medications being later put into his name, even a few months after God told her to stop taking the meds in 1977, as she wrote in her Bible.

I talked about the fateful early 1980s car accident between Alvin's father in the business truck and the Polk Brothers Concrete truck. I conceded that this was considered a minor accident, by all accounts—except by Alvin Ridley and his mother—whose litigation went on for years.

This, of course, ultimately resulted in Chief Land's counterclaim and temporary seizure of Alvin's Chevy van. I conceded that this was the moment that Ridley's Zenith went under, but also suggested to the jury that perhaps the technology transformation from picture tubes to solid-state circuitry played a big role in that as well.

I reminded the jury that Alvin was very literal in his thinking, and that I had forgotten that myself a few times, but that he did have deep and abiding love for Virginia, his wife of thirty-one years, and perhaps his only true friend in the world. This literal way of thinking led to the seemingly cold answer when I asked him about what he had lost, and that he replied "funeral bill." I wanted to get ahead of Buzz on this, as I knew he would bring it up.

I explained that Alvin and Virginia alternately lived in his parents' home, and in his business building right across and down the street from the courthouse, in the years when the Hickeys were "searching" for Virginia.

I got a few smiles when I told the jury about Alvin's feuds with a group of children, the Gass boys, and how I wasn't expecting Alvin to describe specific incidents. The fact that one grew up to be his arresting officer, while his father also testified, and that there was an old feud with the new coroner. It was just how things were in a small town where everyone knows everyone else.

I went through the events of the morning when he found his wife facedown in the bed, his attempts at "Alvin CPR"—not advisable, but sincere, and the cascade of suspicion that fell upon him the moment the coroner walked into his house.

I told about Virginia's writings, and how he didn't trust me with them. I didn't mention the roaches, as they were obvious with all the stomping I had been doing, and the word was all around the courthouse about them.

I spoke about Alvin talking to the authorities, and trusting them, even more than he did his own lawyer for months.

I reminded them that I had let Alvin tell his story, once he insisted on telling it, but that they had also heard his fears and Virginia's fears. While she wrote about all that was going on with Alvin, she always seemed so very supportive of him, praying to God and appealing to the U.S. Congress, and even to presidents.

She proposed a script for the *Unsolved Mysteries* television series, about her father-in-law's accident. She wrote about *The Waltons* television series, and seemed to have been a fan of TV's Ron Howard, the child star who grew up to be a director and producer.

She wrote poetry and about her love for her husband, and while I reminded the jury that she wrote about her views on marriage, they were most definitely Old Testament views, not unlike those of the family she was born into. On the other hand, Alvin didn't seem to be affiliated with any one denomination or sect. He went to wherever he was welcome, until he had drained them of their goodwill and their donations, usually to "fix Mama's roof," which he never really got around to fixing.

On cross-examination, I reminded the jury, the state didn't gain much ground with Alvin. Buzz struggled, as I had for months, in dealing with Alvin's thought process in gaining his cooperation, and Buzz struggled in getting him to answer questions the way that he wanted. The prosecutor harped on Alvin's show of emotions at trial, and the lack of said emotions on the morning of his wife's death. The district attorney completely missed the realization that some people around here had beds in their living room, the warmest part of the house, near the stove. He also was discombobulated by the fact that Alvin slept in his clothes, with his pocket change always on the ready.

I summed up my closing argument, reminding the jury of what was being asked of them, hoping they felt as I did that they deserved the "highest and best evidence" before they should be asked to convict a person of any offense. Poor photo quality, mishandled personal property, the creation of postmortem artifact, all were examples of how the state had failed in providing the quality of evidence they should demand before convicting a citizen.

I thanked them for their attention, then sat down next to Alvin. He stared ahead and Buzz stood to deliver his remaining fifty-eight minutes, the last words the jury would hear before getting the charge of law from the court. Alvin's pocket change started jingling again, until I put my hand on his arm. Then all was quiet as my colleague started asking the jury to convict my client of all charges.

22

I was watching the clock, as I wasn't going to yield one extra minute to the prosecutor. He spent his first ten minutes, as I had, with his strongest suit. For me, it had been Dr. Braxton Bryant Wannamaker. For Buzz, it was the disaster of Dr. Robert Goldberg, his greatest glory in this trial being his cross-examination, a figurative evisceration of the expert witness for the defense.

I was glad Goldberg wasn't here to hear this. The district attorney tore into him, calling him "a hired gun" for the defense. My mind went to the moment I was between an armed Goldberg and an armed Alvin as we viewed Alvin's "scene" near his bed. Buzz went through his "greatest hits" on Goldberg in that cross-examination.

He spent three minutes trying to discredit Dr. Wannamaker for not being a forensic pathologist, but I was confident he would get nowhere attacking one of the nation's premier neurologists and experts on epilepsy, particularly SUDEP. The lowest of lows with Goldberg's cross didn't overcome the quality of Wannamaker's testimony—and he had solved the final puzzle, the mystery of Virginia's compulsive writing.

Buzz rambled on, then tried to distinguish the issue of eye petechiae from other petechiae.

I was frantically taking notes on the time the prosecutor spent on each subject. I don't know exactly why, unless he said something improper, and I wanted the reference for appeal.

I scribbled on the far right of my legal pad, for Alvin to read, elbowing him to look at what I wrote: *He's losing them right _now_.* Alvin read it, but didn't react.

I stopped noting the times the prosecutor was using on each issue he discussed around the halfway point of Buzz's remaining time.

He began to cite a nonfiction self-help book *The Gift of Fear: Survival Signals That Protect Us from Violence* by Gavin de Becker. He began to describe, in great detail, violence from other cases found in the book.

I stood and interrupted his closing, a risky thing some jurors could consider rude. "Your Honor, under *Bell* versus *State,* the district attorney is making an improper argument to the jury and injecting extrinsic and unrelated evidence about a violent event—in terms of whatever he is talking about. And I ask the court to instruct him not to make such an improper argument."

The judge, obviously listening, commented, "Mr. de Becker's book is not in evidence."

The prosecutor defended its use, saying, "Judge, it's not about that, it's about how people judge things and how they react to things."

Judge Van Pelt said, "Well, he can certainly make that argument."

"Your Honor," I argued, "he's describing a case with violent evidence that is totally unrelated to this case, and the *Bell* case is right on it!"

I had cited a case that I knew the court had read, *Bell,* a 1994 Georgia Supreme Court case where a prosecutor in Fulton County had in closing made references to violent acts that happened in unrelated cases. The appellate court reversed the conviction, which was something that Judge Van Pelt did not want to happen here.

The judge looked a bit uncomfortable, but he knew if he didn't corral the district attorney's closing, I would have a significant ground on appeal, if Alvin was convicted.

"Sustained" was all that was said. Buzz was stopped from quoting from the book.

Buzz shifted his closing argument to the well-worn subjects of rigor mortis, livor mortis, and Dr. Hellman's unique take on pete-chiae.

"There was no testimony at all that she had a seizure" was a statement made in closing that I took great exception to—but I couldn't do anything about it. Alvin had called it a "spell," but it should be clear enough that in terms of the woman who had severe epilepsy since age nine, "spell" meant seizure.

Buzz's theme evolved to "The World According to Alvin Ridley," and how he had interpreted family problems, obsessed over various things, and had no money for medicine and doctors, no money for anything. It was a reference to the same self-imposed poverty that I had noted in Alvin for years, an unexplained suffering that continued, even after I had gotten him on Social Security disability.

"Alvin the Liar" was the next broad theme cited by the prosecutor, referencing all the times, he said, Alvin had not told the truth.

He finished by going over the charges, as I had, and as the court was about to do in its charge of the law to the jury. He focused on the second count, felony murder, which, he emphasized, did not require an intent to murder. That worried me.

As Buzz wrapped up, it suddenly fell upon me that, for all intents and purposes, the trial was over. There was nothing more either lawyer could add, or react to. Any exceptions to the charge of the court would be discussed out of the presence of the jury, and preserved for appeal.

I put my hand on Alvin's shoulder. He had fallen into a deep, for lack of a better description, funk. He was quiet, not talking much, and obviously worried. The court announced our lunch break, but neither of us had an appetite. Lori had some things to keep my blood sugar from plummeting, as it was apt to do if I didn't eat.

Just before we reconvened, Alison came up and told me that her best friend, Beverly Edge, the court's law clerk, was going into labor. I'd been prepared for it, and I knew the emotions that were in her heart because we'd been trying now for almost eight months to get pregnant. That is, as much as anyone can try to have a baby while representing Alvin Ridley. I knew Alvin did not kill his wife, but he was guilty as hell of killing our libido at home. I either came home smelling like him or I came home talking about him. I was obsessed, and my obsessive nature had me hyper-focused on the trial. "I promise, we are getting out of town after all this," I reminded her. She said she was going to stay as long as she could before going to the hospital, as Beverly was just reporting early labor pains.

The jury was brought back in, now to listen to the long instruction and charge of the law from the court, which they would apply to the facts as they heard and saw, and in this case probably smelled, as defendant's exhibit 97, collective, Alvin's pillows, still reeked from the garbage bag.

"Good afternoon," the judge addressed the jury, and then the audience. "Ladies and gentlemen, those of you in the audience, the doors are about to be locked again for approximately thirty minutes while I instruct the jury. If you don't think you can sit still or be quiet for thirty minutes, you need to leave now."

Alvin began to jingle his change again, until I touched his arm. I turned to see that Alison stayed in the courtroom.

"All right," he said as he focused on the twelve jurors and two alternates. "Ladies and gentlemen, you are considering the case of the *State of Georgia* versus *Alvin Eugene Ridley, Case Number 98-CR-00836*." The court did not read the entire indictment to them, but did read each count.

The court went on the delicate path of instructing a jury in a criminal trial. Deviation from the tried-and-true language could cause an appeal, and a reversal of a hard-fought conviction. Judge Van Pelt had been a prosecutor for most of his career, so he was very careful.

The state's burden of proof was another critical message I hoped all the jurors were absorbing. "There is no burden of proof upon the defendant whatsoever, and the burden never shifts to the defendant to prove innocence when a defense is raised by the evidence. The burden is on the state to negate or disprove it beyond a reasonable doubt."

I was thinking how in this case, the defense submitted almost three times the physical evidence than the state did, mostly from Virginia's thirty-year journal.

The judge continued: "A reasonable doubt means just what it says. It is the doubt of a fair-minded, impartial juror, honestly seeking the truth. It is a doubt based on common sense and reason. It does not mean a vague or arbitrary doubt, but it is a doubt for which a reason can be given arising from a consideration of the evidence, a lack of evidence, a conflict in the evidence, or any combination of these."

Then this part: "If after giving consideration to all the facts and circumstances of the case, your minds are wavering, unsettled, or unsatisfied, then that is a doubt of the law and you should acquit the defendant, but if that doubt does not exist in your minds as to the guilt of the accused, then you would be authorized to convict the defendant. If the state fails to prove the defendant's guilt beyond a reasonable doubt, it would be your duty to acquit the defendant."

I always was fascinated by the subtlety of this instruction. Words like "should acquit" if minds are "unsettled," and "authorized to convict," if they are not. I liked these words. And especially the "duty to acquit" part. There is never a duty to *convict*. I hoped the jury caught that.

The court instructed on the credibility or believability of witnesses. I thought we were in good shape in that department, other than the disaster of Goldberg.

The charge to the jury ended sometime around two o'clock in the afternoon. I noted it on the outside of the original case file. Now all there was to do was wait.

23

Waiting with a client for a jury to come back is one of the strangest times in life. Normal conversation among people very often involves their plans for the near and the distant future. From what you are going to eat tonight, what you are going to work on next, where you want to get out of town to escape. In the middle of these conversations, invariably, you realize that your client's next meal may be at the county jail, and for the rest of his life, the State of Georgia may be feeding him. What would happen to his house, his cats, Kitty and Meowy? His beloved but untouched Chevy van?

Alvin was very quiet. Not talkative at all. He didn't respond to my reliable team that kept him so well distracted during breaks. He was affected by knowing his fate was being determined in the jury room. While I really wasn't worried anymore about him running away, I could understand better now the pressures that made him think that there was no hope for him in this town, in this county.

"Let's go over here, Alvin," I said as we left the women from the office and went to the window on the defense side of the courtroom, which looked down on the front porch and lawn of the courthouse.

"You know, Alvin, I was out there in 1984 when you gave your speech at the candidate rally, when you were running for sheriff," I told him.

"You were?" he said. At least I had him talking now, but I noticed that his hands were shaking.

"Yes, I was there," I went on, "and I think you gave the best talk of all of them!" I reminded him of his ingenious playing of the national anthem, which goaded all, naysayers and hecklers included, to stand up for the first two minutes of his allotted time. He didn't say anything back, totally distracted by his fate, which was being determined a few yards away in the jury room.

I stood there, shoulder to shoulder, an arm around his back to his opposite shoulder. "Alvin," I asked, "can we pray?"

He dutifully bowed his head, his hands clasped in front of him. Almost every week for several months, I had employed "prayer" in my repertoire of Alvin—control since the first day that my agonizing "Oh, Lord!" exclamation at the start of one of his tirades had shut him up. As he thought I was starting a prayer, I ran with it. But this time, I really wanted to pray. I hoped I had done everything I could have done for him, but I wasn't that confident. I had been messing around in politics and the legislature, and I hadn't spent a great deal of time in the courtroom.

"God, we thank you," I began, "for the witnesses that came out for Alvin, and for the courtroom still full of people who are here to support him." Alvin turned around quickly, peeping to verify that they were all still there, then swung around to his prayer mode again, eyes shut tight. "Lord, take care of Alvin Ridley, whatever your plans for him," I prayed. "We don't know what your plans are for him, but we know that he is one of your children, God, and that you will look out for him wherever he may go." I added, "God, forgive his accusers, too," something I added to shield anyone from being "given up to the Lord" in the last minutes.

I stood there, just holding on to Alvin's shoulder. There was a time that I would recoil at the idea of touching him, of shaking his hand even. This was just over a year ago, when he would only meet me at the same intersection of street and sidewalk, when his calls in the middle of the night were screams about the injustices he faced. I continued my own prayer silently.

I motioned for the team to come and surround him, and this time, Alison joined the women from the office in comforting Alvin, while I walked back to those of my family members who were still sitting in the courtroom.

I hugged my father and mother and sat with them for a minute. I wondered if I could even remember as a boy ever being with my father this late in the afternoon when he wasn't three sheets to the wind. Today he was sober. And I would take that, as they say, one day at a time.

I went back to Alvin when there was some activity with the bailiffs. Was it a verdict? We sat down, and the court notified us, "They have a question."

It was 3:40 p.m., and they had been deliberating just over an hour.

The jury was brought in. It seemed obvious that Kurt Pulver was acting as foreperson, but you could see with her position and body language that Kimberly Clark-Barnes was also assuming a leadership position with the jury. It was just a natural confidence that they both possessed and carried themselves with—the type that will get you elected as foreperson.

Joe Randles would be proud. I thought of him in the hospital. *I need to go see him,* I thought.

The "question" was more of a request. The jury wanted to know if they could hear the recording again of Alvin's interview. The court told them no, they could not hear it again, and had to rely on their memories alone; and no, they could not have the transcripts of those tapes, either.

The jury filed back out to continue deliberations.

Alvin and I again found ourselves at the window. I shared with him that on that front porch down below us, I had not only watched him campaign, but I had campaigned there as well, just four years later and every two years since, until 1996.

"We both campaigned there," he said, adding his signature observation, "What do you think about that?" Then the gravity of the moment made him silent again.

We stood there, together, not saying much, for twenty more minutes.

Then the activity again at the side door. Next we got the informal word, the jury had a verdict.

"All right," the judge announced. "Ladies and gentlemen, I understand from the bailiffs that the jury has a verdict. I don't know what it is. I want to make it clear to everyone that I don't want any outbursts, verbal or otherwise, from anyone. And I particularly don't want anyone doing anything to one of the jurors while they are here in the courthouse, or complaining or talking to them in what could even be remotely conceived to be a threatening manner because of their verdict, whatever it is. If anyone thinks that they can't keep quiet and be calm while the verdict is being published, then I need you to leave now."

No one stirred.

"All right," the judge instructed. "Bring the jury in."

It was 4:10 p.m. The jury filed in. I tried to read their faces, but I could not read anything into any of the faces before us. By tradition, the Clerk of Superior Court, or one of his deputy clerks, takes the verdict form from the jury foreperson, and hands it to the judge for review. If the form was properly and clearly filled out, no matter what the verdict, the judge would hand it back to the clerk for "publication" or public announcement.

Norman Stone, the "Voice of God," was on duty. This was a big case, and he was an elected official in his own right, but this was also the verdict of Alvin Ridley, who for years had frustrated Norman to no end; the clerk having outright accused Alvin of stealing a document from the court file fifteen years ago. Alvin flinched when he saw that Norman was going to touch the verdict.

"Calm down," I whispered. "He's a good man and will play by the rules."

"All right," the judge announced. "Let court come to order. Ladies and gentlemen of the jury, I understand from the bailiff that you've reached a verdict, is that correct?"

Kurt Pulver, the foreperson, said, "That's correct."

"Have you reached verdicts in all three counts?"

"Yes, sir," the foreperson answered.

"And have they all been expressed in writing on each count?"

"Yes, sir."

"Have you dated it and signed it as foreperson?"

"Yes, sir."

This is excruciating, I thought.

"Okay," the judge instructed. "If you will give it to Mr. Stone, he'll hand it to me and let me review it, and then I'll have it published."

Norman, using his one arm, walked with his one good leg and one prosthetic over to the bench, handing the verdict form to the judge. The judge reviewed it, poker-faced. What was obviously seconds seemed like several long, drawn-out minutes.

"I'll have the clerk, Mr. Stone, publish the verdicts."

Norman took the paper from the judge, then positioned himself to project his booming baritone voice, utilized every Sunday morning and Wednesday night in his church, in what every lawyer described as the most fearsome presentation of verdicts in the world.

"In the Superior Court for the County of Catoosa, State of Georgia . . ." he began, his voice booming and clear to probably everyone in the building. "*Criminal Action Number 98-CR-00836,* the *State of Georgia* versus *Alvin Eugene Ridley* . . ."

Alvin and I were standing at our table, while Buzz and Detective Bilbrey stood at theirs.

"Verdict. 'We, the jury, after due deliberation unanimously find the defendant . . .' "

Jesus, please . . .

" 'Count One, not guilty.' "

" 'Count Two, not guilty.' "

" 'Count Three, not guilty.' "

" 'This fifteenth day of January, 1999, signed Kurt A. Pulver, Foreperson.' "

Against the admonition of the court, the defense side of the courtroom erupted in emotion. I was still squeezing Alvin, then turned him toward me.

"You won, Alvin! Not guilty."

Real tears of relief and joy came flowing from his eyes. He fell into his chair.

The judge spoke. "Any question as to the form of the verdict?"

Buzz announced, "Not on behalf of the state."

"No, sir!" I announced.

The judge thanked the jurors, excused them, then turned to Alvin. "Mr. Ridley, the jury having found you not guilty in this case, you are hereby discharged."

At this point, Alvin started sobbing again, totally washed in relief.

For several minutes, there was an outpouring of joy, and I can say, without contradiction, that more genuine affection was shown to Alvin Ridley by more people than he probably had ever experienced in his entire life.

We gathered up the pillows, forever marked "D-79, collective" in the black garbage bag they came in, and stuffed the other exhibits into either the bag or the suitcases. At some point, my father approached Alvin, whispered something in his ear, and then gave him a big hug. I never knew what was said between them.

When I hugged my father, he said, "I'm so proud of you, son." And for some strange reason, for the first time in my life, I felt I had earned it. My eyes became watery. A line of people formed along the bar to congratulate both attorney and client.

Alison quickly excused herself to go attend the birth of the first child of our friends Beverly and Chris Edge. That left me with Alvin to celebrate this great victory.

Alvin and I walked outside the front door and stood on that front porch facing Nashville Street while his crowd—much more enthusiastic for him than the one at the All Candidate Rally in 1984—waited for us. This porch, those steps, so much had happened there in my life. The television cameras were rolling, and I felt that I needed to say something on his behalf, to get things started.

"Ladies and gentlemen, I give you Alvin Ridley, a free man and an innocent man," I said, totally off the cuff, "and he wants to immediately begin to rehabilitate his name," I added optimistically.

We gave some awkward interviews, Alvin's first since his wife's death. "I've always been innocent, I loved my wife. I want to say God bless everybody that supported me." A Chattanooga television reporter started grilling him about what appeared to some as a somewhat-recent embrace of religion, after talking to the Buckley family, Alvin's latest church supporters. The reporter, microphone in Alvin's face, asked, "I'm hearing that you are not really a regular churchgoer."

I felt the need to defend him still, injecting, "There's a difference in going to church, and studying . . . you know—"

Alvin interrupted me, "I go to church regularly." I jumped back in, waving my hand toward the Buckley family, who had come from Alvin's latest church in Chatsworth. "Here are some of Alvin's church family . . ."

The reporter continued, "I know, that's why I say that, because I talked with them beforehand, and this is fairly recently that you've embraced the Lord, is it not?"

Alvin, characteristically, said, "Right."

The reporter followed, "The last two years, three years?"

Alvin said, "The last six months." Of course, he found the Lord again right after his indictment and arrest.

Why am I still defending him? I thought.

When the reporters were finished, and the last supporters started moving away, I turned to Alvin. "Of course, I'll take you home," I said, "but, Alvin, we won! Alison is away with her friend who's having a baby. This is the biggest win I've ever had, and I'd like to go celebrate! Come on, Alvin, I'll take you out for a steak anywhere you want to go in Chattanooga!"

He looked at me, then said, "How about Hardee's?"

"Hardee's? We have that here in Ringgold. Are you sure you don't want to go get a nice steak or anything you want in Chattanooga?"

"Hardee's is fine," he said.

I was amped up. Alvin was, well, Alvin. His emotion was flat. As we got into the Jeep, I was trying to have him fully realize what this victory meant for him. "Alvin, you thought you couldn't get a fair trial here in Ringgold, and today twelve jurors just said you're innocent!"

I continued, "What I mean, Alvin, is that not everyone is out to get you, like you think. I think you should start opening up more to people, I mean, start talking first and not just staring at them, waiting for them to talk first, do you understand?"

"Yeah" was all he said, but I soon learned that he was, unfortunately, listening.

We walked to the back of the line of the one-register fast-food restaurant. Before I could ask him what he wanted, Alvin tapped the shoulder of the woman in front of us. She turned around, startled.

"Hey," Alvin said, "I'm that feller they said kilt his wife, but I didn't kill my wife, and the jury just said that I didn't kill my wife!" Then he did his characteristic spring back, hands on hips, as if saying, *What do you think of that?*

The woman turned and fled the establishment.

"Okay, Alvin," I said, "that was a good start. Just don't sneak up on 'em like that next time." I added, "And don't lead with that you were accused of murder."

We sat at Hardee's and enjoyed our meal, and then I took Alvin Ridley, a free man and an innocent man, home.

EPILOGUE

*M*uch has changed, of course, in the quarter century that has passed since the events of this book took place. Catoosa County's population has continued to explode. Some involved in the case have endured in their same roles, some have moved on to other things, and some are no longer with us. If I learned anything from this experience, it is that we all prejudge, and we all make mistakes. This case made me realize how many innocent—but misunderstood—people probably end up in our prisons.

Joe Randles, the old-school court reporter who taught me much about trying cases, passed away the day after the verdict. While Leigh Ann McBryar did an excellent job covering for Joe in Alvin's trial, I still miss Joe's signals, subtle and otherwise, of when to shut up and sit down in court.

With one passing in our close-knit legal community, we gained another. After going into labor during my closing argument, Beverly Edge, our superior court's law clerk, and Alison's best friend, gave birth to a son, Henley. Alison left the celebration of our victory to attend the birth, joyous for her friend.

My father, McCracken King Poston Sr., had ten great years of sobriety after attending Alvin's trial, until the onset of stroke-like conditions hospitalized him in 2009. A subsequent hospitalization, in the place where he was first inducted into the military in Fort

Oglethorpe, revealed a brain tumor. He passed after just a few days, surrounded by all six of his children and his wife of nearly seventy years. His last years, sober, were a gift.

Barbara Sumners Poston, my mother, lived another ten years, alone, in Graysville, loved and cherished by her children, grand-children, great-grandchildren, and so many others in her orbit. She passed just before her ninety-seventh birthday; in her last hours, also surrounded by my five sisters and me.

At this writing, as with every Monday morning for many, many years now, I will get a phone call from Alvin Ridley, to plan our weekly lunch outing. Now at eighty-one years of age, he cried at the passing of both my parents as if they were his own. Had it not been for that turkey plate they asked me to take to him on Thanksgiving, 1998, this story might have turned out differently.

In 2021, Kimberly Clark-Barnes, the journalist who served on the jury, told a podcast creator that she suspected that Alvin was on the autism spectrum. Kimberly had long ago left newspaper work and had become a nurse in Alaska. She had thought of the case for many years, and her suggestion set off a thousand realizations as I thought back over the difficult times that I had with my former client. I took Alvin to Atlanta to a leading expert on autism for testing.

In the late 1990s, it seemed that no one was talking about autism in adults. His 1998 psychiatric evaluation had suggested only a "paranoid condition." Alvin asked me to sit in on the first part of the 2021 autism testing. The doctor asked him to describe how a couple of sentences made him feel. The sentence "He has gotten under your skin" made him shiver because he took things so liter-ally. "He wears his heart on his sleeve" caused an excited Alvin to interject, "I know that one—he has an artificial heart!" While I had often joked that I wore my pancreas in my right front pocket, I knew that Kimberly was onto something. Sure enough, Alvin's eval-uation and testing revealed that he was very much on the autistic spectrum, and had been his whole life.

This information explained everything. His childhood difficul-ties, and particularly his being taunted and bullied by the other boys at school, while never acceptable, are better understood when considering this was rural Northwest Georgia in the 1950s. His aversion to bathing was because he did not like the sensation of water on his skin. His preternatural ability with picture tube technology and television repair is a regional legend, no doubt because of a mind that, in some respects, is not as limited or clouded as my own neurotypical one. The transactional nature of everything to him, the grudge holding and suspiciousness, all of this could now be explained. With Alvin's permission, I let the community know about his diagnosis, and people in town have opened their hearts and minds to him more.

A succession of legal secretaries after Lori moved on to other employment continued to assist me in helping Alvin over the years, but none more than my current secretary, Carlene Renner Rogers.

Elizabeth Cheek grew up, went off to school, and now works with autistic children in Murphy, North Carolina. Benita Jay Johnson and Misty Walker remained in the community, raising their families.

J. Michael Giglio, R. Kevin Silvey, and I bought an office building together on Nashville Street, the main drag, across the street from the Catoosa County Courthouse, and we continued to run our solo law practices. The county razed our old, converted ranch house with the cheap plastic bubble letters spelling out our names, and now it serves as a much-needed parking lot.

Buzz Franklin switched parties, like pretty much everyone else around here, and finished his distinguished career as district attorney, retiring in 2020. Alvin told me that he long ago forgave Buzz for prosecuting him, as "he was just doing his job."

Vanita Hullander became an excellent coroner for Catoosa County, with a particular focus on preventing drug overdoses, and served for many years in that role until her successful run for the county commission. Alvin, who got registered again, supported her in her race and said he voted for her, also long forgiving her role in the case, and he has asked forgiveness from her for going after her on that day long ago with a broomstick.

Johnny Gass left the Catoosa County Sheriff's Office to run for the chief magistrate judge of Catoosa County, where he has served with distinction for several terms. Again, Alvin long forgave and continued to support Judge Gass, who was just a boy when the majority of his encounters with Alvin took place. Alvin still likes to tell how Johnny's father, pharmacist Harry Gass, saved his life, *"Twiced!"* Transactional as he is, once someone shows kindness toward Alvin Ridley, they merit his "They like me!" status, and, in turn, Alvin likes them. Harry Gass passed away, and Alvin cried.

Dan Bilbrey left the Catoosa sheriff's department to become the chief of police of Ringgold after the retirement of Chief Charles Land. There he served with distinction until internal city politics forced him to retire. I vigorously represented him in his efforts to hang on to his job as chief. He was a credit to law enforcement.

Patricia "Trixie" LeCroy, Alvin's sister-in-law, bravely fought a long battle with cancer, passing on Thanksgiving Day, 2022. While her parents were listed as having predeceased her, there was no mention of her sister Virginia in her obituary. Alvin cried, absorbing and projecting the emotion of the Hickey family's loss.

Dr. Braxton Bryant Wannamaker retired and remained near Orangeburg, South Carolina. I credit him for saving Alvin Ridley.

Superior Court Clerk Norman L. Stone, the "Voice of God", passed away in 2011. I will always miss his voice while announcing verdicts. Dr. Fredric Hellman left the Georgia crime lab to take the position of chief medical examiner for Delaware County, Pennsylvania. In his twenty-one years there, he served with excellence as chief medical examiner of the September 11, 2001, tragedy involving United Airlines Flight 93 in Shanksville, Pennsylvania. He also distinguished himself during the COVID pandemic. He recently retired and returned to Georgia.

My views on Dr. Robert Goldberg, Alvin's favorite *f-o-r-e-n-s-i-c p-a-t-h-o-l-o-g-i-s-t,* have softened over the years. He was certainly enthusiastic and willing to be anything for the case, in any discipline that we needed. Any expertise at all! While a juror in the case wrote to me her opinion that putting him up was the only mistake I made in Alvin's trial, Alvin is more generous and wishes him well. And so do I. The last thing I saw about him, he was quoted in a tabloid where he was opining about the late Princess Diana's autopsy. I guess that this was likely another referral from the Vidocq Society.

Bobby Lee Cook passed at the age of 94 at his home in Cloudland, Georgia. He died as he was preparing for a murder trial.

Judge Ralph L.Van Pelt Jr. recently retired, after over two terms as district attorney and over four terms on the bench. He returned to private practice.

My first ex-wife, Reva, became a very successful marketing executive in Chicago, where she remarried and later moved to Los Angeles. When I learned of the birth of her daughter, Erica, it made me feel at peace that our six years together had not derailed her life, and maybe because of the timing of things, it might have just put her in the right place, at the right time, for her daughter.

Alison and I did become parents, but not in the way we expected. After two failed rounds of IVF attempts—and I am now so thankful that they failed—in the year 2000, we became parents in two regions in the Republic of Kazakhstan, just a few weeks apart, to our daughter, Alina, and our son Mac. Six years later, we all returned to Kazakhstan to bring our son Cal into the family. Being dad to these three children gave me a wonderful way to work out my childhood demons, in part by obsessively going to absolutely every possible school performance and sporting event they ever had—to the point where I have been instructed by all three to keep my enthusiasm in check. They have taught me much about the influence of nurturing over nature. I am told that each of them "inherited" a lot of my expressions and my personality. They have brought joy into my life, and they continue to reward me as they make their own ways in life.

My marriage with Alison did not last. I know now that a major contributing factor was my struggle with childhood issues that led to my obsessive need to micromanage—an obsession to make sure everything is always smooth and even-keeled—along with a continued struggle maintaining close personal relationships. Six years after our divorce, Alison became a mother again, to Graeme, a bright and beautiful son. Graeme's very presence put everything in perspective for me. And since he is my three children's little brother, I feel that I truly gained another son.

In going through two divorces, I learned a lot about myself and about the impact that alcoholism had on my childhood. My father was, even in the throes of alcoholism, the sweetest and most loving father one could ever want. This might have made things even worse because I could never find any room for hatred in my heart. Instead, as a child, I looked inward and always tried to keep the waters calm while somehow blaming myself for his need to drink. In writing this book, I had to explore the depths of that experience. A photo of my father reading every word of the Chattanooga newspaper, as he did every morning, the one time of day when he was consistently sober and at his best, made me realize what likely has fueled my reputation as a lawyer who always took on big, newsworthy cases. Perhaps, subliminally, it was to be seen by him, to make him see me, and be proud.

After the trial, I asked Alvin what had made him stalk me on the street until I agreed to help him. In response, he brought in a VHS tape, one with a label that bore signs of use and reuse. My name was on the paper residue of the torn-off label, written in the now-familiar hand of his late wife. While he would not let me keep it, he let me play it once with the VHS player in my office. It was a grainy, fuzzy recording of the only televised debate in my congressional race. "She liked you," Alvin offered, before taking it away.

The twentieth anniversary of Virginia's death landed on the date of one of our weekly lunches. We took some flowers and visited the grave. For the first time, I saw what Alvin had told the tombstone company to put on his stone. Where I had suggested he put something like, "An Innocent Man," Alvin instructed them to put on his tombstone just how he wanted to be remembered: TV REPAIRMAN.

In hindsight, it's easy to see how Alvin's autism went undiagnosed in the late 1990s. The case was just five years after autism was first recognized as not one, but a spectrum of conditions. However, a crisis of undiagnosed or misdiagnosed developmental disorders in the criminal justice system continues to date. Better funding for psychological evaluations with a broader scope of testing is critical, and needed, for the ends of justice. An untold number of undiagnosed adults remain in our world and in the criminal justice system.

Today, Alvin Ridley seems to enjoy his best life, basking in the warmth of a more understanding community. Last year, he started threatening to live to the age of 110 so that we will have thirty more years of having lunch together every week. And while it is something I never believed I would say, that would be a wonderful thing.

ACKNOWLEDGMENTS

The night of January 15, 1999, I first thought that what I had just experienced in representing Alvin Ridley would make a good book. But neither I nor the story was ready. Yet, this story wanted to be told, and I tried to tell it, as I then understood it, through several featured national platforms. Others have tried to tell the story, too, with and without our blessing.

It wasn't until I met Bonnie Hearn Hill, the first editor and mentor who encouraged me to include *my* story, and not just Alvin's, that it got traction. From the start, Bonnie *got* the story, and she helped me develop a proposal and put together a curated list of agents to pitch it to. And that is how I found Linda Konner, my agent. Thanks to Linda's brilliant work, we soon got the attention of Michaela Hamilton, the talented editor-in-chief for Citadel Press at Kensington Publishing. Before long, we were in business. Without the combination of these three women, along with Robin Cook, Stephanie C. Finnegan and Shannon Plackis, and the graphic designers, interns, publicists, and assistants at Kensington, this book would not exist. And my deep thanks go to the early readers who gave input and endorsements. A special thanks goes to Ann Pryor, Deborah Kohan, Penny Sansevieri, Amy Cornell, and Natasha Walstra. It truly takes a village to educate an author and put out a book.

The next five important women I want to thank are my big sisters: Mary Poston Tanner, Carolyn Poston Towns, Jan Poston Poole, Katie Poston Stuckey, and Nancy Poston. Every man should have sisters, *plural*. I love these five women more than they will ever know. They have all helped guide me in life, by lesson and example, and helped me interpret an often-confusing childhood provided by loving and very well-meaning, yet beautifully flawed, parents. And what parents they were, McCracken King Poston Sr. and Barbara Sumners Poston. Under less-than-ideal conditions, they both shone brightly at just the times and in just the ways they needed to.

To my children, Alina, Mac, Cal . . . and Graeme, who have experienced my parenting flaws, and who have endured hearing this story, ad nauseam, their whole lives, I love you. You each gave me a new purpose in life.

Learning from me that Kazakhstan was the original home of apples, Alvin brought infants Alina, Mac, and later Cal apples from the flea market as gifts when they first came to America, even though, between them, they didn't have a single tooth in their heads. Thank you, my children, for the kindness and understanding you've always shown my neurodiverse friend.

Thanks to professional photographers Tommy Eason, Phil Farmer, Alex McMahan, John Rawlston, and Robin Rudd for help in locating the troves of trial photos they took that are used in this book, as well as to my old friend James Curtis Barger for my author photograph. Thanks to the other photograph contributors as well, as credited in this book, and to Tracy Knauss, for helping me get it all together for the publisher. Also, thanks to the folks at the University of Tennessee at Chattanooga Library, the Chattanooga-Hamilton County Library, and the Bandy Heritage Center at Dalton State College, for preserving our history.

I want to thank the many people who have encouraged and helped me, including my friends Mark Bailey and Rory Kennedy, who first saw the real potential in this story. And thanks to Jon Meacham and Jonathan Karl, whom I am so proud to have known since very early in their incredible careers, and who, along with Rory, all gave this project a great boost by writing blurbs. Thanks also to Jamie Malanowski, Martha Ray, Bill Torpy, Dylan Schaffer, Dan Cogan, Liz Garbus, David McCormack, Bridget McCarthy, David Kopple, Brian Cuban, Eve Reiland, Deborah Spera, Alex Flaster, Joe Rosenberg, Will Davis, Sue Ann Pressley, Pam Lambert, Fannie Weinstein, and especially Merideth Finn for believing in my earlier visions for the story. Being human, I know I have left some folks out, so please forgive me.

Many thanks to Mark Connell, another Graysville School alum, for almost three decades of getting me online and keeping me there for campaigns, my law office site, and now my book site. And a special thanks to Valerie, Hannah, and especially Jessica Brooks and the gang at Autistic Interpretations.

I want to thank my Georgia Capitol Gang, including Ray Holland, Doug Teper, Ron Fennel, Curtis Jenkins, Andy Freeman, and many others, for keeping in touch and reminding me that our short time in Georgia politics was not time wasted. We did some good.

To everyone who taught, guided, and corrected me at Graysville Elementary School, Ringgold Junior High, Ringgold High School, the University of Tennessee at Chattanooga, and the University of Georgia School of Law, I thank you. A special thanks to the University of Georgia School of Law's Class of 1985, too many friends to mention, but especially to the late Doug Baxter, my friend and classmate from junior high through law school. Fifty years ago, he, the late Clay Tucker, and Curtis Barger first taught this Graysville boy how to navigate the big city of Ringgold, Georgia, first introducing me to some of its most notable characters; I miss my old friends.

My secretary Carlene Renner Rogers and Juvenile Court Administrator Tammy Hardin deserve thanks for helping me find the precious commodity of time in order to write. Carlene and Christi Groce, her daughter, along with Jessi Giglio, deserve medals for helping me keep Alvin healthy and happy, from doctors' office trips to his post–cataract surgery eye drops. To all my secretaries and interns who have helped Alvin, while enduring the micromanager in me, and I thank Ashton Meers and Stephanie Corbitt.

Thanks to Kevin Silvey and Mike Giglio, both high school buddies for almost half a century, and longtime law office–sharing friends, and to their staff, past and present.

To Team Alvin, Benita, Lori, Elizabeth, Misty, and others who helped, I give great thanks. If my client had fled the courtroom, as he was always threatening to do, things could have turned out differently. By keeping Alvin calm and in the courtroom, you helped us win.

Thanks to my intern Alli Parker.

To all who ever supported me in the decade of my political life, and for believing in me and my public service, I give thanks. I also give thanks to all the citizens of Ringgold, Catoosa County, Georgia, and Georgia's Old 9th District who voted *against* me in 1996, and to then-Congressman Nathan Deal for beating me soundly enough to put me out of politics. It seems God had bigger plans for me, and for that, I needed to be in Ringgold, Georgia. Later, in the role of our governor, Nathan Deal did more through legislation to help convicted felons get their lives back on track than anyone had, in my memory. And for that, I never told Alvin where he lived.

To everyone who ever misunderstood Alvin Ridley and who may have at first jumped to the wrong conclusions about him, I thank you for coming around with your views. I am no better than you. I just got to know him better, sooner. The beauty of Alvin is that he has long forgiven all of us.

To the two best ex-wives a guy could ask for, Reva and Alison. Thank you both for putting up with me and then sending me packing. Erica and Graeme are proof the Lord works in mysterious ways, in this case by sending us our separate ways.

I am thankful to the late Virginia Gail Ridley for creating the treasure trove of writings over thirty-one years that explained to the world that she was busily engaged in praying, reading, cooking, watching TV, and loving her husband.

Finally I give thanks to my *very* significant other, Jacqueline. From day one, she knew I wanted to write this story, and gave me the space and encouragement to do it. And to her children, Zoe, Jackson, and Elle, I thank you for sharing your mother with me.

And lastly I want to thank my friend Alvin Ridley, now eighty-two years young at time of publication. I now look forward to his frequent office visits and our increasingly more-than-weekly lunches. Alvin, challenging as he was, gave me a second act in life, and maybe even now a third, and I am eternally grateful.